*Everyday Democracy*

# Chicago Studies in American Politics

A series edited by Susan Herbst, Lawrence R. Jacobs, Adam J. Berinsky, and Frances Lee; Benjamin I. Page, editor emeritus

∴

# Everyday Democracy

∴

LIBERALS, CONSERVATIVES, AND THEIR
ROUTINE POLITICAL LIVES

Jeffrey M. Berry, James M. Glaser, and
Deborah J. Schildkraut

THE UNIVERSITY OF CHICAGO PRESS

CHICAGO AND LONDON

The University of Chicago Press, Chicago 60637
The University of Chicago Press, Ltd., London
© 2025 by The University of Chicago

Published 2025


34 33 32 31 30 29 28 27 26 25     1 2 3 4 5

ISBN-13: 978-0-226-84508-1 (cloth)
ISBN-13: 978-0-226-84510-4 (paper)
ISBN-13: 978-0-226-84509-8 (ebook)
DOI: https://doi.org/10.7208/chicago/9780226845098.001.0001

Library of Congress Cataloging-in-Publication Data
Names: Berry, Jeffrey M., 1948– author | Glaser, James M., 1960– author |
   Schildkraut, Deborah J., 1973– author
Title: Everyday democracy : liberals, conservatives, and their routine political
   lives / Jeffrey M. Berry, James M. Glaser, and Deborah J. Schildkraut.
Other titles: Chicago studies in American politics
Description: Chicago : The University of Chicago Press, 2025. | Series:
   Chicago studies in American politics | Includes bibliographical references
   and index.
Identifiers: LCCN 2025013811 | ISBN 9780226845081 cloth | ISBN
   9780226845104 paperback | ISBN 9780226845098 ebook
Subjects: LCSH: Democracy—United States | Right and left (Political
   science)—United States | United States—Politics and government—21st
   century
Classification: LCC JK31 .B47 2025 | DDC 320.473—dc23/eng/20250401
LC record available at https://lccn.loc.gov/2025013811


Authorized Representative for EU General Product Safety Regulation (GPSR)
queries: **Easy Access System Europe**—Mustamäe tee 50, 10621 Tallinn,
Estonia, gpsr.requests@easproject.com
Any other queries: https://press.uchicago.edu/press/contact.html

# Contents

# Illustrations

## Figures

# Tables

## CHAPTER ONE

# Ideology and Everyday Democracy

On January 6, 2021, President Donald Trump led a rally in front of the White House where he made unfounded claims that the 2020 election was stolen and encouraged supporters to "fight like hell." And fight they did. After the White House rally, people marched to the US Capitol, where the House and Senate were convening to certify the Electoral College vote. Their work was violently interrupted by rioters who stormed the building, attacked law enforcement, vandalized offices, and roamed the halls looking for elected officials. As shocking as it all was, the events of that day did not spring out of nowhere. And while President Trump helped incite the riot, he was able to succeed only because there were enough people ready to believe that the election was stolen or ready to abandon long-standing norms of democratic governance, such as the rule of law and the peaceful transition of power.[1]

Many scholars agree that Trump has been as much a symptom as a cause of democratic backsliding.[2] Political elites and features of American political institutions set us on a path toward crisis that started years before Trump decided to run for president.[3] And the American people bring their own proclivities that bolster or undermine democratic governance.[4]

There are many analysts and observers whose work focuses on the broad theoretical underpinnings of democracy.[5] Others have written on the types of behaviors directly associated with events like those on January 6.[6] And of course, there is exhaustive research examining the differences in how liberals and conservatives feel about specific policies and how the two sides in American politics feel about each other.[7] Our mission here is to complement those works by studying the views of the American people on a set of factors that we consider to be the tangible day-to-day manifestations of democracy, such as engaging in discussions with one's political opponents and giving politicians license to compromise. In short, we analyze what we call "everyday democracy": attitudes, behaviors, and processes that people experience in daily life and in their routine considerations of politics and community. Crisis moments get lots of attention, and rightly so, but it is the ordinary political moments that constitute much of politics, and we contend that these ordinary moments can lay the foundation that shapes if, when, and how crisis moments unfold.

We recognize that many of the challenges facing American politics today require elites to do better at practicing forbearance, respecting the institutional boundaries laid out in the Constitution and subsequent policymaking, and upholding democratic principles. Our political system could also benefit from structural changes such as reforms to party primaries and to institutions like the Electoral College. However, we also recognize that such changes are unlikely in the short term. Additionally, we believe that everyday citizens are an essential part of efforts to right the ship. We think it is timely and important to consider the degree to which the American people exhibit democratic proclivities in the normal course of daily interactions.

Given the nature of polarization in the United States today and the extraordinary political events of the past several years, we focus on whether one side of the ideological divide is more (small-d) democratic than the other. We seek to uncover when and where there might be similarities between liberals and conservatives in their daily democratic practices.[8] We also aim to identify where and how they are different. When we do find differences by ideology, we seek explanations. Even when we cannot identify the root of the ideological differences, describing and documenting them is valuable, particularly in our current political moment when it often feels like our democracy is coming apart at the seams.

## Trifling Habits

In perhaps its simplest form, democracy can be understood as a government in which parties lose elections.[9] There's a tendency to think about democracy as being about winning elections, but losing is also a critical part of the equation—as is the behavior of the loser. There are two primary components to this straightforward view of democracy: institutional arrangements, such as rules governing elections and the transition of power; and norms, whereby candidates for office choose to abide by the formal constraints on their behavior.[10] Beyond the rules determined and followed by elites, many democratic theorists believe that the fate of democracy additionally rests with the people. Again, starting with the most basic formulation that democracies involve parties losing elections, it is the people who determine *which* parties lose elections at any given time in a democracy.[11] Once we accept that premise, it immediately becomes clear that the role of the people involves far more than merely picking one candidate or party over another when election day rolls around. How is it that the people determine their prefer-ences in elections? Are some forms of preference formation "better" than others? What other skills or habits do people need to build and possess so they can do their part in upholding democracy? How do they build them, and to what degree do they possess them?

There is a long line of scholars and theorists before us who have laid out some answers to these questions.[12] In this book, we identify specific sets of attitudes and behaviors that map onto some of the general skills and habits that such theorists have argued are desirable for a populace in a democracy to develop. Our primary goals are to consider the extent to which people possess them and to consider similarities and differences by ideology. The list of potential manifestations of a democratic way of being, what we call "everyday democracy," is long, and we do not claim to provide an exhaustive account. Rather, we focus on a set of attitudes and behaviors that capture some of the individual-level orientations undergirding a healthy democratic society and relating to the subjects of our own prior research and expertise.

Our notion of "everyday democracy" may seem casual, since it is not a common term in political science. But if the term is unfamiliar, the idea has a rich history in scholarship. We build on the work of others who have used different language but focused on the same concept of personal capacities for citizenship. Democratic theorists construct arguments about how such capacities can develop so that people may contribute to a strengthening of democracy; we identify several individual-level manifestations of those capacities and assess them.

Our entry into the concept of everyday democracy begins, as does so much of political science, with Alexis de Tocqueville. His *Democracy in America* proceeds along many dimensions, but political scientists contin-ually return to one overriding theme in the book: how the freedom and mores of American culture nurture ordinary people doing ordinary things as they pursue the betterment of their community. In one evocative pas-sage, he writes: "The cares of political life engross a most prominent place in the occupation of a citizen in the United States; and almost the only plea-sure of which an American has any idea, is to take a part in the government, and to discuss the part he has taken. This feeling pervades the most trifling habits of life."[13]

In Tocqueville's eyes, these "trifling habits" are the very foundations of democracy. He returns to this argument over and over, and at one point he says that if readers do not understand how the "practical experience," the "habits," and the "manners" of Americans maintain the institutions of democracy, then his book is a failure.[14] The examples he uses throughout *Democracy in America* make it clear that he means "habits" in a very literal sense. These are instinctive experiences, not people consciously thinking "I need to do this because I want to be involved in politics." Everyday experiences, beginning with just paying attention to one's community, are critical to democratic vitality.

Scholars have used Tocqueville's synonymous term "habits of the heart," rather than "trifling habits," in analyzing how Americans interact with each other in their community. In *Habits of the Heart*, their monumental study of the relevance of Tocqueville to modern America, Robert Bellah and colleagues examine "habitual practices," emphasizing how cultural mores continue to guide everyday behavior across religion, political participation, and economics.[15] These behaviors are not taught, but rather are what we learn through everyday experiences without realizing that we are learning.

Like James Madison in *The Federalist Papers*, Tocqueville views the formation of associations as a natural outgrowth of freedom.[16] But unlike Madison, Tocqueville considers associations to be a "bulwark" against antidemocratic forces rather than the embodiment of self-serving interests.[17] "In no country in the world," writes Tocqueville, "has the principle of association been more successfully used."[18] To illustrate, he describes a hypothetical case involving an obstruction in an intersection. Immediately and without other prompting, citizens would begin deliberating together on how to solve the problem and would then form associations if the matter was not quickly resolved.[19] The experience of working inside an association teaches people how to better engage in politics. It is learning through doing.

Tocqueville's enthusiasm for how associations help to form citizens is shared by Robert Putnam in *Bowling Alone*. The book is Tocquevillian at its core, and Putnam pays homage to the Frenchman in analyzing behaviors that are modern-day "habits of the heart."[20] Putnam calls Tocqueville the "patron saint of contemporary social capitalists."[21] For Putnam, everyday democracy has its roots in the production of social capital. Social capital comes from the "connections among individuals," and such connections build trustworthiness and norms of reciprocity.[22] Simple activities that have apparently nothing to do with politics, such as joining a book club or baking a cake for the church supper, generate social capital and promote a norm of reciprocity. Like Tocqueville, Putnam views these behaviors as unthinking habits that we form over our lifetime.

Putnam argues that declining social capital threatens American democracy. With the withering of associations come fewer opportunities for people to enhance their personal capacities to engage in both political and nonpolitical activities. Like Putnam, we are concerned with taking stock of the habits associated with good citizenship. In the pages that follow, however, we do not restrict ourselves to activities that generate social capital.

As we explain further below, we concentrate on individual-level thoughts and behaviors that provide additional routes for forming democratic habits of the heart.

Habits of the heart cross social classes, as the mundane activities of everyday life can teach us all. In effect, the reason Putnam's book is not *Golfing Alone* is that while bowling is broadly perceived as generally popular, it is especially notable for its legacy as a working-class sport.

Yet not all political activity grows out of the social interactions and connections of one's life. And, again, social capital is declining, which further motivates our concentration on behaviors that are individualistic in nature. Our goal is not to reinvigorate social capital–producing associational life. We take people where they are. Or to use the vocabulary here, we concentrate on habits of the individual heart and not habits of the community. There are many attitudes and behaviors that citizens can practice in their day-to-day life that nurture a democratic mindset. But do they?

## Our Considerations of Everyday Democracy

We are primarily interested in the attitudes and behaviors people carry with them in their daily lives as they encounter people with views that differ from their own, consider whether and how to get informed about current affairs, work with other people (or not) in their communities, and think about how best to connect with different levels of government. As we explain later, we believe that the United States is at a critical point where an assessment of these habits of the heart is warranted and where reflection on realistic ways that such habits can be enhanced is needed. And as we discuss in more detail below, the current level of ideological division in American politics leads us to believe that examining the relationship of ideology to these attitudes and behaviors is particularly important. Because we focus on individual-level attitudes and behaviors that people have opportunities to improve upon every day and not just at election time, we group them under the label of "everyday democracy."

As we conceive of it, everyday democracy refers to a set of attitudes and behaviors that are important for individual citizens to develop and possess in a healthy democracy. While we do not want to diminish the importance of elites—and indeed, addressing some of the more severe threats to the American political system, such as increasingly prevalent minority rule, will require elite action—our focus here is on the mass public.[23] We deliberately emphasize what individuals can do on their own, since such tasks can be easy to actuate—for example, trying to become better informed or making a donation to support a nonprofit in the community. These stand in contrast to some of the more structural or elite-level reforms that are also critical for the ongoing stability of American democracy.

So what are some of the specific qualities we might wish for in our neighbors and in the polity writ large if our goal is to have a peaceful and stable democratic society? Given the importance placed on working with neighbors in the literature described above, we look at community by asking which Americans take actions to sustain and improve their communities and which, conversely, sit on the sidelines. More specifically, the research questions we ask in that portion of our analysis are *Who gives to charity and who volunteers for nonprofits?*

But these aspects of commitment to community form just one of the threads of our inquiry. Our other primary topics are more focused at individual-level thoughts and behaviors, such as compromise (*Who prefers compromise and who prefers to stand on principle?*); federalism (*Where in our governmental structure should authority and responsibility lie? What level of government, if any, is generally trusted to do the right thing? Are people consistent in their views on these questions?*); engaging the other side (*Who listens to those whose views differ?*); and information seeking and group conflict (*How much trust do people have in the media and how do viewers respond to racialized content?*)

More of us surely prefer that we live in a society in which people are willing to compromise. If people are not willing to compromise, gridlock looms, and distrust prevails.[24] It is also generally believed that we should be open to talking to those on the other side and to speak with civility whether we are talking to them directly or on social media. Along those same lines, most say that polarizing media, such as cable and talk radio, make it harder for people to compromise, to trust government, and to interact respectfully. In this vein, does partisan media work against building racial tolerance and respectful deliberation? What about mainstream media, such as broadcast news? When observers say it would be better if trust in the media were higher, do they need to be careful in what they wish for? How consistent are people in their preferences for how power should be dispersed throughout the political system? Is it even preferable for them to be consistent, or is it preferable to prioritize policy outcomes, even if that means trusting the central government more at some times and state governments more at others? Finally, there is universal agreement that it is best to live in a society where citizens are generous and help those in need, whether with our money or our time; how well do Americans embody that ideal?

These manifestations of everyday democracy that we examine—compromise, civility and engagement, federal versus state power, polarizing media, and charity and voluntarism—do not exhaust what we would need to know to fully assess the democratic condition of the American people. Yet together, this collection of attitudes and behaviors can provide considerable evidence about the prevalence of the democratic habits of the heart among the American people at this point in time. And importantly, these topics build on the areas of expertise each of us has developed throughout our careers as scholars and university leaders.

We recognize, however, that while the themes we examine are important for democracy in their ideal forms, there may be times when violating the virtues that they embody is more of the prodemocratic choice. For example, how does one compromise with someone who wants to seize election machines or storm the legislature? How does one remain consistent in their beliefs about government power if the policies advanced by the level of government they normally prefer constrain rights and freedoms? What type of consistency (means vs. ends) should we value? Why should people continue to engage with friends and family members who promote racist or sexist beliefs? Unfortunately, while we can agree in the abstract about general principles that nurture and protect democracy, it is not so simple to specify when violating those principles is the better alternative for democracies.[25] As Nathan Kalmoe and Lilliana Mason argue, parties should not compromise for the sake of peace when the compromise in question means accepting or ignoring the authoritarian and violent impulses of the other side: "If advocating for democracy causes conflict, so be it."[26] Nonetheless, for many people most of the time, choosing to engage, compromising, holding consistent preferences, and the like are often the more democratic options.

## Everyday Democracy and Ideology

Political scientists' fears about threats to American democracy rose before the 2020 election. Even before President Trump took office in 2017, scholars sounded the alarm, emphasizing his authoritarian instincts and the antidemocratic vision of government he so powerfully articulated.[27] In their widely read *How Democracies Die*, Steven Levitsky and Daniel Ziblatt offer a chilling warning: Democracies today are overthrown not by military coups or through revolutions, but instead by the steady erosion of democratic norms and institutions.[28] A slightly different tack is taken by Suzanne Mettler and Robert Lieberman, who emphasize that American democracy has been threatened many times throughout our history. Even so, they conclude that the Trump-era danger is unique, for it exhibits a larger concentration of antidemocratic threats occurring at the same time than in earlier periods of agitation.[29]

The fact that this project took its first steps before the first Trump presidency may make us seem prescient. Alternatively, it may seem that we were simply motivated to promote the arguments of one side of the ideological spectrum. Like Mettler and Lieberman's, though, our concerns grew out of a broader sweep of history. The sharply antagonistic attitudes that became apparent in the 2016 election did not emerge out of nowhere, because segments of American politics were already badly polarized before then. Many scholars have concluded that the latest period of growing antipathy toward the "other" began with Republican Newt Gingrich's ascension in the House of Representatives.[30] He became Speaker in 1995, and he expressed the same beliefs that the other side cheated and connived that Trump would later espouse.

Central as Gingrich is to the unfolding wave of polarization in our country's immediate history, the politics of the early to mid-1990s seem tame in comparison to the present moment. We thus realized that when it comes to assessing the American people's habits of the heart, it is important to consider whether such habits align with ideology. We focus on ideology rather than party because for decades, our discipline considered one's ideological self-identification to be grounded more in ideas and worldviews than partisan identification, which was viewed as more of an identity.[31] We recognize that ideology has taken on more elements of an identity in recent years and that the correlation between partisanship and ideology has increased.[32] That said, we have made a conscious choice here to study ideological differences in democratic thinking, seeking to understand how ideological ideas and democratic ideals are interconnected. Such an investigation is valuable as a descriptive exercise, and the insights it provides can be useful when it comes to developing recommendations for enhancing democratic habits of the heart among Americans who are most engaged in politics.

As worldviews, ideologies are both descriptive and prescriptive; they help people determine what *is* and provide guidance about *what should be done*. As Christopher Federico writes, "Ideologies can be thought of as shared belief systems that reflect a group's understanding of the social world and its vision of what that world should ideally look like."[33] Parties are organizations that field candidates and focus on winning elections in addition to being connected to individuals' sense of self, strongly affected by socialization. Ideologies, by contrast, primarily provide directives about how people and leaders should act. Given that our concern is with daily acts of democracy, ideology strikes us as a compelling dimension along which citizens may differ when it comes to democratic habits of the heart, because

it can offer principled guidance on what people *should* do. And as we discuss in the substantive chapters that follow, there are elements of ideological thinking, such as perspectives on the value of preserving the status quo
or comfort with ambiguity, that pertain directly to the specific democratic
habits at the center of our inquiry, like willingness to compromise or engage
in discussion with political opponents. Thus, by considering ideological
differences, we can come to a deeper understanding of the reasons some
people are more or less likely than others to embody everyday democracy.

Given our current political moment, we surmised that, on balance,
it would be liberals who generally embody more of the building blocks
of democracy.[34] The reality, as we will show, is more complicated. Upon
reflection, it is hardly surprising that our findings are nuanced and do not
all fall into place neatly. Liberals do better on some tests and conservatives on others. Conservatives, for example, show more consistency than
liberals when it comes to thinking about the locus of power in a federal
society, and they are more willing to engage with people that disagree with
them than are liberals. On the other hand, liberals are more likely to make
a donation to charity and to support political compromises. There are also
cases where liberals and conservatives appear to be similar—for example,
liberals and conservatives volunteer at about the same rate. Yet beneath this
aggregate finding is a distinct difference: Conservatives tend to volunteer
for their church, while liberals tend to volunteer for secular nonprofits. Voluntarism is also interesting in that there is no public opinion opposition to
it—everyone supports voluntarism. One value of public opinion research is
that it can identify areas where, in spite of deepening polarization, conservatives and liberals may come together to support new policies. In the case
of charity and voluntarism, there are important provisions of the tax code
that can incentivize (or discourage) such behavior.

A related line of inquiry was to gain a sense of what contemporary liberalism and conservatism look like. We all have a general impression of what
it means to be a conservative and what it means to be a liberal, but in today's
contentious political world it is insufficient to rely on historical generalizations. Classic conservatism, for example, is characterized by a foundational
preference for small government and low taxes. But the first Trump administration placed little emphasis on small government and nevertheless was
immensely popular with conservatives and Republicans. And conservatives show no hesitation in supporting strong governmental intervention
on behalf of policies that they care about, such as restrictions on abortion
or prohibiting discussion of racism. Our own analysis in chapter 2 confirms
that a significant proportion of conservatives are not that conservative
in the classic sense. Using a battery of questions about attitudes on both

economic and social issues, many self-described conservatives hold views that are moderate or even liberal. Liberals, in contrast, are more consistent in hewing to policy positions that are widely accepted as liberal.[35]

Yet we also find that liberals are not necessarily liberal in the classic sense of the word either. Traditionally, liberals have favored a stronger federal government relative to the states, since the federal government was in a better position to enforce equality, develop and sustain the welfare state, and protect civil rights and liberties, hence the "big government" criticism lobbed at liberals from their opponents.[36] Our analysis indicates that when it comes to thinking about where governmental power should be concentrated, liberals tend to be instrumental. They view government power as a means to achieving policy ends; sometimes that results in a desire for giving more power to the federal government, and other times it results in wanting to give more power to the states. Liberals' instrumental nature sets them apart from conservatives, who show some tendencies toward instrumentalism but are generally more consistent in their preferences regarding the distribution of power, with a clear tilt toward the state and local level.

Finally, another notable feature of our approach to assessing contemporary meanings of liberalism and conservatism is that we are primarily concerned not with policy preferences, but with attitudes about governance; we concentrate on politics, not policy. In the end, many of our findings surprised us. And therein lies the value of this book: Our portrait of American politics does not always fit what we think we know about our fellow citizens.

## Motivating Questions and Approach

We have put forth numerous questions and identified trend lines that lie at the heart of our inquiry. All of these lead us to an overriding question: How well do regular Americans who consider themselves to be liberal or conservative contribute to the well-being of democracy? And there are other important subsidiary questions. What are the levels of support for the different manifestations of democratic governance that we examine? Are there ideological asymmetries in that support? Do liberals and conservatives support different components of everyday democracy? If and when they differ, can we explain those differences? What do our findings mean for our assessment about the state of the democratic condition in the United States?

Of course, these questions carry an assumption that differences will be found, but one important possibility to consider is that maybe the sides are not as far apart as many people would expect. Recent research indicates that most Americans have a distorted view of how polarized the American people are and of how different they are from one another when it comes to politics.[37] Most Americans do not disdain the other side to the degree that media coverage would lead us to think, nor do they routinely share their political views on social media.[38] Perhaps they are not that different when it comes to being willing to engage with people different from them, or donating time and money to addressing problems facing their communities, or wanting politicians who are willing to compromise, or trusting the accuracy of the media. If so, that would be an important set of findings to promote, as the recognition of commonality on commitments to everyday democracy could be one part of the project of shoring it up.

Our approach to examining these questions has us exploring a wide range of national public opinion surveys that span nearly two decades. We introduce questions that we placed on Cooperative Election Study (CES) in multiple years, which allows us to dig deeply into the phenomena that we consider. For example, rather than asking people general questions about their trust in the media, we can explore trust in specific media outlets, including ones that respondents consume and ones they do not. Not only can we assess whether people end friendships over politics, we can examine several possible reasons why they would do so, including emotional responses to political disagreement and general orientation toward conflict. And we can identify reasons that liberals and conservatives think differently about the devolution of power and responsibility in our political system because we ask about it directly. Most of our original data collection took place during the first Trump presidency. We therefore complement our survey data with surveys that were commissioned by others, such as the Pew Research Center, the General Social Survey, or Gallup. Our broad time horizon allows us to consider whether patterns are consistent (they generally are) and to see whether it matters which party controls the White House (sometimes it does, and sometimes it does not).

In some chapters, we move beyond our surveys to additional data sources, including content analyses of cable news and social media posts. These additional datasets allow us to see whether information on self-reported engagement behavior on surveys aligns with actual behavior on social media (it generally does) and whether perceptions of the similarities and differences between conservative media and liberal media (such as Fox News and MSNBC) are accurate (they generally are).

While we use our introductory chapter to tell readers what we aim to do in this book, it is also valuable to comment on what we do *not* do. Importantly, we focus on those Americans who consider themselves liberal or conservative. For the most part, we put moderates aside. We focus on people who identify as liberal or conservative because many of the pathologies that allegedly plague the American people are laid at their feet. And as we noted earlier, we want to explore whether the content of ideological worldviews provides insight into the attitudinal and behavioral patterns that we uncover. We recognize that doing so means that a nontrivial portion of the population is not examined deeply here.[39] In some of our analyses, we set moderates to be the reference group, and we direct our inquiry on whether liberals and conservatives differ from them, which, by extension, lets us test whether liberals and conservatives differ from each other. In our concluding chapter, we offer more thoughts about the role of moderates in our inquiry.

We also do not explore in depth or detail how our findings for ideology are conditioned by one's racial group membership. Practically speaking, most of our datasets are majority white. In many instances, we distinguish white respondents from nonwhite respondents, but our opportunities for finer grained analysis of nonwhite racial groups are limited. Conceptually, we also note that what it even means to be liberal or conservative can vary substantially by race, a reality that grows out of complex historical factors.[40] Racial politics are central to the trajectories pertaining to partisanship and polarization that characterize our current moment and that make assessing our democratic condition imperative. In this vein, we analyze media consumption and content, and we illustrate how people's media habits may exacerbate intergroup conflict. We document how "trust in the media" is not always all it is cracked up to be, especially when it comes to people's relationship with "their" media and how that relationship shapes racial attitudes.

## This Urgent Time

There is surely no more frequent defense of the importance of studying politics than "this is a unique period in American history." How often have we heard pundits say that "we're at an inflection point"? Poetic license aside, such arguments seem cogent because there are so many times in American politics that *do* seem like turning points. In the last hundred years the country has experienced the Great Depression, the Second World War, the Cold War, McCarthyism, the civil rights movement, Vietnam, Watergate, the Reagan revolution, September 11, the election of the first Black president, and, most recently, Trumpism. Indeed, it is hard to think of a "normal," relatively quiet time in American politics. The 1800s were just as tumultuous. And before that there was a revolution. It is probably always a good idea to assess Americans' commitment to attitudes and behaviors that are supportive of democracy, but it is especially so in times when they seem to be particularly

tested. Our current moment, like many moments throughout American political history, feels as though it has a sense of urgency in this regard.

Upon Nixon's election in 1968, which certainly seemed profound at the
time, the journalist and political strategist Kevin Phillips boldly concluded
that it was a decisive turning point, a realigning election similar to McKin-
ley's new Republican majority in 1896 or Democrat Roosevelt's cataclys-
mic 1932 win.[41] However, no long-term Republican majority emerged in
the wake of Nixon's election, and instead of realignment, scholars would
soon be talking about dealignment, a decline of both parties and the rise
of a more independent electorate. Phillips's book shows the risk of writing about history as it happens, concluding from recent events that seem
momentous that enduring, far-reaching change is taking place.

Phillips's misconception about 1968 gave us pause when we began our
research for this book. It seemed that America was undergoing something
more than the normal vicissitudes of politics, but were we witnessing trends
that would endure? By the time we ended our research, however, scholars
were talking about a true crisis of democracy. We had come to believe that
the nation was experiencing a powerful challenge to democracy and not
a more transitory uprising. Writing in 2020, Suzanne Mettler and Robert
Lieberman concluded: "We face the weakening of the checks and balances
that prevent democracy from sliding into tyranny. The rule of law, long
taken for granted by Americans, has been eroded by a president who sees
the government as an instrument to advance his own personal and political
interests. Elections, the foundation of democracy, are becoming less free
and fair due to the distorting influence of money, misinformation, and foreign meddling."[42] Their comment about the erosion of the rule of law seems
even more timely at the start of Trump's second term as president than it
was when they originally wrote it in 2020.

There are many puzzles regarding how democracy in America seemingly
went into decline. The task here is a bit more modest. We do not underes-
timate the central importance of elections, nor the campaigns of interest
groups, nor the power of activists who go to meetings, contribute campaign
funds, or even run for office. But most people, most of the time, engage in
politics only in a peripheral sense. Yet ordinary acts—the instinctual habits
of the heart—aggregate into powerful political forces. Beyond the culpa-
bility of elites who traffic in polarization, and beyond the malfeasance of
institutions, is the broader citizenry.

Foremost in our minds is the widespread belief that modern American
politics has become dangerously toxic. And what is thought to be especially destructive is the language used by some when they talk about politics. A common complaint is that caustic rhetoric full of name-calling and

invective has come to define online, and even offline, interaction. Today, the proverbial list of all the things that are wrong with American politics would certainly point to the ease with which the internet facilitates hostile interaction among rank-and-file citizens. Recall Tocqueville's example of the obstruction of the intersection and note that the activity that commenced was face-to-face—neighbors working together to solve the problem. By way of comparison, consider a modern transportation snafu in 2024, when a shipping vessel knocked the Francis Scott Key bridge into Baltimore Harbor and led to the deaths of several members of a road repair crew. Accusations then erupted online blaming the infrastructure failure on the influence of diversity, equity, and inclusion (DEI). As ridiculous as this charge was, it was covered in *The Washington Post* and other major media outlets.[43]

The anonymity allowed by the internet makes it easy to be as nasty as one might like without the opprobrium that would come from saying the same things face-to-face, though a concern in today's political landscape is that even face-to-face interactions have become too unpleasant. And even for those who are open about their identity and may actually benefit from being outrageous, the internet gives them the freedom to do so from the safe distance of their home office or kitchen table. Divisive and polarizing political speech has always existed, but never has there been so much disturbing content put forth, so easily accessible, and so rapidly disseminated as there is today.

This question about civility leads to a familiar question about what it means to be a good citizen. Part of our common civic training is that we should all take the responsibility of citizenship seriously. "Good citizenship" is not quite what we mean by everyday democracy. It is more formalistic and task oriented, with an emphasis on voting, writing one's legislators, becoming active in associations, and so on. Yet, the basic concept of being a responsible citizen overlaps with our own idea of being a good everyday democrat.

At the end of the book we look at the degree to which the literature on virtuous citizenship corresponds to our lines of inquiry and what our results show. But while our investigation is designed to objectively measure specific behaviors and attitudes, we certainly began with normative concerns. For example, one hope was that we would find that everyday democrats were generally tolerant people and not racially antagonistic nor prejudiced against marginalized sectors of the population. But that was what we hoped to find. After a period in which the president of the United States frequently uses racist language, such as referring to Mexican immigrants as rapists and calling African and Caribbean countries "shitholes," we wondered whether this poisonous rhetoric affected attitudes in the broader population.

As outlined in the previous section, our investigation touches upon tolerance in several tests we conduct.

Again, in contrast to Putnam, our approach studies individuals doing ordinary things without generating significant social capital. We also recognize that a strong democracy must contain strong communitarian foundations as well. People can hold attitudes that are individualistic while embracing others that are communitarian. Citizens can have strongly tolerant views on race but never engage in any collective action to further such views. Even for more communitarian activities in our investigation, though, we focused on instinctual individual habits rather than on more demanding forms of collective behavior.

Habits of the heart are typically conceived of in positive terms: attitudes and behaviors that demonstrate concern for one's neighbors and one's country. It is possible, though, that our nation's habits of the heart have turned into hardening of the heart. Pessimism about the future of the country is widespread, but as we said above, America often appears to be at a crossroads. Are we at a real inflection point, or are our political problems enduring ones with new veneers? And as American democracy faces its contemporary challenges at this urgent time, can we know whether this country's citizens are reliable everyday democrats?

## Plan of the Book

We start with a basic building block of everyday democracy, looking at the degree to which liberals and conservatives engage each other and discuss politics across the ideological divide. We consider both online and offline engagement. Regardless of the type of engagement in question, we find that self-identified conservatives are more likely than self-identified liberals to report having ideologically heterogeneous social networks, whereas liberals are more likely than conservatives to report that they have ended friendships or blocked people on social media because of their political views. We confirm the asymmetry in ideological avoidance by analyzing the ideological makeup of followers of liberal and conservative political elites.

Our effort to explain why this asymmetry exists yields incomplete answers. We consider whether emotions play a role and find that feeling anxious or exhausted amid political disagreement makes avoidance behaviors more likely, but those emotions do not affect the overall ideological asymmetry.[44] We get the same pattern of results when we consider people's general propensity to embrace or avoid conflict. Ultimately, we find that the asymmetry can be reduced by focusing on people whose self-identified ideology matches their ideological preferences. Specifically, when we separate conservatives with conservative policy preferences from conservatives with moderate-to-liberal policy preferences, we find that "consistent conservatives" look more like liberals in that they are more likely to avoid the other side. The asymmetry does not disappear, however.

Despite our inability to fully solve the puzzle of asymmetric ideological avoidance, we do end the chapter with one bright note. We include a content analysis of politically relevant tweets across two time periods (one with Obama as president and one with Trump) to consider whether there is an ideological asymmetry in the use of uncivil discourse. We find none, and we additionally find that the overall level of incivility was rather low, with most tweets consisting of retweets of news articles.

As we think about beliefs and behaviors that contribute to our current concern with everyday democracy, a central question is, where does information that nurtures such views come from? Political socialization, enduring beliefs, and political identity form the core of personal attitudes and behavior. But there is also an ongoing stream of information that people are exposed to that can affirm and possibly alter their views. We noted earlier that the architecture of this information flow has changed dramatically in recent years. It is in this vein that we examine news consumption. One of our central findings is that the conventional wisdom that Americans mistrust the media is wildly inaccurate. By disaggregating "the media" and asking respondents about their individual sources of news, we show in our data that people have enormous trust in the media with which they engage.

If Americans trust the news they select to receive, is it also the case that they believe the stories they read, watch, or listen to are relatively accurate? The data demonstrate that people do believe their curated news. Trust in the media and faith in its accuracy are argued to be important for democracy, for they enable citizens to keep watch on elected officials and hold them accountable.[45] But trust in some sources is perhaps more important than in others. To consider this possibility, we seek to determine how such trusted information affects beliefs, with a specific focus on the impact of cable television news and network broadcast news. We show that at least some of the divisiveness in American politics can be traced to those companies that market polarization as a product. Our chapter includes a content analysis of MSNBC and Fox News stories, which illustrates how their programming focuses on politics over policy and how Fox News in particular casts people of color as villains. We then show that consumers of Fox News have higher levels of racial resentment. Specifically, conservatives who watch Fox are more racially resentful than conservatives who do not (and nearly 70 percent of conservatives in our analysis watch Fox, compared to only 18 percent of liberals). For its part, mainstream media news consumption enhances support for compromise and opposition to gratuitous insults. Given how routinely the mainstream media are criticized, we think this is an important finding. America can survive with a significant amount of mistrust in its institutions, but it is threatened by the robust market for polarized political commentary. When observers say it would be better if trust in the media were higher, do they need to be careful what they wish for?

Next, in chapter 4, we turn to our study of political compromise. How people think about the process of politics, about how to sort out a society's many differences, interests, and beliefs, is a critically important everyday-democratic attitude, one that contributes to functional democratic governance. We find, as do others, that liberals are more sympathetic than conservatives to compromise in politics. They are more likely to approve of those politicians who engage in compromise than those who "stick to principle" and are more willing to like the outcomes of compromise by virtue of a more inclusive process. We explore this asymmetry and, embracing Daniel Kahneman and Amos Tversky's prospect theory, make the case that it is a function of how much liberals and conservatives view compromise as leading to a loss versus a gain. Given how powerful the loss frame is in decision-making, it is not surprising that conservatives, who more often than liberals view political change as loss, would be less supportive of compromise. We also show that the asymmetry is driven by differences in how well-educated liberals and conservatives think about compromise. Education contributes to acceptance of compromise for everyone, but for conservatives it also contributes to disdain and distrust of government, attitudes that short-circuit the acceptance of compromise and compromisers. If one does not like government, then compromise that facilitates effective government is less appealing.

Another question we explore in these pages is where power should lie in a democracy, with a strong central government or with the states (chapter 5). Whether power should be distributed broadly or centralized is one important manifestation of such thinking. The founders first argued that democracy on a large geographic scale, one that enabled significant regional differences to coexist, was only possible with a federalist structure, where each constituent part retained its ability to control many of its own policies even while combining into a nation. Of course, they aimed to get the balance right between central power and state and local control after experiencing the dysfunction of the Articles of Confederation. This remains resonant as we consider how our democracy should function. And, for our purposes, it is a question that has separated a liberal from a conservative point of view, both theoretically and in practice. In this chapter we consider the following questions: How consistent are people in their preferences for how power should be dispersed throughout the political system? Is it even preferable for them to be consistent, or is it preferable to prioritize policy outcomes, even if that means trusting the central government more at some times and state governments more at others?

We show that the study of attitudes toward federalism and the devolution of power to state and local governments is complicated by the fact that attitudes about ends and means are intertwined. In this chapter we also look at the question of the devolution of governmental responsibility and use the pandemic as the vehicle for studying which level of government people think should take the lead in implementing solutions to a public health crisis. We find that support for a principled division of power can diminish somewhat on both sides when doing so makes it more likely that one's policy aims will be achieved. But we also demonstrate that liberals are more likely than conservatives to display this tendency. In other words, liberals are more comfortable with the locus of power moving around if that helps them achieve their desired policy ends, while conservatives are more likely to be guided by their preferred division of power even when it does not yield their preferred policy outcome. It is a demonstration of a conservative attachment to a particular democratic principle that is foundational. While we recognize that it is important for people to maintain principled support for the institutional arrangements of their political regime even when they do not get the policy outcomes that they like, we find that the conservative consistency in support for federalism is undergirded, in part, by racial resentment, a finding that complicates the benefits that otherwise come from regime support.[46]

In chapter 6 we consider voluntarism and philanthropy, which have always been at the center of Americans' conception of a virtuous and democratic society. Our Tocquevillian notion of the United States being a nation of joiners is widely seen as confirmation of how we Americans take citizenship seriously. By working with our neighbors, contributing time and money to good deeds, we build community and make neighborhoods and larger entities stronger. Despite this consensus over the necessity of charity and voluntarism, not all Americans donate money or time to charitable organizations.

If not all Americans are charitable, can we distinguish sectors of the population that are more or less so? What types of nonprofit organizations do Americans donate to? And how much do they contribute? A similar set of questions involves volunteering. Strong patterns are evident in both dimensions. Liberals are more likely to donate to charity, though conservatives are more likely to give to one particular sector of the nonprofit world, their churches. Liberals and conservatives volunteer at roughly the same rate, though again, conservatives direct their energies toward their own congregations. Liberals are far more likely to spend time volunteering for secular organizations. Even in the realm of charity, liberals and conservatives are divided. Tocqueville's argument that America remains a country of joiners and of people concerned about their communities remains true today, though there are sharp differences shaped by ideology in the organizations Americans rally around. These findings help us understand how ideologues think more broadly about everyday-democratic notions of what a good society is, about our responsibilities to each other, and about how individuals contribute to a bigger and better whole.

We conclude with chapter 7, where we take stock of our findings and connect them to some of the broad challenges facing American political life today. When all is said and done, what is our ultimate judgment on the questions we posed at the outset? Are the levels of support for the everyday manifestations of democracy that we document sufficient? Are there asymmetries between liberals and conservatives? Does one side consistently do a better job than the other, or are there some democratic ideals that are more dear to conservatives while others are more embraced by liberals? What do our answers to these questions mean for the health and future of American politics?

To put it simply, we conclude that things are both okay *and* not okay. We find that many Americans across the ideological spectrum exhibit attitudes and behaviors that support everyday democracy. But there are many who do not. Although we think there are notes of optimism in our findings, the country is clearly in a precarious situation. Events in recent years have made clear that a small group of people can destabilize the entire enterprise, even if they are not representative of the views of their co-partisans or co-ideologues. The question is, what do the rest of us do in response? And how do we keep small groups bent on undermining democracy from getting bigger?

There are many unrealistic changes that would have to happen for some of our current political problems to get better. Some analysts argue that we need to move away from our two-party system and our first-past-the-post single-member elections.[47] Others argue that we need to eliminate institutional mechanisms that allow minority rule, like the Electoral College or the Senate.[48] Changes of this nature, however, are unlikely anytime soon. And in the face of these structural and institutional barriers to democratic stability, citizens can only do so much. But they can still do a lot. In our concluding chapter, we offer some specific, feasible recommendations derived from our empirical investigations that are geared toward citizens, with an eye toward helping them become, or remain, strong everyday democrats. Most of them come down to staying true, modeling good citizenship, and doing the day-to-day work.

We recognize that it is easy for people to say that they want to do the things that are necessary for good citizenship and that it can be another thing to muster the motivation to actually do it, especially if they feel like no one else is. Here too we see a role for our book. As academics, we have a responsibility to highlight the problems and challenges that face American democracy. We also have a responsibility to highlight what is working. There are a *lot* of people who hold ideas and engage in everyday practices essential for democracy. They support compromise. They engage with people that disagree with them. They volunteer their time and act philanthropically. They do not immerse themselves in reactionary, partisan news sites. The people we are describing here are not just moderates or political independents; our analysis finds many liberals and conservatives, those most engaged by politics, who think and act in ways that are deemed important for democratic stability. Pointing this out is not exactly a solution to the challenges of our time, but we hope that it reminds people that there are many Americans who seem to be doing their part. That knowledge in and of itself might inspire hope as well as a renewed commitment to continuing to believe that American democracy is worth working for, and it can let people who feel that way know that they are not alone.

## CHAPTER TWO

# The Asymmetry of Ideological Bubbles

In June 2018 Sarah Huckabee Sanders, former press secretary for then-President Donald Trump, went to dinner with a group of people at the Red Hen restaurant in Lexington, Virginia. Several of the restaurant's staff members were uncomfortable with her presence, either because they had moral objections to White House policies generally or because they felt that some of the administration's policies threatened them personally. They approached the restaurant's owner, Stephanie Wilkinson, who, after some discussion with her staff, asked Sanders to leave. Sanders complied. According to Wilkinson, the exchange was civil and polite despite its awkwardness. The story, however, took off on social and news media the following day and spawned a national conversation about free speech, civility, and our seeming inability to engage with people with whom we disagree. This incident came on the heels of other Trump administration officials' being confronted while dining by people who disagreed with the administration or its policies, and so it seemed to fit a narrative: Liberals and progressives were bent on shunning conservatives.[1]

On one side of the reaction to this incident were people who cheered and celebrated Wilkinson, including a sitting member of Congress.[2] Even *Glamour* magazine weighed in, with a senior editor writing, "When people in the future want to know what we did, I don't want to tell them that we cleared Sarah Huckabee Sanders' dessert plate and thanked her for the tip. I want to say we threw sand in the wheels whenever we could."[3] Defenders celebrated Wilkinson's decision as an act of civil disobedience and a repudiation of the notion that our democracy rests on our ability to maintain polite interactions despite our political differences. They maintained that confronting and shunning are sometimes necessary.

On the other side were people who called Wilkinson's action disgraceful. Some of her critics called the incident a slippery slope, fearing that anyone can now reject interaction with anyone else over any political disagreement; those critics advocated for greater toleration for and interaction with one's political foes.[4] Others took a more hostile and aggressive approach, posting Wilkinson's home address and phone number and sending hate mail.[5]

This episode and others like it struck a nerve with political observers because it tapped into phenomena that many people feel to be true: that Americans are less willing to talk about politics with people who disagree with them than they used to be, that they prefer to inhabit so-called ideological bubbles, and that others are increasingly comfortable with aggressive retaliation. This story additionally captured the imagination of the political punditry because it fit the narrative that many observers sensed: that it is liberals who are particularly likely to call for shunning the other side, while conservatives revel in getting a rise out of their opponents.

The "OK boomer" meme of 2019 also illustrates avoidance brought on by frustration and suggests an ideological asymmetry. As an essay exploring the meme put it, "OK boomer implies that the older generation misunderstands millennial and Gen Z culture and politics so fundamentally that years of condescension and misrepresentation have led to this pointedly terse rebuttal and rejection."[6] In other words, the older, more conservative generation seeks to engage by telling younger people what's what, and the younger, more progressive generation wants none of it. The younger generation rolls their eyes at those they see as closed-minded, resistant to change, and unsympathetic toward the global challenges that young people today face. They raise their palm and turn away.[7]

Another example of ideological asymmetry with respect to political engagement with the other side can be seen in the phrase "own the libs," a phrase initially adopted by conservatives to describe behavior that involves saying and doing things to get under the skin of one's liberal opponents.[8] In 2017, for example, the Keurig company said it would withdraw its sponsorship from Sean Hannity's show on Fox News. In response, people began destroying their Keurig coffee makers and posting videos of the destruction online. One such post read, "Liberals are offended by this video of a Keurig being thrown off of a building. Please retweet to offend a Liberal. #BoycottKeurig."[9] Conservatives brandishing a hat or shirt or COVID face mask that says "F*ck Your Feelings" also demonstrate this attitude of enjoying getting a rise out of the ideological other. The lack of equivalent phrases on the left suggests that liberals have not been particularly interested in provoking conservatives, at least not to the same degree as conservatives and not enough to develop a catchphrase. That said, "own the libs" later became used by liberals who sought to mock conservative attempts to anger them. For example, liberals might say "getting COVID to own the libs" to ridicule conservatives for not getting vaccinated against COVID-19 and then getting sick.[10]

The examples described here embody the inquiry in this chapter, where we explore whether liberals and conservatives do in fact differ in their engagement with one another and attempt to identify factors that contribute to people having ideologically homogeneous social networks.[11] Before progress can be made on pressing issues of the day, opposing sides must first come together. Such coming together can thus be seen as a precursor to most other facets of everyday democracy.[12] Our first goal is therefore to see whether a systematic analysis would support the anecdotal sense that conservatives are more willing to interact with the other side, what we normally consider to be an everyday virtue. Many scholars of democracy agree that deliberation across lines of division is an important element of democratic governance.[13] While many would also agree that deliberately provoking outrage is not a productive form of engagement, avoidance is, on balance, problematic.[14] Understanding the patterns and causes of avoidance is therefore also a worthwhile effort.

We rely on self-reported responses to survey questions as well as an analysis of Twitter activity (now X) to illustrate that liberals are indeed more likely than conservatives to report having ideologically homogeneous social networks and to engage in what we call bubble-sustaining behavior, such as blocking friends on social media or ending friendships because of politics.[15] After confirming that ideological asymmetry in bubble-sustaining behavior exists, we examine factors that might explain it, focusing on three in particular. First, we consider whether liberals are more likely than conservatives to report feeling unpleasant emotions during political debates.[16] We find that they are, but ideological differences in bubble-sustaining behaviors remain even after we account for these emotional reactions. Next, we consider whether liberals are more likely than conservatives to exhibit a general tendency of conflict avoidance.[17] We find that they are not, and again, ideological differences in bubble-sustaining behaviors remain even after we account for conflict avoidance.

Finally, we address the fact that people who call themselves conservative often do not hold particularly conservative policy preferences, and we consider whether this ideological inconsistency explains why conservatives do not feel the same need to avoid engaging with the other side as liberals. We find that conservatives are more likely than liberals to be ideologically inconsistent (to have policy preferences that do not align with their self-reported ideology) and that this inconsistency can explain some of the asymmetry in bubble-sustaining behavior, yet we also find that ideological differences remain even after taking ideological inconsistency into account.

Of course, engaging with the other side just to anger them is hardly a deliberative ideal.[18] Our investigation therefore also examines whether political discussion among conservatives on social media seems to be more provocative than political discussion among liberals. Importantly, we find that conservatives who use Twitter to express thoughts on a range of political issues are not more likely than liberals to use toxic language.

## Why Ideological Bubbles Matter

At the core of this inquiry are widely held normative assumptions about the characteristics of a democratic society and of the good citizens who propel it forward. In this theorizing, good everyday-democratic citizens are ones who deliberate.[19] That is, they talk to others, listen to both like-minded and contrary views, and truly think about the issue at hand. They are engaged, and, at least at a minimal level, active through some forms of participation. As Peter Levine writes, "If more Americans were involved in constructive and empowered ways, we could make progress on [our most important] problems. Put more positively, as active citizens, we could help to build a better commonwealth."[20] As Nicole Curato and colleagues put it, "Participation and deliberation go together."[21] Engaging across lines of disagreement is therefore foundational to democratic governance. At election time, citizens must be open to hearing arguments across the political spectrum if they are to succeed in their role of holding officials accountable. In between elections, engaging with the other side in one's everyday life allows people to practice and hone this difficult skill.[22]

Although we can become more informed through solitary activity—reading a newspaper, for example—we do not deliberate if we do not have others to deliberate with. Deliberation at work, through voluntary organizations, and through networks of friends and family leads one toward a possible next step, which is collective action. Deliberation entails exposure to various viewpoints, and talking back and forth requires reflection on what is heard. Exposure to those who are not like-minded might lead to a better understanding of our own arguments as we are pushed to consider why we believe what we believe. At the same time, exposure may lead to a greater understanding of arguments that are different from our own. Another possible consequence is that broader exposure leads to increased general tolerance toward others in the political system.[23]

Despite the many virtues of deliberation, it collides with human nature. Most of us desire harmony in our lives. Indeed, pioneering research on social networks established that people generally try to construct politically homogeneous networks.[24] Additionally, exposure to cross-cutting political views can be uncomfortable, particularly if that exposure comes with conflict or incivility.[25] Being confronted with contrary views at work or at a meeting may lead individuals, consciously or not, to avoid putting themselves in the same situation again. It is often easier to say nothing and go on with our day. And, of course, there are larger societal dynamics that teach us to be silent or apathetic.[26]

At the same time, people often misperceive how homogeneous their social networks are, and they overestimate how unpleasant engaging with the other side will be.[27] As Robert Huckfeldt and John Sprague show, such misperceptions can stem from people, consciously or not, avoiding political topics with certain people and from the fact that their friends might misrepresent their own views in the presence of others with the goal of avoiding conflict (1987). Many people have close friends across the partisan and ideological spectrum, and reminding them of that fact can reduce one's dislike of the other side.[28] In light of findings such as these, we see value in providing a descriptive picture of just how avoidant people actually are. People should know if avoidance is not as widespread as it is commonly portrayed. One goal of this chapter is therefore to document and assess the generalizability of the examples described at the outset.

Finally, it is important to note that we recognize that opportunities to deliberate can introduce opportunities to reinforce socioeconomic inequalities and power structures.[29] As Arthur Lupia and Anne Norton write, "Many people who advocate for deliberation take for granted that deliberation is preferable to violence. But what if deliberation simply reinforces the experience of oppression? . . . Are there some statements to which a society's best response is to, at minimum, stop the conversation?"[30] While we approach this inquiry from the stance that engagement with the other side is often an essential element of everyday democracy, we recognize that there may be times when engaging with the other side merely gives oxygen to ideas that are threatening to democratic outcomes. We acknowledge this fact as well when we consider attitudes about compromise later in chapter 4.

## Why Might Liberals Avoid Engagement More Than Conservatives?

In addition to documenting patterns of engagement and avoidance, we consider whether there is an ideological asymmetry to such behaviors. First, there is a societal perception that such asymmetry exists, as detailed in the examples at the opening of this chapter. We therefore assess the validity of that perception. Second, to the extent that there is an ideological asymmetry, we consider whether there are elements of the differing ideological worldviews that help us understand why some people are more prone to curating an ideological bubble than others.

Conservatives being more likely to engage with other side than liberals might initially strike some as counterintuitive, because surveys show that people who align with the ideological right tend to be more likely to rely only on conservative news outlets and avoid mainstream and liberal outlets, whereas people on the left tend to rely on both liberal and mainstream news outlets.[31] In terms of media exposure and consumption then, it is conservatives who are more "bubble-prone." But maybe that tendency itself feeds a reverse asymmetry when it comes to *interpersonal* engagement, particularly if the media that conservatives consume encourage them to feel angry and righteous (which it does), as anger is an "approach" emotion.[32] As Davin Phoenix puts it, "When angered, people engage the fight response to the threat."[33] Anger also makes people feel like they are able to affect an outcome, which could further make people who are riled up more likely to engage with people who disagree with them: Perhaps they are more likely to feel like they can change minds.[34] In short, conservatives may be more likely to engage with their ideological opponents because their political ecosystem has primed them to feel outraged and angry, feelings that have been shown to promote action and feelings of efficacy.

It also may be useful to consider the reactionary nature of conservatism, which has been described well by others as being driven by a concern over a perceived loss of power and changing societal morals.[35] As we discuss in chapter 4, this concern about loss is powerful, and conservatives, feeling a sense of alarm about changes they see in society, may feel more of an urgent need to try to get others to see the threats that they see, which could make them seek out the other side more than liberals. For their part, liberals have been shown to be less threatened by change and ambiguity than conservatives and have less of a need for closure.[36] Together, these attributes may make liberals feel less of a need to reach a consensus or resolution to political disagreement, which could make them more likely to avoid potentially unpleasant or conflictual discussions with people with whom they disagree.

Thinking through the dynamics described in this section complicates the normative assumption that more engagement with the other side is necessarily better. Presumably, engagement fostered by manufactured outrage or by a difficulty coping with inevitable change is not the kind of engagement that deliberative theorists have in mind when they extol the virtues of having conversations with one's political opponents. Nonetheless, we think it is reasonable to posit that liberal avoidance is far from ideal as well, for reasons discussed throughout the book.

## Online and Offline Engagement

One of the challenges of thinking about civic engagement in the online world is to understand how it differs from face-to-face interaction. We can criticize, even insult, those in our online networks or feeds in ways we would not consider in a face-to-face context. Given the nature of Facebook, Twitter, and other online platforms, considerable interaction is with those with whom we have "weak ties."[37] Both exit and voice seem easier with those who are peripheral members of one's own network.[38] One distinguishing feature of the online world is the low barriers to entry. On Twitter, for example, it is usually the case that anyone can follow anyone else. Still, not all tweets are created equal. As online participants, we most value those tweets that come from somebody we regard as trustworthy.[39] This is all to say that we expect that the asymmetric patterns of interactions outside one's bubble between liberals and conservatives will generally be similar whether they pertain to online or offline interactions.

At the same time, however, we argue that political discussion online, especially on Twitter, is a particularly rich representation of the politics of us-versus-them. A critical characteristic of Twitter and other online platforms is that they greatly facilitate taking up arms to fight the "thems." Additionally, the messaging is a means to promote oneself. In the marketing world, being an online "influencer" is a profession, while in politics, would-be influencers play an unpaid sport. Even so, there are still real rewards for building large online political followings. The belief that one possesses a significant voice in the political world is obviously satisfying for those whose passion is politics. It is much more difficult to become such a voice outside of the online world—not everyone can become a legislator, a party leader, a wealthy contributor, or a newspaper columnist. Anyone can become somebody on Twitter. And having a following inherently signals being part of a group, an "us."

If one is not already well-known in the political world, a common approach for building an online following on social networking platforms is to be outrageous. And to be outrageous is to be more than witty or sharp—it is to heap ridicule on the "them" that the people you want to encourage to follow you despise. A related strategy is that online platforms allow one to be anonymous by using a made-up identity. For those who might not like the blowback from saying controversial things, the online world allows them to say what they really want to say about the other side. QAnon accounts, for example, commonly rely on pseudonyms. One might not want one's boss, neighbors, or family to know that one's loyalties lie with a conspiracy movement. One account is @YourAnonNews, which has amassed 6.7 million followers at the time of this writing by posting provocative tweets such as those claiming that the English royal family killed Princess Diana and that Donald Trump allegedly raped a thirteen-year-old girl.

Another attribute of online political engagement is that it is a usual subtext of political posts that those who post believe they are speaking on behalf of a larger community rather than simply offering a personal perspective. In contrast, consider a letter to the editor in a newspaper or an in-person political discussion among friends: Such forms of engagement are not connected to anyone else. The dynamic of posting online is communal not only because posts are distributed to one's followers, but they can also go to people who are not followers but who the site's algorithms believe would be interested in that particular missive. A post invites followers to engage in a dialogue, a dialogue that may appeal to them because of a shared hatred of those on the other side. Posts that succeed in provoking those who are in the "them" camp are proof of one's effectiveness in being a spokesman for the larger community of "us." Thus, it is plausible that people's engagement patterns differ when it comes to online versus offline interactions. The survey measures discussed below allow us to consider this possibility.

## Survey Evidence for Asymmetrical Bubble Behavior

There are ample data across multiple years to indicate that self-identified liberals are more likely than self-identified conservatives to disengage from political interactions with the other side. Surveys show that this disengagement holds for both online and offline interactions. A Pew survey from 2016 asked, "Do most of the people you know have similar political beliefs, different political beliefs, or a mix of various political beliefs?"[40] Liberals were slightly more likely than conservatives (34 percent to 31 percent) to report that most of the people they know have similar beliefs. In 2017 Pew asked about party in particular: "How many of your close friends are of your own party?"[41] Here a ten-point gap emerged, with 67 percent of Democrats and 57 percent of Republicans saying that "a lot" of their friends share their partisan affiliation.

Regarding intentional avoidance, a 2014 Pew survey asked respondents if they had "ever stopped talking to or being friends with someone because of something they said about government and politics." Ending a friendship over politics is not the usual thing, but it is more usual for liberals than conservatives: 17 percent versus 9 percent.[42] Family members cannot be dropped as easily as friends, but they can be avoided. Here, again, there is a yawning gap between liberals on the one hand and conservatives on the

other. In a December 2016 poll from the Public Religion Research Institute, 17 percent of liberals but only 3 percent of conservatives said yes when
asked, in "this holiday season, have you decided to spend less time with
certain family members because of their political views?"[43]

Purposeful disengagement is also measurable by asking about online
behavior, and here again we see that liberals are considerably more likely
than conservatives to pull out of a social media relationship if they are
offended by something that someone has posted on Facebook or some other
social media site. In the 2014 Pew survey, 33 percent of liberals responded
that they have "hidden, blocked, defriended, or stopped following someone
on a social networking site because [they] did not agree with something that
they posted about government and politics." Just 22 percent of conservatives did the same. The 2016 presidential election heightened this difference
even further, with 41 percent of liberals in the Pew survey and only 26 percent of conservatives "changing their settings to see fewer posts from someone in [their] feed" because of something related to politics, and 41 percent
of liberals versus 26 percent of conservatives "block[ing] or [unfriending]
someone because of politics." We also note that for both liberals and conservatives, reports of avoidance seem to be higher for online interactions
than for offline ones. Using data from 2018, Jeff Spinner-Halev and Elizabeth Theiss-Morse find that Hillary Clinton voters were more likely than
Donald Trump voters to say that they have taken actions to restrict their
engagement with the other side, such as blocking someone on social media
or ending contact with a family member or friend.[44]

One might think that the ideological differences are attributable to the
fact that liberals lost the election, making them more sensitive to commentary from the other side. Yet data from 2012 suggest that even when Obama
was in office, liberals were more also likely than conservatives to "unfriend"
someone because of their political views.[45] It therefore does not seem that
this pattern is unique to the Trump era.

On the 2018 and 2020 Cooperative Election Studies,[46] we fielded questions similar to ones used by Pew. Figure 2.1 shows the results by ideology.[47] A few noteworthy trends are evident. First, in both years, liberals are
more likely than conservatives to inhabit an ideological bubble or engage
in bubble-sustaining behaviors, like blocking someone or ending a friendship over politics. Second, all types of avoidant behavior were more common in 2020 than they were in 2018 for both liberals and conservatives.
Third, avoidant behavior is again more common when the action in question involves social media. When asked about ending a friendship over politics, fewer than half of the respondents report doing so for both ideological
groups in both years.

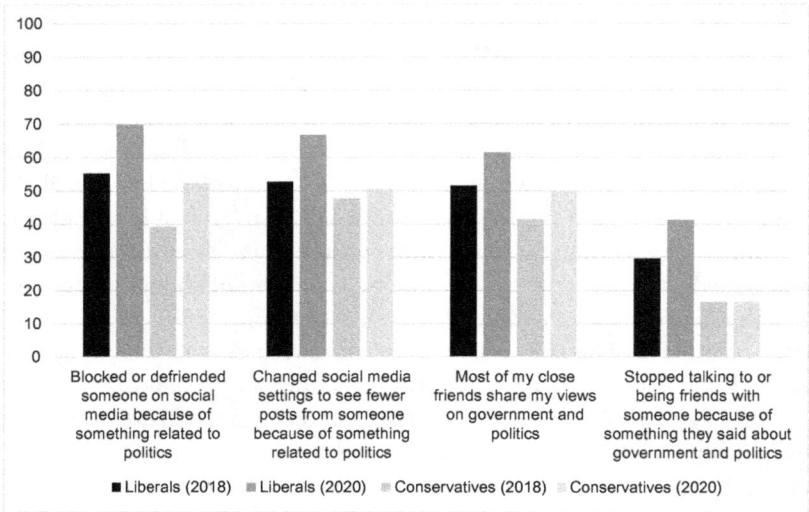

FIGURE 2.1. Liberals are more likely than conservatives to reduce social interactions with the other side, especially online (2018 and 2020)

Source: 2018 and 2020 CES

## Asymmetrical Bubble Behavior on Twitter

The survey data tell a clear and consistent story, but they all rely on self-reported behavior. What about actual behavior? To see if actual behavior aligns with self-reported behavior, we turned to an analysis of Twitter. Twitter users have control over the accounts that they choose to follow. Additionally, Twitter algorithms extend exposure to those who appear to be like other followers in any user's network. What this means is that the universe of tweets that a person sees will reflect the ideological makeup of the accounts that they choose to follow. These dynamics of Twitter and the survey research we described thus far led us to expect that liberal and conservative networks would be distinctive. More specifically, we expected conservatives' Twitter networks to be more heterogeneous in their ideological makeup than liberals' Twitter networks. We tested this hypothesis by analyzing the followers of elite actors. In particular, we expected that the followers of conservative elites will themselves be conservative, whereas the followers of liberal elites will come from a broader range of the ideological spectrum. Put another way, ordinary Twitter users who are conservative would follow both liberal and conservative elites, while ordinary Twitter users who are liberal would inhabit more of a bubble, following liberal elites but not conservative elites.[48]

To test this hypothesis, we randomly selected a minimum of two thousand followers from twenty-six elite actors (thirteen liberal, thirteen conservative) who were prominent in either electoral politics or political commentary in 2018.[49] We then used an ideology estimator developed by scholars at New York University, which is available as a package on GitHub.[50] The tool has preestimated ideologies for more than one thousand elite political accounts and media outlets, and it can estimate any user's ideology by looking at the composition of elite accounts that they follow. User ideologies that earn a negative score are considered "likely liberal," while ideologies that earn a positive score are considered "likely conservative." Our final sample for this portion of the analysis includes 202,613 Twitter users.[51]

The results in table 2.1 confirm our hypothesis that the conservative elites have a more homogeneous following among our randomly selected set of followers than liberal elites. Recall that with the ideology estimator, positive scores are considered conservative and negative scores are considered liberal. The scale ranges from −2.36 to +2.36. Table 2.1 shows that the mean score for followers of conservative elites is 1.185, while the mean score for followers of liberal elites is −0.362. These results indicate that followers of conservative accounts are concentrated on the conservative side of the spectrum, while followers of liberal accounts are closer to the midpoint. In other words, liberal elites have followers who are both liberal and conservative, while conservative elites have followers that tend to be conservative. The larger standard deviation for liberal elites is further indication that their followers are more likely to span the ideological spectrum than followers of conservative accounts.

Figures 2.2 and 2.3 provide another illustration of this finding. Figure 2.2 shows the distribution of ideology scores for followers of conservative elites. It clearly demonstrates that followers are concentrated on the positive (conservative) side of the $x$-axis. Figure 2.3, on the other hand, shows

TABLE 2.1. Ideology of Twitter users as estimated by the elite accounts they follow

| Account type | Mean | Median | Std. dev. |
|---|---|---|---|
| All conservatives | 1.185 | 1.476 | 1.152 |
| Conservatives (politicians) | 1.054 | 1.341 | 1.135 |
| Conservatives (commentators) | 1.414 | 1.751 | 1.146 |
| All liberals | −0.362 | −0.553 | 1.543 |
| Liberals (politicians) | −0.078 | 0.385 | 1.543 |
| Liberals (commentators) | −0.844 | −1.341 | 1.419 |

Note: Cell entries are ideology estimates of a random subset of followers of elite accounts. Larger positive scores are more conservative; larger negative scores are more liberal.

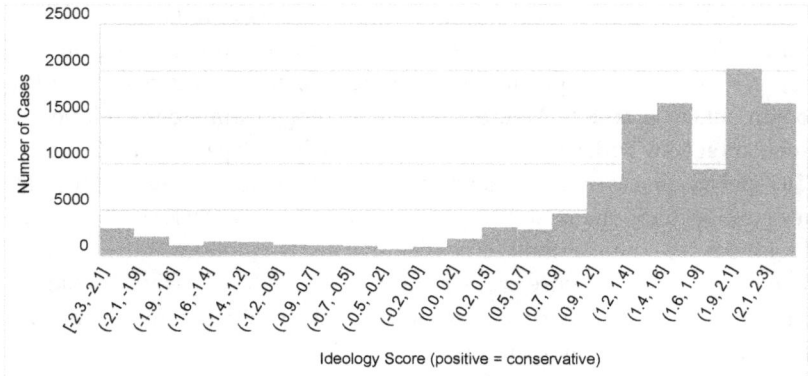

FIGURE 2.2. Conservative elites on Twitter have followers who are mostly conservative

Source: Twitter sample compiled by authors

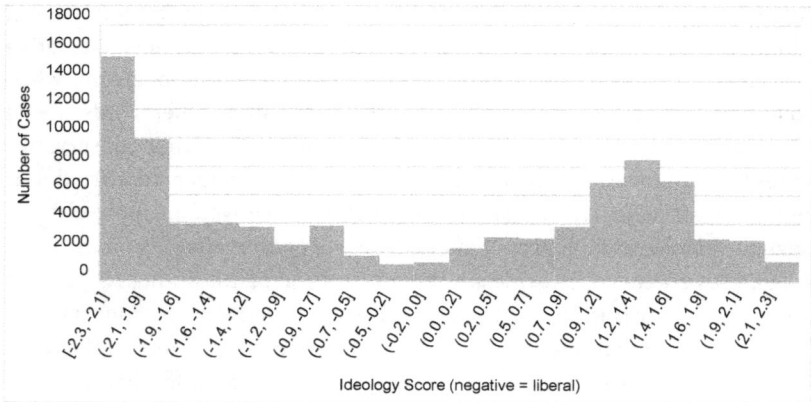

FIGURE 2.3. Liberal elites on Twitter have followers who are liberal and also conservative

Source: Twitter sample compiled by authors

the distribution of ideology scores for followers of liberal elites. Although most followers are on the liberal end of the scale, there is also a cluster of followers on the conservative side as well.

Table 2.1 also breaks down the elite accounts by profession, separating politicians, such as Donald Trump and Hillary Clinton, from commentators, such as Sean Hannity and Rachel Maddow. We find that the overall pattern holds: The means for conservative politicians and pundits are further from zero than the means for liberal politicians and pundits. Additionally, the standard deviation for conservative politicians and pundits is smaller than the standard deviation for their liberal counterparts.

Overall, our analysis of followers of elite accounts leads us to conclude that actual behavior on Twitter corresponds to self-reported behavior in public opinion surveys: Liberals are more likely than conservatives to try to seal themselves off from exposure to people with whom they disagree. Analysis by Gregory Eady and colleagues using alternative methods to analyze Twitter users reaches a similar conclusion.[52]

## What Explains Asymmetrical Bubble Behavior?

### DIFFERENCES IN EMOTIONAL REACTIONS TO POLITICAL DEBATE

What explains asymmetrical bubble behavior? We considered the possibility that liberals might have different emotional reactions to debating political issues with people on the other side than conservatives do. Recall that anger is an "approach" emotion that leads people to be more likely to take action. Other emotions can affect political engagement as well. For example, anxiety can lead people to be risk-avoidant and withdraw, while enthusiasm, like anger, can promote engagement.[53] In general, people expect political engagement with the other side to feel unpleasant, and such expectations are associated with greater levels of avoidance.[54] When asked about how they feel when they engage in political discussions, liberals may be more likely to report feelings associated with withdrawal, and conservatives may be more likely to report feelings that promote engagement. What we know about the media environment and political style of conservative elites supports this possibility.[55]

To assess the role of emotions in this phenomenon, our 2018 CES module included the following survey battery: "When you debate political issues with people who have different views than you do, to what extent do you feel: excited, angry, calm, anxious, exhausted?" Response options were very, somewhat, and not at all. We included calm and exhausted for exploratory purposes: Calm strikes us as a neutral state that could serve as a useful point of comparison for the positive and negative emotions, and exhausted strikes us as a feeling that is prevalent among liberals but that we believe has not been explored in existing studies.

We speculated that liberals would feel more negative emotions associated with avoidance, which could in turn explain their greater tendency to take steps to minimize interactions with people that disagree with them

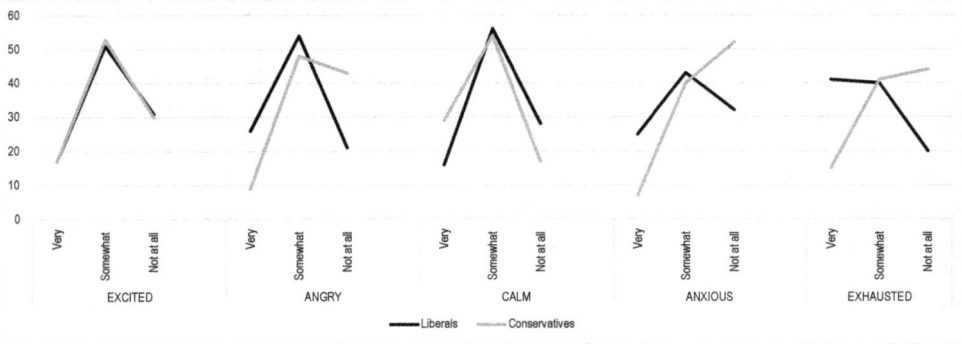

FIGURE 2.4. Liberals report more negative emotional reactions than conservatives when engaging in political debate with the other side

Source: 2018 and 2020 CES

while conservatives might be more likely to feel emotions associated with engagement. As figure 2.4 shows, liberals were more likely than conservatives to report feeling angry, anxious, and exhausted, while conservatives were more likely to report feeling calm. Exhaustion in particular stands out as a feeling that was far more prevalent among liberal respondents. Notably, conservatives were *not* more likely to say that they felt angry. Perhaps they would have been more likely to report feelings of anger had we asked if they feel angry when they think about politics or when they consume news, but when it comes to debating with the other side, it is liberals who appear more likely to report feeling angry.

The next step was to see whether these emotions help explain the patterns of responses to the questions in figure 2.1, and whether including these questions alongside indicator variables for ideology renders ideology insignificant. The results of this inquiry appear in table 2.2. Our model includes dummy variables for liberals and moderates, with conservatives serving as the reference category. Our comparison of interest is between liberals and conservatives. We also control for education, gender, race, and whether the respondent consumes conservative media.[56]

We control for gender because prior research shows that women were more likely than men to unfriend people on social media because of things having to do with politics.[57] Likewise, existing analyses show that nonwhite respondents are more likely than white respondents to unfriend others because of politics.[58] Finally, we anticipated that younger people might be more likely than older people to manipulate their social media accounts, and, as the "OK boomer" meme described at the start of this chapter suggests, younger people may have less patience for engaging with the other side than older people.

TABLE 2.2. Emotions and social interactions with the other side (logit)

| | Blocked or defriended someone on social media | Changed social media settings | Most friends have similar political views | Ended friendships |
|---|---|---|---|---|
| Liberal | 0.889*** | 0.493* | 0.586** | 0.722** |
| | (0.300) | (0.298) | (0.291) | (0.331) |
| Moderate | −0.184 | 0.293 | −0.290 | 0.037 |
| | (0.306) | (0.276) | (0.281) | (0.339) |
| Education | 0.356*** | 0.096 | 0.328** | −0.183 |
| | (0.133) | (0.131) | (0.135) | (0.175) |
| Conservative media | 0.064 | 0.058 | 0.067 | 0.160 |
| | (0.248) | (0.236) | (0.239) | (0.269) |
| Female | −0.034 | −0.059 | 0.119 | −0.466* |
| | (0.207) | (0.208) | (0.211) | (0.264) |
| Nonwhite | 0.167 | −0.397 | −0.222 | −0.243 |
| | (0.289) | (0.276) | (0.294) | (0.410) |
| Age | −0.005 | −0.025*** | 0.009 | 0.009 |
| | (0.006) | (0.006) | (0.006) | (0.007) |
| Not feeling excited | −0.013 | 0.152 | −0.105 | 0.090 |
| | (0.165) | (0.166) | (0.165) | (0.237) |
| Not feeling angry | −0.083 | 0.287 | −0.099 | −0.418* |
| | (0.200) | (0.212) | (0.197) | (0.232) |
| Not feeling calm | 0.001 | 0.065 | −0.254 | −0.234 |
| | (0.183) | (0.169) | (0.182) | (0.214) |
| Not feeling anxious | −0.335* | −0.310* | 0.069 | −0.580*** |
| | (0.182) | (0.185) | (0.189) | (0.200) |
| Not feeling exhausted | −0.044 | −0.274 | −0.450*** | −0.299 |
| | (0.160) | (0.170) | (0.162) | (0.185) |
| Constant | 0.063 | 0.990 | 0.600 | 1.656 |
| | (0.837) | (0.805) | (0.883) | (1.095) |
| $N$ | 552 | 552 | 552 | 552 |
| $\chi^2$ | 47.77 | 37.89 | 36.83 | 38.07 |

Source: 2018 CES.

Note: Standard errors in parentheses.

*$p < .10$; **$p < .05$; ***$p < .01$.

We include conservative media consumption because its following is vast and, as noted earlier, it encourages its audience to feel outrage and anger.[59] The level of trust in these media among its consumers is high. In our 2018 CES module, the proportion of Rush Limbaugh's listeners who trusted him "a lot" or "some" was 88.1 percent. Trust scores for Sean Hannity's radio show listeners and Fox News viewers were nearly as high. As we demonstrate in the next chapter, these outlets scapegoat, mock, and diminish the other side.[60] People who consume this media might be more likely to jump into the fray, though it is also possible that the ire spurred by conservative media promotes disdain, which could make consumers want to limit cross-ideological relationships. We therefore introduce it as a control to see if exposure to outrage encourages or diminishes bubble-sustaining behavior. For our measure of conservative media consumption, we asked respondents if they had watched, read, or listened to several political news and commentary sources in the past month, including Fox News, the Rush Limbaugh Show, and Sean Hannity's radio show. Then we add up the total number of conservative outlets to which they said yes.[61]

For the emotions measure, "not at all" is coded higher, so a positive coefficient means that not feeling that emotion makes the behavior in question *more* likely, while a negative coefficient means that feeling the emotion makes the behavior *less* likely. For example, the negative coefficient on anxiety in the first model means that as one's level of anxiety goes down, so does the likelihood of blocking or defriending someone on social media because of politics. Coding the emotions in this manner may seem awkward, but we felt that all coding options were awkward in some way. Our discussion of the results below therefore walks the reader through the most salient findings.

Among the emotion measures, anxiety matters the most. It is significant at 90 percent in two models and at 99 percent in a third. People who report feeling anxious when they engage in political debate are more likely to block or defriend someone on social media, to say they changed their social media settings due to politics, and to say that they have ended friendships because of political differences.[62] We also find that people who report a feeling of exhaustion are more likely to say that most of their friends share their political views, and reporting a feeling of anger is associated with a greater likelihood of saying that one has ended a friendship over politics. Notably, we do not find that anger stimulates an approach response on any of the measures examined here.

For our purposes, however, the main question is whether accounting for emotions renders ideology insignificant. We find that despite the effects for anxiety and exhaustion, being liberal is consistently significant in promoting bubble behavior relative to conservatives. In three of the four models, being liberal is significant at 95 percent; in the fourth model, it is significant at 90 percent. So although liberals are more likely to report feeling anxious and exhausted than conservatives when engaging with the other side, an ideological divide remains even when accounting for those emotions.[63]

## DIFFERENCES IN CONFLICT ORIENTATION

Maybe a more generalized tendency to want to avoid conflict would explain the asymmetry between liberals and conservatives. Here we build upon the political scientist Emily Sydnor's work on the relationship between conflict orientation and political engagement.[64] Sydnor illustrates that people who are comfortable with conflict ("conflict approaching") sometimes participate more in politics. One's conflict orientation is a relatively stable personality trait that can serve as a resource that enables political engagement.

Intrigued by Sydnor's argument, we added to our module on the 2020 CES a five-question battery that measures conflict orientation to determine whether liberals and conservatives differed in their conflict orientation level and whether ideological differences in bubble-sustaining behaviors disappear in models that control for this orientation. Respondents were asked how much they agree or disagree with the following statements: I enjoy challenging the opinions of others; I find conflicts exciting; I hate arguments; Arguments don't bother me; and I feel upset after an argument.

As with Sydnor, we find that liberals and conservatives score similarly on conflict orientation measures, as illustrated in figure 2.5. But perhaps controlling for conflict orientation eliminates ideological asymmetry? We find that it does not. Using models similar to those used in our analysis of emotional reactions to political debate, we find that liberals remain more likely to engage in bubble-sustaining behavior and to report more homogeneous social networks than conservatives, even after controlling for conflict orientation.[65] The results, shown in table 2.3, also show that among the conflict

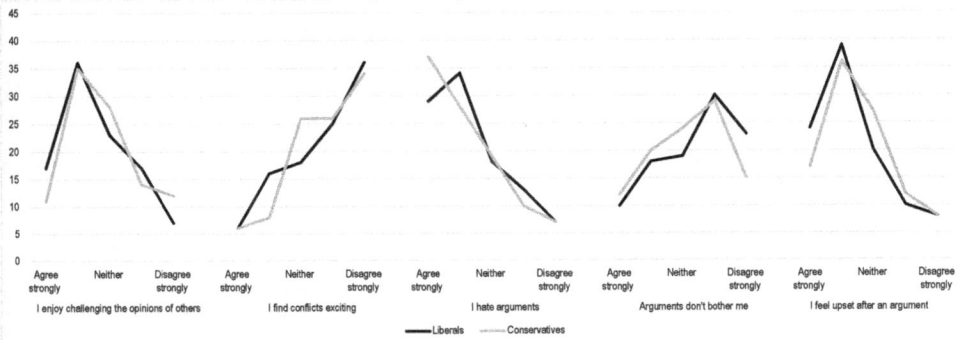

FIGURE 2.5. Conflict orientation does not vary by ideology

Source: 2020 CES

TABLE 2.3. Conflict orientation and social interactions with the other side (logit)

| | Blocked or defriended someone on social media | Changed social media settings | Most friends have similar political views | Ended friendships |
|---|---|---|---|---|
| Liberal | 0.847*** | 0.527** | 0.552*** | 1.136*** |
| | (0.217) | (0.232) | (0.198) | (0.213) |
| Moderate | 0.313 | 0.190 | −0.717*** | 0.557** |
| | (0.232) | (0.246) | (0.213) | (0.253) |
| Education | 0.169 | 0.376*** | 0.218** | 0.262** |
| | (0.117) | (0.121) | (0.101) | (0.117) |
| Female | −0.160 | 0.377* | 0.046 | −0.344* |
| | (0.187) | (0.121) | (0.167) | (0.187) |
| Nonwhite | −0.044 | −0.345 | 0.022 | −0.088 |
| | (0.217) | (0.229) | (0.192) | (0.215) |
| Age | −0.008 | −0.019*** | 0.016*** | −0.008 |
| | (0.005) | (0.006) | (0.005) | (0.005) |
| I enjoy challenging opinions of others | −0.180* | −0.032 | −0.275*** | −0.106 |
| | (0.095) | (0.098) | (0.082) | (0.095) |
| I find conflicts exciting | 0.162* | −0.015 | 0.072 | 0.026 |
| | (0.097) | (0.102) | (0.086) | (0.104) |
| I hate arguments | 0.046 | 0.047 | −0.172* | 0.178* |
| | (0.093) | (0.098) | (0.091) | (0.101) |
| Arguments don't bother me | −0.142 | 0.057 | −0.004 | −0.004 |
| | (0.093) | (0.099) | (0.081) | (0.098) |
| I feel upset after an argument | −0.307*** | −0.148 | 0.089 | −0.274** |
| | (0.095) | (0.101) | (0.092) | (0.110) |
| Constant | 1.251** | 1.104* | −0.420 | −0.797 |
| | (0.613) | (0.618) | (0.554) | (0.678) |
| $N$ | 748 | 739 | 936 | 895 |
| $\chi^2$ | 38.75 | 38.94 | 69.53 | 61.75 |

Source: 2020 CES.

Note: Standard errors in parentheses.

*$p < .10$; **$p < .05$; ***$p < .01$.

orientation measures themselves, people who dislike challenging the opinions of other people are less likely to block or defriend people because of politics and are less likely to report a homogeneous social network (in these models; "disagree" is coded higher). Additionally, people who do not feel upset after an argument are less likely to block or defriend people on social media and are less likely to have ended a friendship over politics.

While some of the conflict orientation measures work in ways that make theoretical sense, conflict orientation is not tied to ideological orientation, nor does conflict orientation explain the robust ideological asymmetry in liberals' greater tendency to avoid interacting with the other side than conservatives'.

## MAYBE CONSERVATIVES ARE NOT ALL THAT CONSERVATIVE

Christopher Ellis and James Stimson have shown that a sizable number of conservatives have long been inclined to support liberal policies.[66] In their terminology, *symbolic ideology* is the label people adopt, while *operational ideology* is the ideological slant of one's policy preferences. They estimate that nearly 30 percent of symbolic conservatives hold nonconservative positions on economic and cultural issues, which is in stark contrast to liberals, where only 3 percent fail to express liberal preferences.

We therefore wondered if a plausible explanation for why conservatives are less likely than liberals to inhabit ideological bubbles is that many self-described conservatives do not hold conservative positions. It could be that these conservatives may be more likely to find common ground with people they encounter and therefore are less likely to feel the need to avoid certain people in their daily lives. Consistent conservatives, on the other hand, may feel that they have more at stake in political discussions and may be less patient when it comes to dealing with alternative viewpoints. We acknowledge, however, that there are reasons to expect that this disconnect might not matter. In particular, among some people ideology is increasingly considered an identity akin to partisanship and other social identities.[67] Among Republicans in particular, the symbolism of conservatism looms large in their understanding of politics and partisan conflict.[68] If one's ideological attachment is an important part of a person's sense of self, it may, on its own, determine whom one engages and whom one avoids, which means the policy preferences one holds may be irrelevant to phenomena under investigation here.

In both our 2018 and 2020 CES analyses, we combined ten policy questions into a scale of operational ideology. In the 2018 analysis, we selected five questions about economic issues or government spending, such as raising the minimum wage, and five questions about social or cultural issues, such as gun control.[69] Owing to changes in the common content questions in the CES, our 2020 measure of operational ideology includes three questions about government spending and seven questions focused more on social or cultural issues.[70] We then created a dummy variable distinguishing consistent conservatives, who are symbolically and operationally conservative, from inconsistent conservatives, who are symbolically but not operationally conservative. Like Ellis and Stimson, we find liberals are more ideologically consistent than conservatives. In 2018, 93.6 percent of liberals were ideologically consistent versus 72.5 percent of conservatives. In 2020, 92.9 percent of liberals were ideologically consistent versus 70.5 percent of conservatives. Since nearly all liberals in both surveys were ideologically consistent, our remaining analysis in this section focuses only on self-identified conservatives.

Figure 2.6 shows responses to our bubble-behavior questions broken down by year and by ideological consistency among conservatives. In nearly all cases, ideologically consistent conservatives were more likely to report inhabiting or curating an ideological bubble than inconsistent conservatives. The one exception is that in 2020, inconsistent conservatives were more likely than consistent conservatives to say that they blocked or defriended someone on social media because of something related to politics. If we recall the data from liberals in figure 2.1, however, we can see that even though consistent conservatives inhabit bubbles more than inconsistent conservatives, their level still does not match that of liberals.

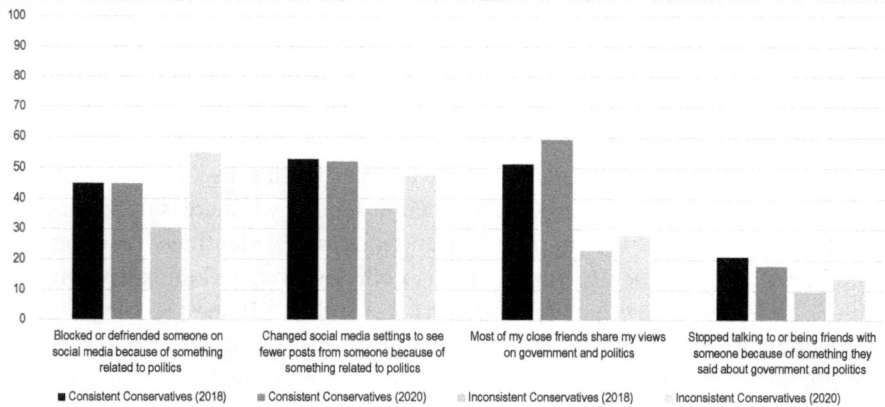

FIGURE 2.6. Consistent conservatives are often more likely than inconsistent conservatives to reduce social interactions with the other side

Source: 2018 and 2020 CES

For example, while 18 percent of consistent conservatives in 2020 said that they have ended friendships over politics (versus 14 percent of inconsistent conservatives), a whopping 41 percent of liberals reported ending friendships. And while 59 percent of consistent conservatives in 2020 say that most of their friends share their views on government and politics (versus 28 percent of inconsistent conservatives), 62 percent of liberals report ideologically homogeneous friend networks.

Next we turn to logit models to determine whether the differences observed in figure 2.6 between consistent and inconsistent conservatives are statistically significant after controlling for additional factors. As before, we control for education, gender, race (white vs. nonwhite), consumption of conservative media (2018 dataset only), and age. The results appear in tables 2.4 (2018 data) and 2.5 (2020 data). In both tables, we see that consistent and inconsistent conservatives differ most clearly in their tendency to report that most of their friends share their political views. In 2018,

TABLE 2.4. Social behavior as a function of being a consistent conservative (2018; logit)

| | Blocked or defriended someone on social media | Changed social media settings | Most friends have similar political views | Ended friendships |
|---|---|---|---|---|
| Consistent conservative | 0.652* | 0.499 | 0.885** | 0.629 |
| | (0.353) | (0.345) | (0.351) | (0.501) |
| Education | 0.489*** | 0.572*** | 0.051 | 0.090 |
| | (0.181) | (0.176) | (0.190) | (0.285) |
| Conservative media consumption | −0.530 | −0.329 | 0.705** | 0.642 |
| | (0.345) | (0.342) | (0.358) | (0.599) |
| Female | −0.324 | 0.100 | −0.032 | −0.129 |
| | (0.299) | (0.290) | (0.316) | (0.486) |
| Nonwhite | 0.366 | −0.103 | −1.163** | −0.507 |
| | (0.448) | (0.411) | (0.476) | (0.682) |
| Constant | −1.330*** | −1.325*** | −1.367*** | −2.505*** |
| | (0.455) | (0.423) | (0.471) | (0.670) |
| N | 291 | 291 | 291 | 291 |
| $\chi^2$ | 15.07 | 14.33 | 22.80 | 10.59 |

Source: 2018 CES.

Note: Standard errors in parentheses.

*$p < .10$; **$p < .05$; ***$p < .01$.

TABLE 2.5. Social behavior as a function of being a consistent conservative (2020; logit)

| | Blocked or defriended someone on social media | Changed social media settings | Most friends have similar political views | Ended friendships |
|---|---|---|---|---|
| Consistent conservative | −0.294 | 0.203 | 1.238*** | 0.163 |
| | (0.340) | (0.340) | (0.318) | (0.390) |
| Education | 0.202 | 0.352* | −0.045 | 0.286 |
| | (0.194) | (0.199) | (0.166) | (0.223) |
| Female | −0.327 | 0.016 | −0.130 | −0.671** |
| | (0.312) | (0.316) | (0.273) | (0.339) |
| Nonwhite | 0.650 | 0.216 | −0.414 | −0.363 |
| | (0.417) | (0.443) | (0.361) | (0.446) |
| Constant | −0.018 | −0.504 | −0.709 | −1.675*** |
| | (0.404) | (0.415) | (0.356) | (0.460) |
| N | 224 | 220 | 301 | 292 |
| $\chi^2$ | 6.49 | 4.32 | 23.06 | 10.04 |

Source: 2020 CES.

Note: Standard errors in parentheses.

*$p < .10$; **$p < .05$; ***$p < .01$.

consistent conservatives are also more likely to report having blocked or defriended someone on social media because of politics.[71] In the remaining models, the differences between consistent and inconsistent conservatives are not statistically significant.[72]

From the analysis in this section, we conclude that some of the asymmetry between liberals and conservatives in bubble-sustaining behavior is attributable to the fact that many self-identified conservatives do not hold particularly conservative policy positions. Conservatives who do hold conservative policy views are more likely than their moderate or liberal-leaning counterparts to curate an ideological bubble. But their bubble-sustaining ways still do not match those of self-identified liberals.

## Owning the Libs?

Thus far we have documented that although many people who consider themselves to be liberal or conservative take steps to limit engagement with the other side, and that such actions may have been more common in 2020 than in 2018, we also documented that many do not, particularly when asked about offline behavior. We also verified that liberals are in fact more likely than conservatives to establish ideological bubbles both online and in person. We considered several possibilities that might explain this ideological asymmetry: emotional reactions to political discussion (including consumption of conservative media), conflict orientation, and ideological inconsistency. The only one with supporting evidence was that many conservatives hold liberal policy preferences, though accounting for this pattern did not eliminate the asymmetry. At this point in our study of political discussion, we have one more question to consider: whether conservative political discussion is more likely to be provocative or uncivil than liberal political discussion. How much do conservatives really seem driven to "own the libs"? Recall that we started this inquiry out of an interest not just in asymmetries in engagement but also in asymmetries in the nature of that engagement. Civility is broadly accepted as a core norm of democratic deliberation, but, of course, incivility is part and parcel of a free society, and there are certainly times where calls for civility are veiled attempts to preserve existing power structures. For social scientists, one concern is that incivility can degrade the democratic processes and change the way citizens regard government.[73] With the rise of social media, concerns about incivility have intensified as millions of Americans have become direct participants in back-and-forth uncivil behavior and as their own representatives have done the same.[74]

Beneath this broader trend of increasing interaction, we wondered whether conservatives and liberals exhibit differential behaviors. We have already shown that conservatives are more likely to engage with the other side than liberals, and conventional wisdom holds that conservatives seek to provoke, as exemplified by the phrase "own the libs." It also could be that an asymmetry in uncivil discourse fuels the asymmetry in engagement analyzed thus far: If liberals expect people on the other side to be uncivil, they may preemptively disengage.

We therefore sought to test whether conservatives are more likely to be uncivil than liberals. We also take civility to one of its confrontational ends, name-calling. The term "name-calling" may seem to be overly vague, but we follow a content-analysis template that defines it as "words and context that make the subject look foolish, inept, hypocritical, deceitful, or dangerous."[75] We sought to test whether conservatives more frequently utilize such language in taunting opponents, clearly not an everyday-democratic practice.

For this portion of our analysis, we used a web-scraping tool to randomly select tweets that met certain date and keyword criteria. First, we selected tweets in English that were posted in March 2013, 2014, 2017, and 2018 from accounts based in the United States. These periods were selected to create comparable political contexts. The periods occur during the first two years of President Barack Obama's second term and President Donald Trump's first term, a time when postelection momentum fueled the presidents' agendas. We randomly selected times within each day of each selected month and then randomly selected tweets that related to seven topics we identified as particularly relevant during the period, using keywords associated with the following categories: discrimination, environment, fiscal issues, government, gun violence, health care, and immigration.[76] We then dropped any user who was included in the list of more than one thousand elites in the ideology estimator tool discussed earlier, in order to increase the likelihood that our sample consisted mainly of ordinary Americans on Twitter. Once duplicate tweets and elite accounts were dropped from our sample, we had a database of 11,156 tweets.[77] This dataset allows us to sample political discussion on Twitter that is initiated by everyday users.

To estimate a user's ideology, we use the same ideology estimator tool described earlier. To estimate the level of incivility, or toxicity, of a tweet, we use Perspective API, a tool developed by Jigsaw and Google's Counter Abuse Technology team. Perspective uses machine learning to detect toxic posts, which it defines as "a rude, disrespectful, or unreasonable comment that is likely to make you leave a discussion."[78] Perspective assigns a continuous score between zero and one, ranging from highly unlikely to be toxic to highly likely to be toxic. Finally, to assess the degree of name-calling in our sample, we searched the tweets in our database for a set of keywords associated with political insults.[79]

To establish the validity of both the toxicity and ideology estimators, we think it is instructive to review some of the tweets in our dataset and their corresponding ideology and toxicity scores. Table 2.6 lists tweets for each topic at both high and low levels of toxicity.[80] We believe that a quick skim of the tweets establishes the face validity of the estimators used in this study.

We find that across all issues and all time periods in our database, the mean toxicity score for all Twitter users was 0.265. This number did not vary with the ideology of the user. There are two points to take away from this result. First, the overall toxicity score is rather low, an encouraging sign for those who may be worried about the tone of political discourse in the United States. We suspect one reason the average toxicity score is low is that when we skim through the content of the tweets in our dataset, we see that many consist of tweets that share links to news articles, a phenomenon that has been documented elsewhere.[81] Second, we do not find that conservatives are more likely to post toxic tweets than liberals are.

TABLE 2.6. Face validity of tweet toxicity measure

| Tweet | Toxicity | Ideology |
|---|---|---|
| Targeting immigrants, imposing tariffs, harming our environment, racism, killing wildlife, KEEP AMERICA GREAT, MY ASS! | 0.953 | −2.326 |
| I have one question. . . . Where do you draw the line for who can marry who or "what" in marriage equality? | 0.091 | 2.054 |
| One just said global warming isn't real because it's so cold. What even? I can't, you're so stupid, I hate you. | 0.966 | −1.405 |
| Man can do as much about Earth's Climate Change as Jupiter's . . . but don't tell a liberal they will pass a Trillion $ Jupiter Aid package! | 0.159 | 2.326 |
| but, she is collecting unemployment benefits, so technically, isn't she paid by the gov't to be a bitchy, stupid troll? | 0.933 | 2.326 |
| It seems to me the only issue is our debt. We can't afford to pay for Medicare Medicaid & social security & yet Rs & D's refuse to address! | 0.106 | 2.326 |
| Obama is the worst President in the history of the United States of America and 51 % of you idiots elected him twice. wake up America! | 0.952 | 2.054 |
| I hear so often: "nothing's gonna change no need to vote". Let GOP have both House & Senate there will be change-none can live with. | 0.074 | −2.326 |
| Are all Americans Stupid or just the fucking Republicans? Yes I said it! How can the Surgeon General's nomination turn into a NRA issue? WTF | 0.953 | −2.326 |
| Do republicans know that when the 2nd amendment was written there were only muskets? Someone should tell them! I did. | 0.129 | −1.341 |
| #DearMrPresident, trumpcare is disgusting,$600 blln gift to rich,higher costs to older n poorest,kill Medicaid,u r worst pres in history | 0.872 | 0.806 |
| Why no mention of the more than 5 million of us who've lost our insurance and can't afford #Obamacare? | 0.116 | 2.326 |
| All these #republican pricks talkingShit about "illegal" immigrants are the 1st ones to take advantage of the cheap labor immigrants provide | 0.764 | −2.326 |
| Why is that Dreamers get access to Congressmen and Congresswoman and their Staff and the Voter does not ? RT Please | 0.071 | 1.476 |

These patterns are replicated when we zero in on name-calling. Our search yielded 277 tweets (2.5 percent of total tweets) that involved name-calling.[82] As with our mean toxicity score, it is perhaps encouraging that the percentage of tweets that used name-calling was not higher. Not surprisingly, the overall toxicity of tweets involving name-calling is high, with a mean of 0.75, a finding that provides further validation of this tool. Our main question, however, was whether conservatives would be more likely to use name-calling than liberals. They were not: 2.7 percent of liberal users in our database posted a tweet that involved name-calling versus 2.4 percent of conservative users.

Like other contemporary scholarship, our research here suggests that the image many of us have of what political discussion is like for most people is not all that accurate.[83] Our findings suggest that the perception that conservatives seek to own the libs may be driven by the attention given to some elites who engage in this behavior, like Donald Trump, but that the behavior is not widespread among ordinary conservative Americans. Of course, we come to this assessment from one analysis of social media behavior, and we recognize that additional examinations of other data sources and other time periods would be valuable.

## Conclusion

One goal of the analysis in this chapter is descriptive, to illustrate actual patterns of political engagement and examine how they compare for liberals and conservatives. Our findings uphold some elements of conventional wisdom (that liberals are more likely to curate ideological bubbles than conservatives) and call into question other elements of conventional wisdom (that conservatives are more provocative and uncivil than liberals). Another goal is to consider whether one side of the ideological divide is doing better than the other when it comes to embodying the requisites of everyday democracy. With the caveats noted earlier regarding how there may be times when avoidance rather than engagement is the more democratic option, we find that conservatives are more likely to follow elites on the other side, are less likely to avoid the other side in their online and in-person interactions, and appear no more likely to seek to provoke when they use Twitter.

And although we might not be quite as optimistic as Tocqueville in his assessment of the public-spiritedness of Americans, we do find a few glimmers of hope in this chapter that we think are important to highlight. While it may be concerning that levels of bubble-sustaining behavior are as high as they are in our survey results, we also found that avoidance is far less common offline than online, and that toxic behavior is not as common as many people probably fear. We also found that watching conservative media, a format with a business model built on fostering anger and antagonism, did not affect any of the measures studied here.

This is not to say that we let conservative media off the hook. Our next chapter provides a deep dive into the media, where we consider how the high level of trust that people have in their chosen media outlets shapes intergroup relations. Part of the perception many people have that political engagement with the other side is necessarily unpleasant surely comes from the types of political discussion they see occurring in the media.[84] At the same time, pollsters and news headlines regularly proclaim, and decry, that Americans' trust in the media is at an all-time low and still declining. In the next chapter, we examine what kind of information about the other side people are getting from the media that they consume. We show that people trust their own media considerably, and that their consumption patterns affect political division asymmetrically.

## CHAPTER THREE

# Racial Resentment and Mass Media

Critical race theory emerged seemingly out of nowhere as a highly visible and controversial political issue in 2021. There was no precipitating event such as an economic downturn or natural disaster to draw attention to this otherwise obscure academic framework. Critical race theory is more than forty years old and until 2021 had elicited little attention outside of the academy. And for good reason: It is rather straightforward in what it argues. The core idea is that racism is the product of institutions and laws, not simply the result of bad people acting in bad ways. For example, discrimination against members of minority groups by banks is systemic, with inequitable lending practices embedded in institutional norms and in law.[1] At this point this thesis is a rather obvious truism.

What changed in 2021 was that Fox Cable News and other conservative outrage outlets began to emphasize critical race theory, often identifying antiracism efforts by local school districts as evidence of "reverse racism" run amok. In the first six months of 2021 (and, not coincidentally, the first six months of the Biden administration), Fox ran somewhere in the neighborhood of two thousand stories on critical race theory. A guest on Fox equated the evil of critical race theory with the ideology of the Ku Klux Klan and white supremacy.[2] Sharing the screen with a large graphic labeled "Anti-White Mania," Fox's Tucker Carlson told viewers that something needed to be done before the United States "became Rwanda."[3] Since television networks can measure the precise response they receive from specific content they generate, it is safe to conclude that Fox's decision to run two thousand stories on critical race theory in the space of six months signaled a powerful audience response.

The seriousness of contentious racial issues offers a sharp contrast to the seemingly simple, everyday task of turning on the television and selecting a program to watch. Sometimes we mindlessly flip channels with the remote, trying to land on something that captures our interest. The search for news-related content is typically habitual: Unlike the case of entertainment, there are just a limited number of networks to which we might gravitate. But even if the first channel number we push is habitual, it is no less a choice. At an abstract level, when we choose news and opinion to watch, we believe we are fulfilling an important obligation of citizenship: to be informed. In the case of the cable networks Fox and MSNBC, news and opinion come wrapped inside of polarizing content.

As we saw in the last chapter, different sectors of the American population react differently to the idea of engaging in polarizing content. Liberals are more likely to retreat, while conservatives are more comfortable with cross-ideological encounters. Here we extend our analysis to consumption of the mass media, turning from active engagement, arguing, and vilifying others online to the more passive experiences of watching cable television and listening to pundits discuss politics.

A starting point in understanding the differences between liberals and conservatives in their consumption of news is in the structure of the media that caters to them. There is no liberal equivalent of conservative talk radio, which has a substantial listening audience and one that is far larger than Fox Cable.[4] As for cable, Fox has a much larger audience than its liberal rival, MSNBC, often drawing twice the viewers for its prime-time lineup. In short, there is a far greater appetite for outrage content on the right than on the left.

Another important line of inquiry is to ask how liberals and conservatives process the information they receive from cable. As Dannagal Young notes, the precise content of political programming on cable reflects "different psychological frameworks of liberalism and conservatism, which account for distinct psychological traits and aesthetic preferences."[5] Political shows on Fox and MSNBC are designed to provoke viewers and to make them angry. This is not simply a by-product of the polarizing content but the essence of the business strategy to attract viewers. Anger generates "stickiness"—the propensity of viewers to keep watching rather than flipping the channel, and to come back the next night for more.[6]

The Trump era has intensified concerns about misinformation and its impact on political attitudes and behavior. There is nothing new about media-generated misinformation; the history of mass media is characterized by different forms of misinformation emerging from different technological advances and changing business practices.[7] Even so, today is different from earlier periods because of the density of businesses that market polarizing and highly inaccurate content, as well for the rapidity with which misinformation careens unimpeded through the internet and on social media.

Polarization is part and parcel of a free society, where citizens can say what they want about their government and about the opposition party. But polarization has increased in recent years, and there is growing worry that it is having a cancerous impact on the body politic. Cable news is not the only reason, of course, but it is often held as the prime example of what is wrong with politics today. The rising anxiety by scholars over President Trump's behavior and the January 6, 2021, attack on the Capitol generated an impassioned and expanding literature on the crisis of democracy. This literature commonly condemns Fox News for undermining democratic norms. In *Four Threats*, Suzanne Mettler and Robert Lieberman conclude, "The ascent of conservative media has generated an angrier public, undermined trust in government, and stimulated hostility toward those in the other party."[8] Steven Levitsky, a coauthor of *How Democracies Die*, points the finger at Fox as well, arguing that a major reason this country has gone off course is that "a fairly large number of Americans no longer believe anything but Fox News."[9] Still, what Fox *causes* and what Fox *reflects* in terms of underlying polarization already present remain points of scholarly contention.

We combine this research on media use with a policy focus on race. The importance of race needs no explanation: no issue has been so central in the political and social development of this country. Beyond its intrinsic importance, however, we use race because our preliminary research showed that the two ideological networks divided sharply on the way racial issues are portrayed. With this early research in mind, we designed the next stage of our work along two lines of inquiry. First, while the corrosive nature of cable television has been well documented, how Fox and MSNBC handle the sensitive issue of race is less clearly understood. In the first half of this chapter we detail in precise terms just how these two ideological networks frame stories dealing with race. What is distinctive about each network's description of racial problems as well as their discussion of underlying causes and solutions? Beyond particular policy areas such as affirmative action or immigration, what is the image of nonwhite Americans that is conveyed to audiences? Our second question asks, what difference does any of this make? As citizens form and re-form their attitudes on race, how does the messaging on Fox and MSNBC affect what they believe?

We draw on our own databases to shed light on these questions. The content of these news networks is shaped by the underlying economics of cable television, and we provide context here before moving to a discussion of race on the two networks.

## The Business of Cable

The media business is characterized by an extraordinary level of competition for the eyes and ears of those who follow the news. The everyday choices of consumers may not elicit a lot of thought when exercised, but these habits reflect underlying values affirmed by repeated viewing of their shows. Such choices as to which media outlets to use as one monitors and understands the news has enormous implications for democracy. Market preferences of ordinary Americans influence not only the presentation of news and opinion but levels of access to media content. It may seem remarkable that the mundane act of people pushing a few buttons on their TV remote shapes a country's media environment. Despite the broad competition across the media world, for those interested in discussion of politics on cable, there is limited choice. There are only three popular news networks: Fox, MSNBC, and CNN. Two other conservative networks, Newsmax and One America News (OAN) had their day in the sun when President Trump, furious at Fox because of its postelection coverage, encouraged his supporters to watch them.[10] Their ratings bump faded over time, though. OAN is no longer carried by any major cable distributors and Newsmax has struggled to gain revenue from its shows. CNN occupies a different space than Fox or MSNBC as it tries to maintain ideological neutrality during most of the day. Only with its prime-time lineup does it veer to the left. Its evening audience is small, the smallest of the three major cable news networks, with each show's nightly audience drawing under a million viewers. MSNBC has no left-leaning cable networks to compete with, though CNN's evening programs are an alternative for liberal viewers.

The ratings for the programs on MSNBC and Fox reveal modest-sized audiences for the prime-time programs. Using ratings for a representative night in April of 2024, Fox's prime-time lineup had audiences of 2.0 million for Laura Ingraham (7:00 p.m.), 2.6 million for Jesse Watters (8:00), 2.3 million for Sean Hannity (9:00), and 2.2 million for Greg Gutfeld (10:00). MSNBC's audience was smaller, and the network has suffered from the reduced role of its star, Rachel Maddow. The comparable audience figures were 1.2 million for Joy Reid (7:00 p.m.), 1.3 million for Chris Hayes (8:00), 1.2 million for Alex Wagner (9:00), and 1.5 million for Lawrence O'Donnell (10:00).[11]

The nightly network news shows on broadcast TV on ABC, NBC, and CBS (all at 6:30 p.m. Eastern time) provide an interesting basis of comparison. These shows are widely thought of as media dinosaurs, not nearly as central to the daily provision of news as in their heyday when Walter Cronkite, along with Chet Huntley and David Brinkley, ruled the airwaves. Although they have declined in popularity since then, they still maintain robust audiences. The three broadcasts combined (at around the same time period as the audience figures for cable listed above), averaged around eighteen million viewers nightly.[12]

A different picture of cable emerges when we switch from the size of individual program audiences to the public's more general exposure to the cable news networks. In our 2018 CES module, respondents were shown a list of eleven media outlets or programs and asked if they had "watched, listened to, or read" any programming from each of them over the past month (table 3.1). Asking respondents to recall what they watched over a month's time is certainly subject to the imperfections of memory, but even with the error term, the magnitude of the exposure to cable news is impressive. While only a tiny percentage of the adult population is watching an evening political talk show at any one time, 40 percent of the population reported that they viewed Fox over the past month, while 32 percent said the same for MSNBC. Using a different set of measures, David Broockman and Joshua Kalla determine that one in seven Americans watch eight hours or more of partisan TV in a month.[13]

More broadly, these data demonstrate that at least a third of respondents indicate some level of exposure over the past month to all sources save NPR and the two talk radio shows. Clearly, the broader population is not ensconced in a narrow echo chamber. In a sophisticated analysis of Americans' media diet, Andrew Guess concluded that "most people are not habitual partisan news consumers."[14] As for the two cable channels, though, relatively few Fox viewers watch MSNBC and vice versa.

How do we reconcile the modest nightly audiences for cable programming with aggregate levels of exposure that are comparable to those of the nation's leading mainstream media? Beyond the obvious methodological difference

TABLE 3.1. The media diet of CES respondents

|  | Yes (%) |
| --- | --- |
| Fox Cable | 40.0 |
| MSNBC | 32.2 |
| CNN | 44.9 |
| CBS | 35.3 |
| NBC | 36.4 |
| ABC | 33.7 |
| Rush Limbaugh | 14.3 |
| NPR | 24.8 |
| *New York Times* | 33.7 |
| *Washington Post* | 33.1 |
| Sean Hannity (radio) | 16.6 |

Source: 2018 CES.

Note: Survey question: "Please indicate if you have watched, listened to, or read any of the following in the past month." $N = 856$.

of pooling a month's watching over a single night's program, these figures suggest that a good chunk of the audience for cable is fleeting, with people watching only occasionally. The monthly figure also incorporates channel flippers, who may watch a segment here and there but are not reliable viewers. The risk of channel flipping also explains why cable news programs proceed for twenty minutes or more before the first commercial break. Viewers may also gain exposure from seeing clips on YouTube, Facebook, and other websites. The wording of our survey question did not distinguish how people watched. It is also worth pointing out that our data show that over one-third of respondents continued to tune into broadcast networks.

Perhaps even more revealing are responses to questions we asked about the trust and accuracy of the media. Trust in media facilitates everyday democracy: It allows users to make habitual choices and not think about how reliable their sources are. If people are to use daily practices to hone their ability to hold leaders accountable, their media consumption habits and the trust they place in journalists and media outlets are surely relevant. Respondents were asked for each of the eleven media sources, "Please indicate how much you **trust** each of the following" and "Please indicate how **accurate** you think each of the following is" (table 3.2). Disaggregated by

TABLE 3.2. Belief in the trust and accuracy of media sources

| | TRUST A LOT + TRUST SOME (%) | | VERY ACCURATE + SOMEWHAT ACCURATE (%) | |
|---|---|---|---|---|
| | Used in the past month | Did not use in the past month | Used in the past month | Did not use in the past month |
| Fox Cable | 75.2 | 19.9 | 77.7 | 25.8 |
| MSNBC | 83.9 | 29.2 | 87.5 | 37.8 |
| CNN | 74.4 | 26.6 | 81.9 | 33.3 |
| CBS | 83.6 | 42.4 | 87.1 | 51.9 |
| NBC | 81.4 | 40.1 | 85.5 | 48.4 |
| ABC | 78.2 | 43.5 | 84.8 | 51.2 |
| Rush Limbaugh | 88.1 | 19.7 | 89.2 | 26.0 |
| NPR | 87.2 | 41.2 | 89.2 | 52.6 |
| *New York Times* | 81.5 | 36.5 | 86.2 | 46.4 |
| *Washington Post* | 84.5 | 37.9 | 87.1 | 44.1 |
| Sean Hannity (radio) | 88.6 | 20.2 | 89.2 | 27.2 |

Source: 2018 CES.

Note: Survey questions: "Please indicate how much you **trust** each of the following" and "Please indicate how **accurate** you think each of the following is." $N = 856$.

users and nonusers, the pattern is one of enormous trust in the media that respondents utilize. Eight of the eleven sources are trusted by more than 80 percent of their users, including network news. Our data indicate that mainstream news shows, though treated as an anachronism in today's fragmented media environment, are still both consumed and highly trusted by many Americans. Among those who do not read, watch, or listen, both the trust and accuracy scores are considerably lower. These patterns stand in stark contrast to Americans' reliably harsh criticism of the media in general.[15] A recent national survey showed that only 36 percent of respondents say they have "a great deal" or "a fair amount" of confidence in the mass media.[16] Americans seem to believe that the *other* media—the media that they do not use—is the problem, not the media they use, which they trust greatly.

These patterns regarding trust and accuracy speak loudly to the frustration with the growing and menacing problem of misinformation. In this context, the declining readership of newspapers and the declining number of newspapers themselves are particularly alarming, while sources spreading conspiracy theories and outright lies grows. The problem illustrated by tables 3.1 and 3.2 seems to be less that people do not trust mainstream media—a common complaint—but that too many do not engage with it.

Cable news has a devoted following, and its consumer support is not out of line with how people judge other media. Unfortunately, cable news erodes broader consumer confidence because it tells viewers that much of the other media is biased and puts politics above truth and is therefore not to be trusted. When people feel they cannot trust information coming from major media outlets, their ability to hold leaders accountable suffers. Because holding leaders accountable is one of the primary functions of citizens in a democracy, we believe that media consumption choices, and the consequences of such choices, are important components of everyday democracy.

Cable's buoyancy is all the more remarkable given that it is a rather staid vehicle in an era of much more dynamic and interactive media. The prime-time shows on Fox and MSNBC rarely venture beyond two or more people sitting still and talking for an extended period. Cable news is also an industry that succeeds in spite of its demographics, with both Fox and MSNBC attracting an audience with a median age of around seventy.[17] The sweet spot for advertisers is viewers in the twenty-five-to-fifty-four age bracket, because this population has high consumer needs, including home furnishings, cars, clothes, and baby goods. The primary reason the networks prosper in spite of their aging viewers is that they receive lucrative carriage fees from local cable vendors. Cable providers, such as Verizon or Comcast, must pay the networks they carry a per capita fee each month for each residence receiving their service. These fees are passed along in the charge for basic cable, the minimum service that all cable customers must purchase. Thus, all who choose to receive cable must pay for Fox, CNN, and MSNBC, even if they never watch them.[18]

## Race Coverage

To gain a better understanding of how race is covered, presented, and analyzed by cable programs, we undertook our own viewing of them. During the period from mid-September 2018 to mid-September 2019, we selected a randomized sample of six prime-time shows on Fox and MSNBC: *Tucker Carlson Tonight, Hannity*, and *The Ingraham Angle* on Fox, and *All In with Chris Hayes, The Rachel Maddow Show*, and *The Last Word with Lawrence O'Donnell* on MSNBC. This Prime Time Cable TV Data Set consists of seventy-eight one-hour shows, though the units of analysis in this study were program segments, not entire shows. A segment was defined as the time between commercial breaks, and the total number of segments in these seventy-eight episodes was 330, an average of a little over four per show.[19]

### NARRATIVES

At the center of our analysis was an attempt to code each segment as to its narrative arc. Narratives are stories, and storytelling is as old as humanity: Cave paintings, tapestries, and hieroglyphics on temple walls all tell stories. We do not pretend to understand the neuroscience, but narratives fit the way our brains work. Narratives offer order in a complex set of events.[20] The narrative form contrasts sharply with the presentation by the evening network broadcast news shows, which contain only about twenty-one minutes of content and run video-oriented stories in frenetic succession. The hourlong cable shows can tell stories at length, offering their hosts' interpretation and a resolution in terms of truth triumphing over lies.

The narratives in cable stories typically focus on villains. In these dramas, one or more leaders on the other side are doing something that is dangerous or vile (or both). Scholarship on political attitudes provides considerable insight into why these types of narratives succeed. In this highly polarized era, much of the passion of politics is directed antagonistically toward perceived enemies. This is "affective polarization," which Shanto Iyengar and colleagues describe as politics where the "Democrats and Republicans both say that the other party's members are hypocritical, selfish, and close-minded."[21] One reason for such polarization is an increasing tendency among Americans toward identifying with a kindred social grouping and remaining apart from those outside their group.[22] Cable programming feeds affective polarization by its lavish attention to those their viewers hate.

In this vein, on Fox the Democratic Congresswoman Ilhan Omar does not just represent liberalism gone bad; indeed, she is portrayed as embodying the threat of Sharia law. On MSNBC, right-wing domestic terrorism is said to be the new normal. Extreme rhetoric and outsized warnings form the language of cable. One difference with cable in comparison to other forms of storytelling, such as movies or folk tales, is that there is not much emphasis on heroes who will be able to save us from the evil abyss. Cable is decidedly downbeat, and to call attention to heroes suggests that everything will be okay in the end. That is not a good story line when you are trying to convince viewers that Armageddon is nigh. Consequently, the emphasis is on villains, who are far more compelling than virtuous counterparts. In the world of cable news, there is not a Batman for every Joker.

## MINORITY GROUP MEMBERS AS VILLAINS

Since these six shows offer political commentary rather than covering the news, there should be no expectation that the topics addressed each night follow what would be seen on the evening broadcast news or in that day's newspaper. To document what is covered by these shows, one part of our coding scheme identified the primary policy content at the center of each story. A story with policy content was defined as those discussing matters concretely before government. The results may seem surprising: Relatively few segments are devoted to discussion of any policy. Only about a quarter of stories on both networks involve policies being considered by one of the branches of government (table 3.3). For example, despite the centrality of abortion in American politics, only a single Fox story was devoted to this issue, and none were aired by MSNBC. Fox ran no stories on health care, despite the Trump administration's effort to terminate the Affordable Care Act. MSNBC broadcast just two stories on health care during this entire year of our research.

If policy was generally ignored, what were these segments about? In a word, "politics." Such stories were mostly devoted to campaigns, elections, media coverage, the repulsiveness of various politicians, and President Trump's performance. The underlying focus of many such stories was to discredit the other side of the political spectrum. This content is the essence of affective polarization, demonizing the opposition and emphasizing that they are a grave and imminent threat to our political system. There are ideological claims made on these shows, to be sure: Conservatives do not

TABLE 3.3. Issue coverage on Fox and MSNBC

|  | Fox (%) | MSNBC (%) |
| --- | --- | --- |
| Health care | 0.0 | 1.3 |
| Abortion | 0.7 | 0.0 |
| Climate change/environment | 1.4 | 1.3 |
| Foreign policy | 2.0 | 5.8 |
| Economics/foreign trade | 1.4 | 0.6 |
| Immigration | 12.2 | 8.4 |
| Other policy related | 4.8 | 8.4 |
| Not policy related | 77.6 | 74.0 |
| Total | 100.1 | 99.8 |
| Segments | ($N = 147$) | ($N = 154$) |

Source: Prime Time Cable TV Data Set.

Note: Percentages may not total 100.0 owing to rounding.

believe in democracy, liberals are socialists, and so on. Far more provocative, though, are stories about qualities of character. In 54 percent of the segments on MSNBC, either a host or a guest said that those on the other side are liars. This term was only slightly less popular on Fox (46 percent). And by the standards of cable, "liar" is far from the worst insult.

Within this context, the two networks differ sharply in how they cover race. As table 3.3 shows, immigration, which on cable almost always has a racial emphasis, is the only policy area related to race to receive at least a modicum of coverage on the two networks. But race is frequently front and center in Fox's coverage of political (nonpolicy) stories. The race-related stories in the Fox sample were characterized by an emphasis on villainous opponents, irrational behavior of subjects, and events and trends that appear to be spiraling out of control. The network's underlying strategy on race is to stoke viewers' resentment of racial and ethnic minority groups in America and of immigrants trying to get into America. This pattern fits a traditional interpretation of racial attitudes of poorly educated white Americans, one that argues that they are resentful of nonwhite people because they fear a loss of their own status.[23] Fox communicates that Black and Hispanic Americans are unfit as citizens because they act irresponsibly, endangering the country. The network thus raises the status of its own viewers—people it champions as exemplary citizens embodying the spirit of the real America.

The coding recorded the name, race, gender, and position of villains. The vast majority of villains were current or former government officeholders or other officials, while those outside of government, such as journalists, social media figures, or advocacy leaders, were less frequent targets. Above all else, what stood out in these segments is how often nonwhite individuals are the villains on Fox. Our notations identified, in order of appearance in a segment, up to three villains. On Fox, nonwhite individuals were villains between 38 and 46 percent of the time (fig. 3.1). On MSNBC, the first mentioned villain is a person of color just a little over 1 percent of the time; this figure grows only a bit for the second and third featured villain.

Beneath these summary numbers, who are the minority figures that Fox goes after? By and large, those who appear in these stories were not minority politicians who had real responsibility in the Congress at the time, such as Karen Bass, Cory Booker, Jim Clyburn, Elijah Cummings, John Lewis, or Hakeem Jeffries. There was not a single story that featured any of these legislators. Instead, there was an unrelenting focus on three newly elected Democratic members of the House: Alexandria Ocasio-Cortez, Ilhan Omar, and Rashida Tlaib. These congresswomen were constantly mocked, ridiculed, and portrayed as fools. Ocasio-Cortez, for example, was called an "idiotic wind bag" who should be told "to be quiet and take a seat."[24]

The broader stories themselves were relentlessly negative and ominous. The most common theme in segments involving minority groups was the

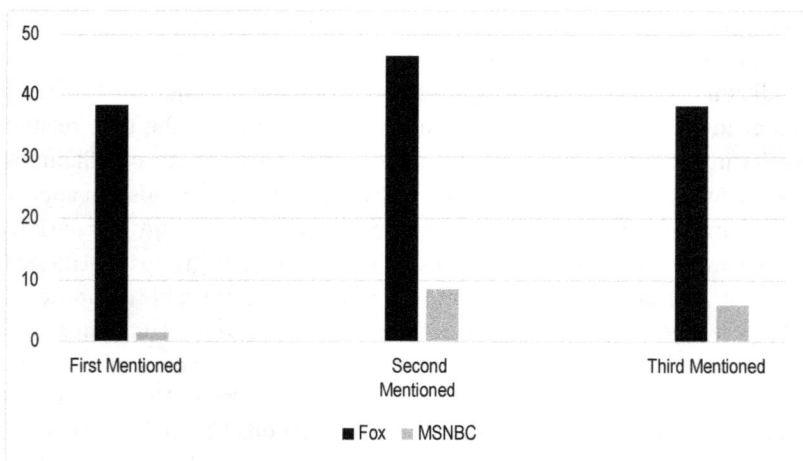

FIGURE 3.1. Fox villains are disproportionately minority

Source: Prime Time Cable TV Data Set

Note: Percentage minority. $N$ = 330 segments.

effort of people from Central and South America to cross the southern border of the United States. Fox's stories emphasized that there was a large criminal element among the "caravans" of people who were walking north in hopes of entering the country. When the Trump White House forced these would-be immigrants to stay on the Mexican side of the border before some were eventually processed, the stories emphasized that this homeless horde was responsible for a great deal of crime. Another line of stories relating to minority groups on Fox described disorder in cities, emphasizing crime and homelessness. One gruesome story on *The Ingraham Angle* used camera footage showing people passed out on the street, disheveled vagabonds, and shabby tent camps. For good measure, Ingraham added that there was human feces on the street.[25]

One reason there are few minority villains in MSNBC stories is because more often than not (61 percent), President Trump was the first villain. Also, there were not many people of color in the administration during this time, though there were a few, such as Ben Carson (Secretary of Housing and Urban Development) and Elaine Chao (Secretary of Labor), for example, whom liberals would have enjoyed seeing skewered. Yet, given MSNBC's demographically diverse audience, one may wonder whether its instincts are not to go after people of color unless a story is too big to ignore. MSNBC's audience is 67 percent white, 24 percent Black, and 9 percent other. Fox does not have to be concerned about offending minority viewers because it hardly has any. Its audience is 94 percent white, 1 percent Black, and 5 percent other.[26] Not coincidentally, the demographic composition of the two political parties is reflected in these network choices on content. When MSNBC does run a story involving race, invariably it is highly sympathetic. For example, when children were separated from their parents at the southern border by US border patrol officers, MSNBC responded indignantly with extensive coverage and visuals of toddlers sobbing and of holding pens described as "cages."

Analysis of the gender of villains showed that minority women were particular targets on Fox. Just under half of all villains on Fox were female, and half of those were women of color. It is hard to know what the precise baseline would be for proportionate representation of villains, but leadership of liberals in and out of government is disproportionately male. In work published elsewhere, we found that the language used to describe minority women on Fox's programming was harsher than that used for male villains.[27] The overall finding is that, more than any other target group, women of color were dehumanized and subjected to crude, hostile descriptions.

## Advertisements

Given the language used by Fox hosts to describe those they dislike, one might wonder why American businesses would run commercials on the network. When Tucker Carlson called Senator Tammy Duckworth, a woman of color who lost both her legs in the Iraq War, a "moron," why would a sponsor want to find itself subject to an inquiry as to why it financially supports such a show?[28] Periodically, liberal advocacy groups like Media Matters or Color of Change do attack Fox sponsors and launch boycotts of specified advertisers. Boycotts are not an idle threat in this age of social media, where consumer campaigns can be initiated with little direct cost.

Over time, various tirades by Fox hosts have, in fact, driven sponsors with brand names off the network. After Carlson savaged Black Lives Matter and called demonstrators "criminal mobs," sponsors such as Disney, Nordic Track, T-Mobile, and Sandals, all of which are prominent brands, pulled their ads from the show.[29] We found in our viewing of the three prime-time Fox programs that the vast majority of sponsors were companies with low brand recognition, and many lacked a brick-and-mortar presence, relying on direct-to-consumer sales. During this period of study, a disproportionate amount of overall advertising on Fox's evening programs came from My Pillow, the company headed by the conspiracy theorist Mike Lindell.

Why do Fox producers, executives, and its board continue to permit such language and themes in their shows when it costs them significant advertising revenue? In an extremely competitive environment, with typical cable households having close to two hundred channels to choose from, standing out from the pack has obvious benefits. Fox's outrage strategy—angering viewers by making them furious with the opposing side—forms the basis of its marketing approach. An outrage approach incentivizes hosts to be ever more outrageous so as to make the audience believe that they will not back down and will tell the truth no matter the consequences.[30] After Carlson replaced Bill O'Reilly, who was pushed off the air owing to charges of sexual harassment, he built his audience by becoming ever more controversial and not being inhibited by advertiser desertions. In the wake of Carlson's firing and Fox's payment of $787.5 million to settle a defamation lawsuit brought by Dominion Voting Systems, Jesse Watters, his replacement, has been more temperate, if still provocative.

If it were not for the carriage fees, the need for more advertising revenue would be imperative for Fox. The three major cable networks are in the enviable position of having landed first in the news space as cable services began to emerge. Although there have been continuing calls for cable vendors to offer à la carte menus for customers to choose from instead of packages of channels, choices of cable bundles continue to be the norm. Once these three networks gained their position in the cable spectrum, cable vendors had no interest in adding more news networks, as that would require them to pay additional carriage fees. Carriage fees are passed on to customers, and resistance to price increases has only grown with the rise of YouTube and other alternatives to cable television. Still, there is advertising on Fox, and in the aggregate it provides substantial revenue. Income from ads across Fox Corporation amounted to around $1.1 billion in 2022.[31]

Although it is harsh in its criticism of Republicans and conservatives, MSNBC is more temperate in its language. As noted above, it typically trails Fox in audience size by a significant magnitude, though the Trump years drove viewership almost as high as Fox's. No less an expert on cable ratings than Fox's CEO, Lachlan Murdoch, noted that MSNBC's viewership went up "because they were the loyal opposition."[32] Murdoch's analysis is right on target: For liberals, the MSNBC hosts and especially Rachel Maddow were the most visible and important voices standing in strident opposition to Donald Trump. They were far more articulate and powerful critics of Trump than the bland Democratic congressional leadership. In the last year of the Trump administration, the net advertising earnings for MSNBC amounted to $720 million.[33] After Biden succeeded Trump in office, ratings slid considerably for the network; it was no longer the opposition, and Biden was pretty bland copy in comparison to Trump. Its ad revenue fell sharply to $530 million in 2022.[34]

## Impact

The incessant drumbeat of racially antagonistic content on Fox can be criticized for its insensitivity, its incivility, and, above all else, its sheer prejudice. Unfortunately, norms of what people believe is acceptable to say in public regarding race have evolved in recent years, and more today think it is acceptable to express their racial animosity in public.[35] As Donald Trump demonstrated, what used to be a dog whistle has become a bullhorn. His open racial animosity in 2016 paid dividends: Voters' racial attitudes were key in moving votes among those who were swayable.[36]

While we can bemoan the corrosive impact of cable on the national conversation, its ultimate impact remains unclear. In the simplest terms, people who watch Fox are conservative, and people who watch MSNBC are liberal. Thus, there is a powerful self-selection bias in who watches cable.[37] This presents a serious challenge to researchers who would like to determine whether the content on cable truly influences viewers or, alternatively, whether it merely offers confirmation of beliefs already held.

To illustrate the starkness of the ideological divide between those who watch Fox and those who watch MSNBC, we draw on a basic question about racial attitudes from the 2020 CES. Respondents were asked whether they agreed with the statement "White people in the U.S. have certain advantages because of the color of their skin." As shown in figure 3.2, close to nine out of ten of those who watched MSNBC agreed with this view of race in America. CNN viewers were only slightly less likely to agree with the statement. In contrast, only 24 percent of Fox viewers believe that white people have inherent advantages in American society because of their race.

Although it surely comes as no surprise that Fox viewers and MSNBC viewers see the world differently, the enormous divide on their respective attitudes on racial discrimination is still striking. These two sets of people see American society as fundamentally different, with opposite views of the relationship between race and life's opportunities. It is not plausible that watching different cable channels in and of itself created such a large gap between these two sets of viewers. At the same time, it should not be assumed that cable watching had no impact on attitudes. Perhaps beyond the selection bias in the choice of cable stations by those who already have

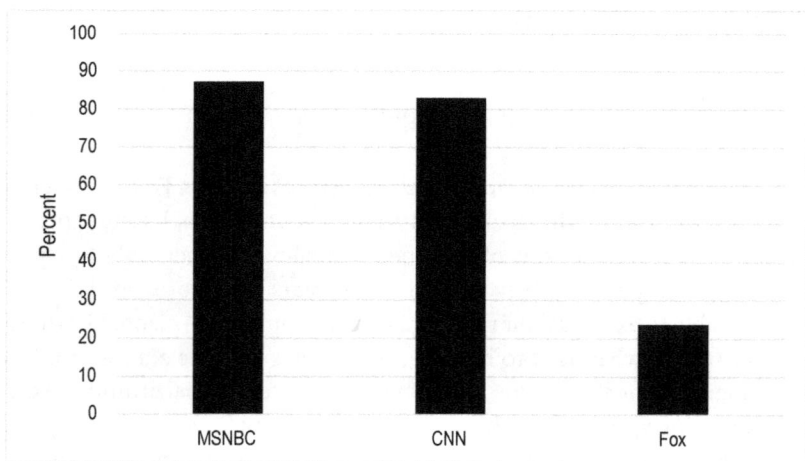

FIGURE 3.2. Viewers' attitudes toward white privilege

Source: 2020 CES

Note: Percentage who strongly agree or somewhat agree with the statement "White people in the U.S. have certain advantages because of the color of their skin." $N = 360$.

strong opinions, there are some respondents who became firmer in their beliefs than before they started watching. For example, a liberal person might have responded that they were in "somewhat" agreement with the statement on race, but after watching Rachel Maddow for a year, they might move into the "strongly agree" camp. And those who were already "strongly agree" could have become even stronger in their agreement.

The hosts of cable programs are watched because viewers believe they have important things to say and offer a unique perspective on politics. The dynamic of the programs is that of a confidence game, where hosts engage viewers by flattering them as being those who actually understand what's going on. The hosts build a sense of intimacy and present themselves as "relatable, reliable friends."[38] Many who watch become passionate fans, feeling that they are part of a community, one that is under attack from the barbarians at the gate. The goal of hosts in this confidence game is to make watching TV something more than a casual experience—to shape the hour into an intense encounter. And, again, the way to accomplish that is by making people angry. Anger can condition a range of political attitudes and values. As Steven Webster notes, "The growth in anger within the American electorate has reshaped political behavior by increasing partisan loyalty and decreasing citizens' affective evaluations of the opposing party."[39]

Can anger move people beyond what might be regarded as their starting point before exposure? A number of scholars have tried to determine empirically whether cable watching has an impact above and beyond confirming existing beliefs. Kevin Arceneaux and Martin Johnson utilized an experimental design where in lab participants were exposed to different treatments in what they watched. They conclude that cable watching had no effect in comparison to control groups.[40] Matthew Levendusky approached the same question and also used a clever experimental design to measure the effect of cable. But his findings differ: he determined that while cable did not change people's minds, it did polarize some of them further.[41]

A close reading of these two books does not reveal an obvious reason why they reach contrary conclusions about the impact. Experimental designs are attractive to researchers because they facilitate analysis of cause and effect; thus, they provide an opportunity to test out hypotheses by holding the overall environment constant while manipulating one or more variables. But therein lies a problem for analyzing the effect of cable television watching. What goes on in a lab does not reflect how people actually watch television in the real world. Viewers in their normal environment will not be hyperfocused on sifting one slice of information while knowing that they will have to answer some questions after exposure to the clips provided to them. And at any given time a cable channel's actual viewing audience will include regular watchers, occasional viewers, and those flipping channels. This mix of attention spans and ideological intensities is the true face of cable audiences.[42]

## Racial Resentment

Despite their rigor, it is clear that lab experiments are limited in what they can tell us about the impact of cable on political attitudes. One alternative is to use survey research, and here we use questions from the 2018 CES to analyze the relationship of cable viewing and political attitudes. The questions about what media sources respondents utilized, featured in tables 3.1 and 3.2, are meant to draw out viewers of Fox and MSNBC. Surveying responses on racial attitudes has its challenges because of the sensitivity of the topic, and to reduce the idiosyncrasies that accompany the response to any one survey question, we rely here on a battery of questions in the CES on race. One qualification is that these questions ask about attitudes toward Black people, so generalizations do not apply to all people of color. There are many ways to measure racial attitudes, but Josh Pasek and Kathleen Hall Jamieson found in their study of race and the 2020 election that "no matter how such attitudes are assessed, they remain a central cleavage in American political life."[43]

Specifically, the questions we utilized asked about personal responsibility. Do Black people not work hard enough? Are they responsible for not doing more to better themselves? Or has racial discrimination held them back? Respondents were asked to agree or disagree with these four different statements:

1.  Irish, Italians, Jewish and many other minorities overcame prejudice and worked their way up. Blacks should do the same without any special favors.
2.  Generations of slavery and discrimination have created conditions that make it difficult for Blacks to work their way out of the lower class.
3.  Over the past few years, Blacks have gotten less than they deserve.
4.  It's really a matter of some people not trying hard enough; if Blacks would only try harder they could be just as well off as whites.

For statistical purposes these four items were combined into a single scale. In the regression in table 3.4, a positive coefficient indicates support for the less charitable view toward Black people (they do not merit any favors, have not been held back by a legacy of slavery and discrimination,

TABLE 3.4. Impact of consuming Fox and MSNBC on racial resentment

| | Liberals | Conservatives | Moderates |
|---|---|---|---|
| Watching MSNBC | −0.371*** | | −1.023*** |
| | (0.111) | | (0.143) |
| Watching Fox | | 0.252* | 0.533*** |
| | | (0.106) | (0.144) |
| Education | −0.168*** | −0.104*** | −0.104*** |
| | (0.037) | (0.031) | (0.048) |
| Age | 0.000 | 0.001 | 0.008* |
| | (0.003) | (0.003) | (0.004) |
| White | −0.105 | 0.277* | 0.450** |
| | (0.122) | (0.134) | (0.145) |
| Constant | 2.915*** | 3.897*** | 2.868*** |
| | (0.212) | (0.236) | (0.297) |
| $N$ | 248 | 295 | 225 |
| $R^2$ | 0.131 | 0.075 | 0.305 |

Source: 2018 CES.

Note: Standard errors in parentheses.

*$p \leq .05$; **$p \leq .01$; ***$p \leq .001$.

have not gotten less than they deserve, and have not worked hard enough). A negative coefficient indicates the opposite point of view. For those in the liberal camp, we calculate associations with those who watch MSNBC. And for conservatives, the analysis focuses on the effect of watching Fox (there were too few liberal respondents who watch Fox and too few conservatives who watch MSNBC to study, so those cells in table 3.4 are blank).

It is unsurprising that liberals who watch MSNBC and conservatives who watch Fox hold views in line with their general ideological leanings, though it is certainly noteworthy that the media choices explain heterogeneity in racial attitudes *within* ideological groupings. Along these lines, the findings for moderates are also revealing. The attitude of moderates who say they watch MSNBC is in line with support for Black people, while those moderates who watch Fox are more likely to believe that Black people are to blame for their lack of progress. That these respondents designate themselves as moderates does not mean there is no selection bias at work here. They still had to make a conscious decision to watch a program, and they are not political tabulae rasae when they hold the TV remote in their hand. The comparison with the ideologues on both sides suggests, however, that there is something more at work than self-selection. The statistical relationships are strong and notably greater than the ones for the ideologues.

Other researchers differ on the impact of partisan media. Some believe that it has little or no impact given the selection bias of who chooses to watch it. For those who are strong partisans, watching ideological cable news offers confirmation of already-held beliefs.[44] But given the size of the audience for the cable news networks, a modest exposure effect from viewing content that is not in line with one's normal way of thinking is of consequence. Broockman and Kalla find that exposure to content that is not in line with content of the ideological networks can influence views. Their experiment incentivizing viewers to watch a channel on the other side of the ideological spectrum demonstrates that a wider range of exposure can overcome motivated reasoning.[45] But outside of experiments, any real-world impact of cable on attitudes is likely to come from moderates who are not wedded to any one channel.

In contrast to the different conclusions of academic researchers, cable producers have a high degree of certainty regarding what works in terms of audience response. Through focus groups, electronic monitoring of viewers' physical reaction, real-time viewership levels that are monitored minute by minute, and overall program ratings, producers and their analytical teams determine what topics, frames, and language are most effective at maintaining audience interest. Their conclusion, clearly, is that polarizing content works really well, and for Fox nothing is more polarizing than race.

## Conclusion

We place cable TV watching within a group of behaviors that are modern-day habits of the heart. Viewers' habitual choices bring them news and opinion, and while this exercise of everyday democracy may seem rather passive, it is one that has important implications for the way we understand the political world around us. We usually read Tocqueville for his flattering view of American democracy and his enthusiasm about the American spirit. But some habits of the heart reflect underlying values that work against the harmony he chronicled in *Democracy in America*. Cable news programs reinforce our existing beliefs, likely hardening them, and may also misinform us, as content is shaped not by standards of journalistic neutrality but by marketing considerations.

Measuring just how we might be influenced is another matter. Assessing the impact of cable on political attitudes has no shortage of methodological complications, and no one study is widely accepted by media scholars as baseline data. Although we do not believe we have provided the definitive analysis of the influence of cable, there are several findings that stand out as central and are strongly supported by our research and that of others. A starting point is to acknowledge that while this genre of research compares Fox with MSNBC, their commonality is limited. To be sure, both networks offer polarizing content aimed at provoking anger in their viewers. But Fox has far different boundaries when it comes to what constitutes acceptable language and narratives.

Fox's marketing strategy is to play on the racial antagonism of many of its core viewers. Nothing was more evident during our year of watching cable than Fox's relentless negativity toward people of color. This hostility was not manifested in an occasional story; rather, it was a constant drumbeat. When Tucker Carlson said immigrants make "our own country poor and dirtier," and the network did not reprimand him, his message was effectively sanctioned by the corporation.[46] There are no time series data that we are aware of on Fox and race, but what is clear from earlier studies is that Fox's harsh treatment of minorities is nothing new.[47] We also know that Fox has long been fully trusted by conservatives, who believe it is the one news source that tells them the truth about politics.[48] There is no equivalent of this crude racism on MSNBC. The liberal network mocks conservatives, questions their motives, and even calls their intelligence into question, but such talk still remains within the norms of conventional, if contentious, political rhetoric.

Measurements of the impact of cable are compromised by the selection bias of who chooses to watch each network. As demonstrated in figure 3.2, this bias is strong. Showing a film clip or a printed story to subjects in a lab setting does not correspond to the way people actually watch cable news and process its content. Its most loyal audience watches a favorite program on a habitual basis, many nights a week, and may tune into other programs on this network at other times as well. The sheer repetition of themes, frames, and language has an impact far beyond that of a one-shot exposure. And repetition is the product of internal analytics documenting what the audience response is to specific content.

Cable news networks operate under an unusual business model in which they receive capitation fees while other competitors are effectively frozen out of basic cable packages. This arrangement gives Fox, MSNBC, and CNN levels of profitability that they would not be able to achieve if they were subjected to à la carte purchasing of each cable channel by consumers. Fox and MSNBC make money with modest audiences, essentially curated for their strong ideological orientations. The hosts of these networks' programs understand that the trust of their audiences is key to maintaining their popularity. Their impressive success at this—recall table 3.2 on trust and accuracy—is maintained by their personal manner and by their understanding of how language and the framing of content keeps people watching. *Hosts and networks are in the polarization business*, and they have every incentive to keep generating the material that pushes people's buttons.

For Fox, the biggest button to push is race. The differences between conservatives and liberals that we analyze throughout this book are at their starkest when it comes to attitudes on race. And these differences are exaggerated by looking at Fox and MSNBC viewers, since they hold more intense and more ideological views than the general populations of conservatives and liberals. Fox pushes race because Fox viewers feel strongly about race. Fox hosts and their guests "teach" viewers what is acceptable to say about minority groups in America, and unfortunately, those lessons are ones of intolerance. One of the consequences, says Sydnor, is that "incivility breeds incivility." She adds, "As citizens see name-calling and vitriol as part and parcel of elite political communication, they are more likely to use it themselves."[49]

It is beyond the scope of our research to assess how cable may influence the political agenda or the decisions policymakers reach in response to issues receiving a high degree of sustained attention on cable. As with the case of critical race theory, discussed at the outset of this chapter, both agendas and public opinion were sharply influenced by Fox's relentless coverage. Critical race theory was not a political issue prior to this coverage by Fox and other conservative outrage outlets. And soon discussion on cable turned into legislation restricting what could be covered in public schools and colleges, most notably in Florida and Texas.

These larger impacts call to mind some of the earliest social science research on media. The two-step flow of communications hypothesized that media could influence political elites, who would then magnify that impact by using the frames from coverage in their communications with constituents.[50] Fox is particularly successful at generating coverage of its shows by mainstream media. Leading newspapers and political websites frequently run stories on highly controversial statements by Fox hosts. Any regular reader of *The Washington Post*, for example, knows that the columnist Erik Wemple continually runs pieces on something a Fox host said that was racist or ignorant or insensitive or all of the above. Websites such as Mediaite and Media Matters are essentially businesses devoted to telling liberals about what offensive things Fox hosts are saying.[51] Fox, the network itself, is news.

We also wondered whether the differences between conservatives and liberals we found in chapter 2 would carry over into the behavior we examined in this chapter. Recall that in chapter 2 we demonstrated that conservatives are more willing to talk to those on the other side than are liberals, both online and off. A common concern about cable television and political media in general is that idealogues on each side live in a "bubble"—a self-imposed media diet restricted to outlets that are in line with their own views. We do not measure bubble behavior of this sort directly in this chapter, though we did find that liberals generally do not watch Fox and conservatives generally do not watch MSNBC. The Pew Research Center, however, has measured the degree to which people exist in a media bubble, and its research shows that an equal number of Republicans and Democrats tend to restrict themselves to partisan media they agree with.[52]

How might we explain what appears to be different patterns between interpersonal interaction on social media and general media consumption? In terms of tweeting versus watching cable news networks, what is probably most significant is that consumers in each cohort come from very different populations. Only 7 percent of those who use X (Twitter) are fifty years old or older.[53] As we have noted here, cable viewers are a geriatric population: The median age for both liberal and conservative cable viewers is around seventy. The interactions we consider in chapter 2 and the media consumption patterns we consider in this chapter are dramatically different in their manner of engagement. Someone on a social media platform is actively engaged, moving through their feed and possibly firing off a post. Posting can be quite impulsive and can be completed quickly. Watching cable news is passive: A viewer can sit on the couch without any active interaction with the medium. One literally does not have to lift a finger until it is time to turn the TV off or change the channel. If a viewer wants to send a clip from the program they are watching that they think a friend or family member might like (or hate), they have to go to a website such as YouTube or that of the network, find the correct clip (which may not be up until later after the program has aired), access it, attach the address to an email, text, or social media account, and then send or post it. In short, it takes some work. The larger point is that in today's world the term "media" covers a huge variety of formats, with widely varying levels of active engagement. Behavior related to one medium may be wholly unrelated to behavior in another. Factors we discuss in chapter 2, such as the prevalence of anger in conservative outlets and reactions to perceptions of loss, likely contribute to the different ways that liberals and conservatives engage in the active interactions considered in chapter 2 but may be less relevant when it comes to more passive forms of media consumption.

Finally, a recurring theme on Fox is that to compromise with the other side is to abandon principle and play politics as usual. It is something RINOs (Republicans in Name Only) do, not true conservatives. Yet in chapter 2 we demonstrated that conservatives are more willing to talk to the other side than are liberals. Are conservatives, despite Fox's gospel, more willing to compromise in real-world politics? We turn to this question in the next chapter.

## CHAPTER FOUR

# Acceptance of Compromise

The budget agreement is a bipartisan compromise. Neither side got everything it wanted. That's the responsibility of governing.

President Joe Biden, after negotiating a bill to raise the debt ceiling and
prevent a shutdown of the government

It [the agreement] doesn't get everything everybody wanted, but . . . in divided
government that's what we end up with.

Former Speaker of the House Kevin McCarthy[1]

Democratic practice is necessarily messy. Different interests, beliefs, and
priorities are articulated in the process of policymaking and get sorted out
as government officials distribute resources, determine which values will be
maximized and whose interests will be served, and set a course for the future. Democratic theory suggests that our presidential, first-past-the-post,
bicameral and tripartite, pluralistic system works because it is designed to
generate political outcomes that both satisfy majorities and protect minorities. The processes of American governance are imperfect—slow, tortuous,
and often conflict-ridden—but somehow they often yield the compromises
required for democratic self-governance.

Of course, not everyone thinks that compromise is a great virtue. The
cost can be high. Representatives must often give something up, sometimes
something important, to come to a resolution on an issue. It sometimes
requires coming to terms with an opponent who is disliked or disdained.
We start with an assumption that compromise is a healthy thing in a democracy, agreeing with Jennifer Wolak when she writes, "Compromise is a democratic norm, one we support not because it benefits our personal stakes,
but . . . because we believe that we should."[2] Yet, as we have workshopped
our ideas, there have been critics who have taken on this assumption, con-
flating compromise with capitulation to the other side and concerned about
giving even a partial victory to a particularly disliked leader.

It is not just that for some people compromise equates with weakness. In
an influential and compelling article, the political scientists John Hibbing

and Elizabeth Theiss-Morse argue that many of the *processes* of policymaking are inherently unattractive to voters.[3] They explicitly call out the open conflict and aggressive performances that can precede compromise, as well as the horse trading and "smoke-filled rooms," and argue that it is the usual political business, as much as the unusual business, that is disdained. Of course, some of the compromising happens in private, where, negotiation theorists argue, "deliberative negotiation" is most likely to be successful.[4] Yet, after the fact, the compromising is uncovered by a free press, and we see and read about how the sausage was made. Additionally, the product of policymaking is editorialized, often with a dose of outrage, which contributes to the phenomenon that Hibbing and Theiss-Morse describe. It is no wonder that citizens are cynical, and that the government is unpopular in such an environment.

Despite concerns that the processes that yield compromises can turn people off, we show, like Wolak, that at the level of principle there is strong support in the mass public for compromise in policymaking.[5] We argue that this reservoir of support for compromise, this acceptance of the concept by everyday democrats, is critically important to the success of our democratic system. If there is broad personal support for the idea of compromise, then there is room for elected officials to forge solutions. It may even create an incentive for public officials to seek solutions to society's challenges via compromise. Broad public acceptance of generalized compromise also makes possible support for specific compromises. If the process is perceived as legitimate, the outputs are more acceptable. The connection of everyday attitudes and the performance of democratic governance in this domain is direct and profound.

In this chapter we focus on how American ideologues perceive political compromise unattached to any particular issue or political actors. Public support for generalized political compromise is high, a finding that extends across a broad time span, across different polls, and across most subgroups of the American electorate. But there is an ideological asymmetry here, as elsewhere in this book. Liberals embrace generalized political compromise more than conservatives—again, a finding that is consistent across time, across various polling outfits, and across different articulations of the question. In the pages ahead, we offer two major explanations for the ideological difference we observe. One of these is based upon the notion that compromise requires loss or gain from one's current positions or one's place in society. As we will show, loss and gain influence how one thinks about the value and efficacy of compromise. The second is that education has a major impact on whether or not one values compromise, but we will show that how education interacts with other ideas held by liberals and conservatives leads to differences of note. As with most political phenomena, multiple forces can be at play, and whichever the more compelling explanation, there are meaningful implications for this difference in how liberals and conservatives understand compromise, what we consider an everyday attitudinal building block for democratic politics.

## Support for Generalized Political Compromise

What do Americans want from their elected officials? It is unsurprising that constituents would support someone who will "re-present" them, someone who will faithfully reflect their own views, beliefs, and principles—where they exist—and then apply them to the various policy issues that arise. Citizens also want elected officials who get things done, who solve problems and move society forward. Here is where the act of political compromise creates tension, because faithfully reflecting views and standing by principles can stand in the way of resolving issues and moving society forward.

In the early decades of public opinion surveys, pollsters did not really inquire much into this tension. It is not that they did not ask about compromise, but it was mostly in the context of a specific issue, often one in the realm of foreign affairs. But in recent decades, the electorate has become more politically polarized. Members of Congress and state legislators are representing ever safer, more politically homogeneous districts.[6] At the same time, competitive primaries are often rewarding politicians who are ideologically pure, if not necessarily the most ideologically extreme.[7] Those on the ideological outskirts of the parties have become more prominent in Congress (and other councils and legislatures), and the question of compromise versus principle has become more relevant. Not surprisingly, in the past couple of decades, pollsters have increasingly included general questions about compromise in their surveys.

We begin by showing responses to a variety of questions about compromise asked by different pollsters, using different wordings and response categories and capturing a period of time in which US politics has continued to polarize. These results can be found in table 4.1. Most striking is that during these years, support for generalized political compromise is high; how high depends upon how the question is asked and how the alternative to compromise is characterized. Utilizing the expansive Roper Poll online survey archive,[8] we selected various questions measuring attitudes toward compromise, looking at questions that evoke the concept in different ways. Some research, like the Pew survey in 2019, simply asks about compromise without offering an alternative: "How important is it to you that elected officials are willing to make compromises with their political opponents to solve important problems?" Other surveys pit compromise against other values that respondents might care about. Do respondents prefer their representatives to compromise to "solve important problems" or "get things done" or do they prefer representatives who "will stand up to the other side," "stick to their positions," or "stick to their principles"? As is apparent in table 4.1, with only two exceptions, strong majorities of all respondents support political compromise as a general principle, even when presented

TABLE 4.1. Liberal and conservative orientation toward political compromise (percentage supporting compromise, with one exception)

| | All | Lib | Mod | Con | Diff., Lib-Con |
|---|---|---|---|---|---|
| ANES (2016): "Would you prefer a government official who compromises to get things done or who sticks to their principles no matter what?" | 63.3 (4,231) | 81.5 (985) | 69.7 (849) | 52.6 (1,288) | 28.9 |
| Pew (2017): "I like elected officials who make compromises with people they disagree with" vs. "I like elected officials who stick to their positions." | 58.9 (8,269) | 72.3 (2,180) | 65.5 (2,815) | 43.7 (3,059) | 28.6 |
| Pew (2018a): "I like elected officials who make compromises with people they disagree with" vs. "I like elected officials who stick to their positions." | 44.6 (1,444) | 50.1 (369) | 40.6 (532) | 46.4 (515) | 3.7 |
| Pew (2018b): "In general, how important, if at all, is it for someone in high political office to do each of the following? Be able to work out compromises." (% essential) | 77.8 (1,233) | 78.5 (377) | 79.6 (452) | 74.9 (374) | 3.6 |
| Institute of Politics and Public Service (2019): "I'm tired of leaders compromising my values and ideals. I want leaders who will stand up to the other side." (% agree strongly)[a] | 57.7 (1,010) | 51.0 (361) | 52.6 (76) | 62.8 (519) | 11.8 |
| Institute of Politics and Public Service (2019): "Compromise and common ground should be the goal for political leaders." (% agree strongly) | 62.6 (1,010) | 65.1 (361) | 78.9 (76) | 58.6 (519) | 6.5 |

| | All | Lib | Mod | Con | Diff., Lib-Con |
|---|---|---|---|---|---|
| Pew (2019): "How important is it to you that elected officials are willing to make compromises with their political opponents to solve important problems?" (% very important) | 65.5 (5,061) | 65.3 (1,379) | 70.7 (1,973) | 59.2 (1,577) | 6.1 |
| AEI (2020): "When it comes to politics today, do you think if one side wins, the other loses, or it is possible for everyone to get something they want?" | 52.3 (4,026) | 55.3 (1,543) | 55.3 (907) | 48.1 (1,121) | 7.2 |
| AEI (2020): "On issues you care most about, which comes closer to your opinion? (1) It is possible to compromise and find common ground with people who agree with you. (2) It is not possible to compromise and find common ground with people who agree with you." | 80.2 (4,028) | 82.6 (1,544) | 85.7 (903) | 76.9 (1,113) | 5.7 |
| ANES (2020): "Would you prefer a government official who compromises to get things done, or who sticks to their principles no matter what?" | 60.6 (8,186) | 71.6 (2,296) | 63.3 (1,845) | 55.2 (2,651) | 16.4 |
| CCES (2020): "I like elected officials who make compromises with people they disagree with" vs. "I like elected officials who stick to their positions." | 52.1 (997) | 67.3 (330) | 55.1 (256) | 38.6 (336) | 28.7 |
| Pew (2021): "(1) Compromise in politics is really just selling out what you believe in. (2) Compromise is how things get done in politics, even though it sometimes means sacrificing your beliefs." | 73.1 (9,955) | 80.9 (3,240) | 80.1 (3,968) | 59.4 (3,240) | 21.5 |
| USA Today (2022): "For a moment I want to empower you to describe the characteristics of the ideal president through your eyes. Forget about who may or not be a candidate in 2024. Would your ideal president stand on principle no matter what, even if it means some things don't get done, or compromise in order to get things done?" | 62.6 (910) | 77.8 (242) | 74.1 (302) | 41.1 (326) | 36.7 |

Note: Sample size in parentheses.

[a] Note that in this question percentages represent the rejection of compromise.

as the alternative to adherence to principle or purpose.[9] The size of that majority fluctuates as the questions vary in construction and are asked at different political moments, but there is no question that Americans favor compromise over intransigence and recognize what President Gerald Ford once said about compromise: that it "is that oil that makes government go."[10]

The two exceptions in the table are meaningful and instructive. In the 2019 survey sponsored by the Institute for Politics and Public Service at Georgetown, respondents are asked to agree or disagree (strongly or not strongly) to the one-sided statement "I'm tired of leaders compromising my values and ideals. I want leaders who will stand up to the other side." A strong majority—58 percent—strongly agree with the statement, a counter to the other findings in the table. However, in the very same survey, researchers also offered a second statement: "Compromise and common ground should be the goal for political leaders." Respondents supported compromise and common ground, and to an even greater degree, with close to 63 percent in strong agreement. Remarkably, almost 65 percent of the "tired" respondents *also* strongly agree that compromise should be the goal for our leaders. The second exception, in a Pew survey from 2018, has overall support for compromise at roughly 45 percent. It is driven by a great momentary erosion of liberal support for compromise, a finding we explore further below.

The conclusion that compromise in politics is valued by a majority of Americans through a period of time of ever greater polarization might defy expectations and parallels some of the findings earlier in this book that show that not every aspect of everyday democracy is so conflict laden. The fact that liberals are more accepting of compromise than conservatives or nonliberals is yet another conclusion one can draw from this exercise. This finding is less surprising and indeed is consistent with what other social scientists have found when looking at ideological and/or partisan differences in the predilection to compromise.[11] Up and down table 4.1, the difference between liberals and conservatives is apparent, often markedly so. This difference waxes and wanes a bit over time, but at no point and in no single survey do conservatives appear more friendly to compromise than liberals, or even equally accepting of it. No matter how the question is asked, no matter who asks it, no matter what dimension of compromise is emphasized or what the counter is, this finding holds firm.

This liberal-conservative public opinion difference has been noted elsewhere, and the conservative reluctance to compromise that we see here aligns with what is easily observable in the contemporary political environment. Both parties have played a role in polarization, but it is the Republican Party that has been the key driver of the phenomenon. As

Thomas Mann and Norman Ornstein write: "However awkward it may for the traditional press and nonpartisan analysts to acknowledge, one of the two major parties, the Republican Party, has become an insurgent outlier—ideologically extreme; contemptuous of the inherited social and economic policy regime; scornful of compromise; unpersuaded by conventional understanding of facts, evidence, and science; and dismissive of the legitimacy of its political opposition. When one party moves this far from the center of American politics, it is extremely difficult to enact policies responsive to the country's most pressing challenges."[12] With the scenario that they describe, it may not be that much of a surprise that conservatives so consistently lag behind liberals in accepting political compromise. It may just be that conservative citizens are simply responding to the politics they observe. Mann and Ornstein wrote *It's Even Worse Than It Looks* in 2016. Since the election of Donald Trump, it's even worse than it was.[13] This trend is not just due to ideological extremism. Over the years, Trump's populism and pugilism have become the party's brand and its style, and it should not be surprising that rank-and-file voters would reflect this stance.

But it also could be that the relationship of elite politics and public opinion is reversed—that conservative politicians are working within the confines of conservative public opinion and indeed are incentivized to be more aggressive to please their constituents. If that is the case, then the important question becomes what lies behind the liberal-conservative difference. What are the origins of conservative distinctiveness? Does this difference say something about the underlying everyday principles or perspectives that define the two sets of ideologues?

As we think about the reciprocal nature of the relationship between elite and mass politics, there is value in looking at the relationship of ideology to attitudes toward *nonpolitical* compromise. If that relationship is strong, then it really may be something in the "natures," the general approaches to other people, of the two sets of ideologues. If a relationship between ideology and nonpolitical compromise does not exist, then we can conclude that it is something about the political context that brings out the difference. Survey researchers do not often ask about compromise outside of a political context, and so we designed and placed a couple of the survey questions on the CES politics survey in 2018 to test for a liberal-conservative difference in nonpolitical compromise. Additionally, we identified a 2018 Pew survey that captured responses to compromise in a business context.

As table 4.2 illustrates, respondents to these questions overwhelmingly support the notion of compromise outside of a political context. Over 78 percent of all respondents, no matter their ideology, believe that being able to "work out compromises" is an essential skill for someone in an important business position to have. Almost nine in ten respondents claim to try to work out compromises when disagreeing with others, and that is also the percentage of people who want their children to compromise when they have disagreements. There is a modest difference between liberals and conservatives on these items, suggesting some psychological difference in an orientation toward nonpolitical compromise. The major conclusion here, though, is that the natural impulse of almost everyone is to value compromise. The much larger differences in attitudes toward political compromise suggest that the political environment affects individuals more than individuals affect the political environment.

So we are left with a consistent liberal-conservative difference on political compromise to elucidate, and in the pages ahead, we offer some possible

TABLE 4.2. Liberal and conservative orientation toward compromise outside of a political context

| | All | Lib | Mod | Con | Diff, Lib-Con |
|---|---|---|---|---|---|
| CCES (2018): "When you find yourself disagreeing with someone else, whether it is at work, with friends or with family, do you [try to find ways to compromise so that both of you get some of what you want] or do you [try to change the other person's mind so that you can get your way]?" (% compromise) | 88.1 (987) | 88.6 (281) | 90.8 (273) | 82.4 (323) | 6.20 |
| CCES (2018): "Suppose you have a child, and your child is playing with a friend, and they disagree over what to play next. Would you encourage your child to [compromise with the friend] or [stand firm to get what he or she wants]?" (% compromise) | 92.3 (832) | 95.1 (246) | 92.9 (226) | 89.9 (296) | 5.20 |
| Pew (2018): "In general, how important, if at all, is it for someone in a top business position to do each of the following? Be able to work out compromises." (% essential) | 78.2 (1,137) | 87.3 (314) | 74.8 (409) | 73.7 (399) | 13.60 |

Note: Sample size in parentheses.

interrelated explanations. The kernel of the first explanation lies in one last big takeaway from table 4.1. While the various items in the table come from different surveys, the shrinking of the liberal-conservative difference in the Trump years and the apparent expansion of the difference in the first years of the Biden presidency are stunning. These changes are not in perfect alignment. The first Pew survey of the first Trump administration a few months after his inauguration still shows a sizable liberal-conservative difference, but the suggestion here is that the difference will ebb and flow as political control of the government changes hands. This variation would be expected given Laurel Harbridge and colleagues' findings that while Americans say that they value the principle of bipartisanship, when presented with an actual policy compromise, they still prefer partisan victories. In other words, people like policy compromise much more when it is the *other* party that must bend.[14] That tendency should lead the partisan difference in compromise approval to grow and shrink as the power relationships in Washington change.

In looking across time, however, there also is value in holding both the pollster and the question constant, looking at responses to a particular question asked identically and repeatedly over time by a single survey organization. Ideally, we would track panel data, looking at the same respondents and tracking their responses over time. Alas, there are no panels that repeat a compromise question. But looking at cross-sectional data over time and looking at liberal and conservative attitudes toward the same compromise question do allow us to draw some conclusions about how political circumstances affect the ideological difference.[15]

In figure 4.1 we look at a series of seventeen YouGov surveys that repeat the question "If you had to choose, would you rather have a member of Congress who compromises to get things done, or who sticks to their principles no matter what?" between 2012 and 2023. Looking at this trend allows us to track liberal and conservative responses across two Democratic administrations and one Republican administration.[16] Replicating what we see in table 4.1 but this time keeping the survey question constant, we see that the difference between liberals and conservatives grows during the Obama and Biden administrations and shrinks during the first Trump administration. However, the size of the difference is more a function of conservative responses than liberal ones. There is some evidence of liberal sensitivity to context: Liberal acceptance of compromise dips to a low point at the very beginning of the first Trump administration and jumps substantially when Joe Biden takes over the presidency. But neither of these changes is enduring, and in all three administrations, on average, roughly three-quarters of liberals prefer compromise. Conservatives, on the other hand, do shift significantly and in a sustained way across administrations. During the two

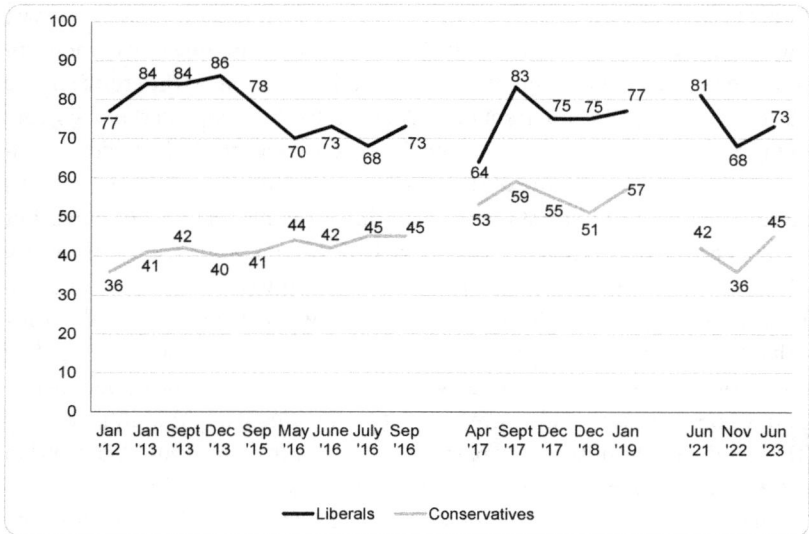

FIGURE 4.1. The difference between liberals and conservatives on support for legislative compromise is enduring but varies in size by administration

Source: YouGov surveys, 2012–2023.

Note: "If you had to choose, would you rather have a member of Congress who compromises to get things done, or who sticks to their principles no matter what?" Data points represent the percentage of liberals and the percentage of conservatives taking the compromising alternative.

Democratic administrations, the average conservative acceptance of compromise is 41–42 percent. In the Trump years, it averages 55 percent.

So there is substantial evidence that this ebbing and flowing is a function of one side or the other having control over the political agenda. This party control is not always complete. The American presidential model is different from a parliamentary model, where one party or coalition controls the legislature and the executive, the government drives the course of action, and the opposition simply serves to counter the majority. For the most part, however, control of the presidency does offer one party much more leverage over the agenda. The fact that liberals respond, at least temporarily, to the administration's changing hands and that a substantial percentage of conservatives are sensitive to which party is controlling the presidency suggests an explanation for why liberals appear to be more friendly to political compromise than conservatives, and that explanation is rooted in a psychological theory that we will discuss in the next section. This argument helps explain why people belonging or sympathetic to the out-of-power party are less likely to want compromise than those controlling the levers of political power.

## Prospect Theory

The theory that informs our argument is prospect theory, which was first conceived and refined by Daniel Kahneman and Amos Tversky.[17] The centerpiece of the theory is the concept of loss aversion, whereby people confronting a decision concern themselves more with loss than with gain. This predisposition to focus on loss, they argue, is heightened in contexts of risk and uncertainty and is especially apparent in situations involving bargaining. They write: "Loss aversion can complicate negotiations. Experimental evidence indicates that negotiators are less likely to achieve agreement when the attributes over which they bargain are framed as losses than when they are framed as gains. This result is expected if people are more sensitive to marginal changes in the negative domain. Furthermore, there is a natural asymmetry between the evaluations of the concessions that one makes and the concessions offered by the other party; the latter are normally evaluated as gains, whereas the former are evaluated as losses."[18] Or, as Jonathan Mercer puts it, "People hate to lose even more than they love to win."[19] This insight is simple, powerful, and well supported in the laboratory. There also is ample evidence of it in the real world, where the standard economic assumption of utility maximization is often overridden by the desire to avoid risk as people make financial decisions. Indeed, prospect theory influenced the discipline of economics so much that Kahneman, a psychologist, received the 2002 Nobel Prize in economics "for having integrated insights from psychological research into economic science, especially concerning human judgment and decision-making under uncertainty."[20]

Given how influential the theory has been in economics, and given its natural connection to negotiation, it is quite remarkable that the literature on political compromise has not "discovered" prospect theory. Mercer argues that the theory simply has not resonated much in political science. The problem, he asserts, is that Kahneman and Tversky's experiments in the laboratory enable them to easily manipulate perceptions of loss and gain, but in the real world of politics it is much more complicated to figure out what is loss and what is gain. Our own empirical review of the prospect theory literature supports Mercer's observation about political science. Kahneman and Tversky's key articles on prospect theory have been cited more than 65,000 times,[21] according to the Social Science Citation Index, but a review of these citations shows very little influence on scholarship about compromise in general and almost nothing on political compromise. Only 281—0.004 percent—of the more than 65,000 citations are from articles with the key word "compromise" in the article title, journal title, or abstract. Further refining the search, only 10 of those 281 articles also had "politics" as a key word.

Thus, the theory has not really penetrated academic discussions of legislative politics or public opinion on politics. But it should. Political compromise inevitably involves a calculus of loss and gain—not only one's own prospective loss and gain, but also the possible loss and gain faced by the other side. It is often negotiated in a context of uncertainty, with the possibility of a successful resolution to a negotiation usually balanced by the risk of giving away too much. Moreover, concern about how the media and the public will assess credit and blame also hovers over political compromises. At its core, then, the act of political compromise would seem to be well understood through the lens of prospect theory, and it should apply as we attempt to understand both how people come to accept compromise in the political realm and why some types of people (e.g., liberals), more than others (e.g., conservatives), would be more inclined to support compromise. Contra Mercer, we argue that in a starkly partisan context, gain and loss are relatively easy to assess. We also argue that the theory helps explain the consistent finding that conservatives are less friendly to political compromise than liberals, because, in general, liberals value change—the "progress" in "progressive"—while the conservative impulse is to protect or "conserve" the status quo.

Conservatives, we contend, are less inclined to value compromise because they are more likely than liberals to view political change through the lens of loss, which is consistent with findings in political psychology showing that conservatives have a heightened sensitivity to loss. Hibbing and colleagues, synthesizing an extensive review of literature, make the case that "variations in physiological and psychological responses to a particular category of stimuli—those that are negative (or aversive)—correlate with political orientations."[22] This reverberates in several ways relevant to our discussion. Conservatives, for instance, find threatening stimuli more distracting,[23] are more likely to interpret ambiguous stimuli as threatening,[24] are more likely to believe that the "world is a relatively harsh place,"[25] and are less risk tolerant as a result.

What is popularly known as the "culture war" illustrates how this orientation toward loss manifests itself in real-world political attitudes. On the left, the term is used to describe how right-wing politicians and strategists have used a whole panoply of social issues—abortion, gay and transgender rights, and race and its treatment in history, among others—as a vehicle for pursuing votes and stimulating the base. Why do these issues resonate so much with rank-and-file conservatives? Our speculation is that it is because these issues spotlight loss—loss in status, loss in a way of life, loss in accustomed values. The *National Review* columnist Dan McLaughlin makes this case as he challenges the idea that conservatives are solely responsible for propagating the culture war:

> Of course, the idea that only one side engages in culture war is not only ridiculous, it is especially dishonest when one takes the position that it is only the conservative party that does this. As a simple matter of history and self-definition, self-identified progressives define themselves around "progress"—in other words, *changing the culture as it exists*. Self-identified conservatives define themselves around "conserving"—in other words, *not* trying to change things, or at any rate, not changing them swiftly and dramatically. While this is an oversimplified view of where the right and left sides of the political spectrum stand on any given issue, the general tendency of progressives to push for accelerated changes while conservatives just want to leave things alone means that progressives will be the aggressors in cultural battles far more often than are conservatives.[26]

Culture war issues are not the only ones that situate the Left as advancing change and the Right as defending the status quo, but whatever the issue, we argue that this gain/loss calculus matters.

If prospect theory applies to understanding political compromise, not only should it explain why conservatives are so consistently less likely than liberals to accept compromise, but it also suggests an explanation for the ebbs and flows of ideological difference on display above. When Democrats control the White House and are driving the change agenda, it is conservatives who would be confronting loss more than gain, and the liberal-conservative difference should be enhanced. When Republicans control the change agenda, that difference should shrink. It is liberals who then face the prospect of loss due to change in a conservative direction. Indeed, this is the pattern we observed in table 4.1 and figure 4.1. A change in the administration does not reverse the results wholly; a generalized conservative hesitancy about political compromise still seems to operate. But new presidents often come with mandates to shift direction, and people respond to that. Even if the idea of a presidential mandate does not stand up to scrutiny,[27] presidents inevitably claim it—"I earned capital in the political campaign and I intend to spend it,"[28] said George W. Bush after his election in 2004—and political commentators often accept the claim. An assertive presidency is bound to be the focal point of voters on both sides of the political spectrum and to influence public opinion in ways that would be predicted by Kahneman and Tversky.

The back-and-forth seen in these surveys, especially in its timing, provides circumstantial evidence of our hypothesis. We offer more direct support for the argument that prospect theory and loss aversion explain the different orientations toward compromise by liberals and conservatives in an experiment we placed on a series of public opinion surveys conducted in Pennsylvania in 2014. Our experiment starts with a survey question designed to investigate individual proclivities toward compromise and to see whether we find the same ideological gap that we observe consistently in the polls discussed above. Our study looks at compromise on the issue of the minimum wage, an issue that brewed throughout 2014 in Pennsylvania and elsewhere. Fourteen states and the District of Columbia raised the minimum wage during 2014.[29] Although the minimum wage was debated in Pennsylvania, there was no successful action on the issue. It was, however, an issue that was very politically relevant at the time of our experiments. It is a particularly meaningful one given our desire to measure just how much people are willing to move toward compromise.

## MINIMUM WAGE RATE EXPERIMENT

Our first study, conducted in the August 2014 survey, begins with a question intended to anchor the respondent in a position. We then see whether our follow-up question can pull the respondent away from that position toward compromise with the position of the other party (with liberals presumed to favor a higher minimum wage and conservatives a lower one). Because political negotiations are generally reported to be between Democrats and Republicans in government, not liberals and conservatives, our initial question reads: "Democrats and Republicans in Washington are debating the minimum wage. The minimum wage is presently $7.25 an hour and Republicans in Congress would like to keep it there. President Obama has proposed that the minimum wage be set at $10.10. Ideally where do you think the minimum wage should be set? Should it be set at $7.25; $7.95; the midpoint $8.65; $9.35; or at $10.10?" Once the respondent has established a position to this question, we ask a follow-up: "Suppose that you were the [Democrat/Republican] responsible for negotiating the final minimum wage rate. Would you stay at [previous answer], or would you be willing to compromise at: [for Democrats] $9.35, the midpoint $8.65; $7.95; $7.25? [for Republicans] $7.95; the midpoint $8.65; $9.35; $10.10?" The survey script automatically asks respondents who are registered with one of the parties to represent that party in the exercise. Respondents who report that they have not registered but who *identify* with one of the parties are also included. Conservative Republicans and Republicans/independents and liberal Democrats and Democrats/independents are thus tracked through the exercise.[30]

Respondents who put themselves at one of the wage end points are offered all the middle-position alternatives in the follow-up question. If they start at one of the in-between positions, they are only offered response categories that lie between their own position and the end-point position of the other side. Thus, if a liberal Democrat places herself at $8.65, she is then asked whether she would compromise to $7.95 or $7.25. It might seem odd to include complete capitulation as a "compromise alternative"—and not a single respondent takes it—but offering the whole span of alternatives allows the respondent to express how far to the other side he or she would be willing to go.

The results of this exercise conform to our expectations, as seen in table 4.3. While 61 percent of liberal Democrats are willing to negotiate and move away from their original preference, only 37 percent of conservative Republicans strike this stance. In a measure that captures both how many people move toward compromise *and* how far they move, liberal Democrats move 48 cents to compromise, while conservative Republicans only move 28 cents. The difference, while not huge, is statistically significant.

The exercise is not over, however. The minimum wage scenario we presented to respondents offers an interesting and not atypical example of an issue requiring compromise. With Republicans defending the status quo and Democrats pushing for upward change in the wage, Republican conservatives face the prospect of loss and Democratic liberals the opportunity for gain in the survey exercise. Applying Kahneman and Tversky's logic to such a situation, one would anticipate that Republican conservatives should hold on to their position more tenaciously than Democratic liberals. While this is not the logic of every public issue, it is the case for those issues—of which there are many—on which progressives challenge the status quo and conservatives seek to preserve it.

TABLE 4.3. Liberal and conservative orientation toward compromise on the minimum wage

|  | Liberals | Conservatives | Difference |
|---|---|---|---|
| Compromise (%) | 61.2 | 37.2 | 24 |
|  | (214) | (253) |  |
| Movement to other side ($) | 0.48 | 0.28 | 0.20 |
| $T$ |  |  | 5.168*** |

Source: Franklin and Marshall Poll, September/October 2014.

Note: Sample size in parentheses.

***$p < .01$.

## INCOME TAX RATE EXPERIMENT

But what if we replicate our first exercise and replace the minimum wage with an issue on which Republicans are pushing for change and Democrats are defending the established position? This is what we have done in the next iteration of the survey, swapping out the minimum wage in the exercise for a proposal to cut the top-bracket federal income tax rate from 40 percent to 36 percent. This exercise mirrors the minimum wage exercise, with the anchoring question offering five response categories (36, 37, 38, 39, 40) and with a follow-up that offers compromise to each tax rate between one's own preference and the end point associated with the other side. Our expectation, derived from prospect theory, is that as the logic of the issue changes, so too should the partisan and ideological responses to that issue. The ideological difference we observe in the minimum wage exercise should reverse in this tax rate exercise, or at least disappear.

Indeed, with income tax rates at stake, the difference between liberal Democrats and conservative Republicans in willingness to compromise essentially dissolves (table 4.4). The fact that the findings are not reversed, that the gain/loss logic of the situation does not lead conservative Republicans to be more compromising than liberal Democrats, creating a mirror image of the original findings, indicates that there is still something else about a conservative mindset that is more intransigent. It also may be that the tax rate reduction we stipulated in our exercise may not have been dramatic enough to evoke the full effect. Our four-percentage-point reduction is not that far from the one proposed by Donald Trump during the 2016 presidential campaign (from 39.6 percent to 33 percent for the highest earners). Nonetheless, this pattern of results suggests that ideological responses to compromise on the tax issue is the reverse of those we see on the wage issue, evidence that Kahneman and Tversky's insight applies. At least some of the ideological difference we observe repeatedly is due to the fact that conservatives are more often concerned about change—and loss—than liberals. We argue that their inflexibility, their lower tolerance for compromise, is as much a response to the prospect of loss as a rejection of the healthy democratic principles required of everyday democrats. The fact that conservatives are more likely to face loss than gain is what often differentiates ideologues on scores of issues that are central to contemporary politics. On top of that, there may be something more—a defensive stance, an aversion to societal change—that explains why conservatives might resist compromise in a more general way, a habit of the heart that experience shows has consequential political implications.

TABLE 4.4. Liberal and conservative orientation toward compromise on taxes

|  | Liberals | Conservatives | Difference |
|---|---|---|---|
| Compromise (%) | 34.1 | 28.2 | 5.9 |
|  | (88) | (78) |  |
| Movement to the other side in tax rate (%) | 0.57 | 0.42 |  |
| $t$ |  |  | 1.145 |

Source: Franklin and Marshall Poll, September 2014.

Note: Sample size in parentheses.

## Education, Ideology, and Compromise

A second explanation for the ideological difference that we so consistently observe on acceptance of compromise involves the interaction of ideology and education.[31] What does it take to enable individuals to embrace, or at least tolerate, political compromise? There are good reasons to believe that education is key. Education is a contributor to civic participation in general.[32] As Michael Delli Carpini and Scott Keeter argue, the political knowledge that accrues from education is "a critical and distinct facilitator of other aspects of good citizenship. A well-informed citizen is more likely to be attentive to politics, engaged in various forms of participation, committed to democratic principles, opinionated, and to feel efficacious."[33] Philip Converse is emphatic: "Education is everywhere the universal solvent."[34] Mikael Persson, after reviewing the broader political science literature, concludes that "the relationship between education and political participation is perhaps the most well-established relationship that exists in research on political behaviour."[35] Education is a powerful independent variable even beyond questions of participation.

How might this translate to a relationship between education and approval of compromise? We know that better-educated people are more likely to be exposed to a larger and more sophisticated variety of news sources.[36] The version of politics they encounter is more detailed and more nuanced. Political sophistication also means understanding and acknowledging the values of others, a recognition that there are other ways of thinking and being.

The education solvent is also thought to reduce the friction of political differences by teaching tolerance, civility, and an appreciation of democratic norms necessary for government to function. One of the most essential norms is that of compromise. It is easier to achieve compromise when citizens regard those on the opposing side to be people of good faith, a loyal opposition rather than the embodiment of evil. Optimally, the compromising mindset should be ingrained in our consciousness as we are educated from a young age on how government works.[37]

If there are reasons to believe that education will contribute to a compromising attitude, there are also reasons to question why it should matter. Some Americans see compromise as abandoning principle. If opponents hold different values than we do, why trust them? Education may make the operations of government easier to comprehend, but even those who are educated can find it satisfying to stereotype adversaries and believe their motives are suspect. Being highly educated may even make us more confident that we know more than our ideological adversaries.

We explore the relationship of education to acceptance of political compromise via three public opinion surveys from the early 2020s: the 2020 American National Election Survey (ANES), the 2020 CES, and a Pew survey from 2021. As before, the idea is to employ survey questions that vary modestly in wording and response categories. To look at the relationship of education to approval of political compromise, we divide respondents into three education categories, looking at those who have a high school degree or did not graduate from high school; those with some college but no degree; and those with a college degree (including those who have done postgraduate studies).

In each of the three cases, on view in figure 4.2, we find clear, simple, and strong evidence of the bivariate relationship we anticipated. Looking at "All" respondents in the surveys, including ideologues and nonideologues alike, each advance in education leads to stronger approval of compromise, the difference being between 15 and 18 percentage points separating the less educated from the well educated.

It is worth noting that the effect of education on political compromise is not a function of the fact that educated people hold their values and policy preferences less dear or are less vigorous in their advocacy of their point of view than people with less education. Indeed, the opposite is true: As studies have shown, better-educated people understand political principles better, can better articulate them, and better understand how various ideas coalesce into belief systems.[38] The point is that the relationship we observe in figure 4.2 is not because the well educated have a looser attachment to principles. It is, we argue, something else, likely a greater appreciation for the mechanisms of democratic government that are required for it to function effectively and produce policy.[39]

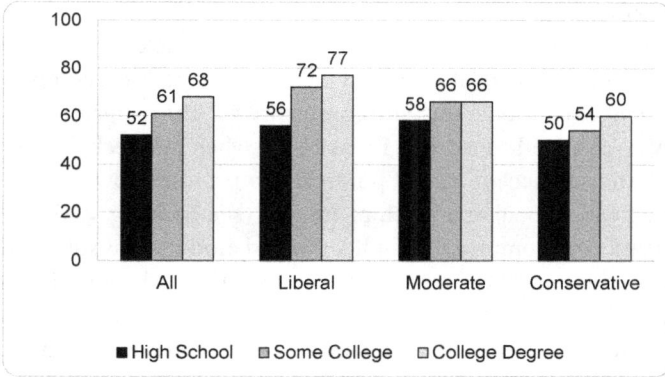

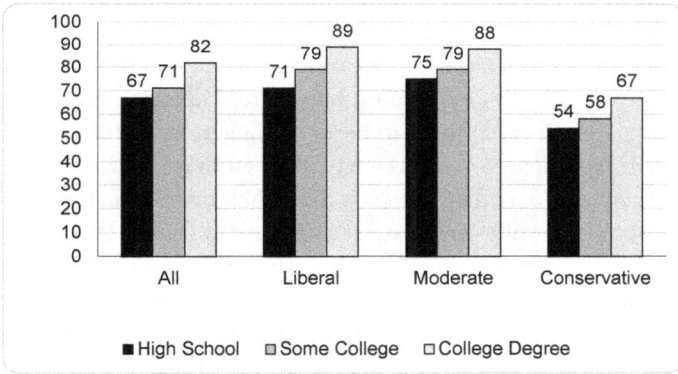

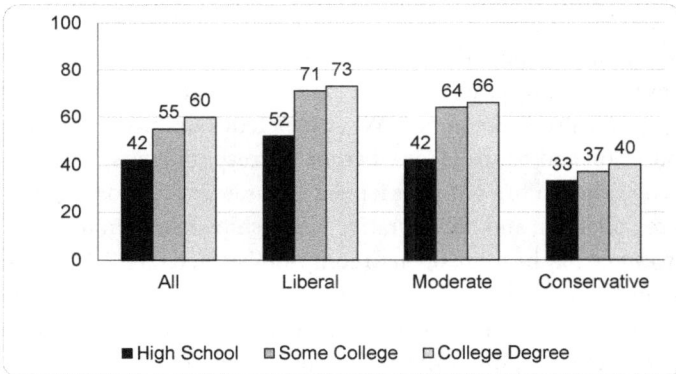

FIGURE 4.2. Education contributes to acceptance of compromise, but for liberals more than conservatives

Note: (*top*) "I prefer officials who compromises to get things done" (ANES 2020). (*middle*) "I like elected officials who compromise" (CCES 2020). (*bottom*) "Compromise is how you get things done" (Pew 2021).

The consistency of this relationship between education and approval of compromise is striking, but then we control for ideology using each of the three surveys. Is the relationship of ideology and political compromise the same for liberals, moderates, and conservatives? The pattern across all three surveys is clear and consistent. In each case, when we break the relationship of education to acceptance of political compromise down by ideology, a stunning conditional relationship emerges (see again fig. 4.2). The impact of education on compromise for liberals and moderates is substantial. Analyzing the 2020 CES, for instance, 52 percent of less-educated liberals desire elected officials who "compromise with people they disagree with" rather than those who "stick to their positions." That percentage climbs to 73 percent for well-educated liberals, a difference of twenty-one points. The difference is even larger for moderates, a twenty-four-point difference. The difference between less-educated and well-educated conservatives, however, is a mere seven points. In the other two cases, the contours are a little different, mostly with moderates, but the relationship is again smaller for conservatives. There appears to be something quite distinctive about conservative attitudes. Not surprisingly, they embrace political compromise less frequently than others, but it is more than this. Education, which matters a lot for everyone else, matters substantially less for them.

To develop this point further, we analyze the relationships in figure 4.2 in a multivariate setting, again employing all three surveys, first testing whether the bivariate relationships we observe in figure 4.2 hold when we control for demographic variables. In our equations, our dependent variables are acceptance of compromise (coded so that positive coefficients are associated with acceptance of compromise). In this first iteration of this exercise, our independent variables include a dummy variable for conservatives that captures the difference between conservatives and nonconservatives, with all else the same.[40] We also include our three-category measure of education and controls for whether the respondent is nonwhite (versus non-Hispanic white), older, or female. It has been argued that women have a more collective and collaborative leadership style than men, suggesting that women may be more open to compromise than men.[41] Older people are often more engaged in politics than younger people and have more experience with politics, which might make them more likely to appreciate compromise.[42] On race, Black Americans and members of other racial minority groups are less likely than white Americans to trust others. In some studies,[43] that difference is large. Other studies show that nonwhite Americans have lower levels of trust in a range of institutions, including law enforcement, healthcare providers, and government.[44] With less trust of other people and with greater skepticism of institutions, nonwhites may find negotiation and compromise—the "oil" of government—more difficult to accept.

The coefficients in the first two columns of table 4.5, with demographics held constant, show that the effect of ideology—conservative versus non-conservative—on the acceptance of compromise is robust and significant. As expected, conservatives are distinctly less friendly toward compromise; the coefficients are strong and significant across all three equations. Also strong and significant are the coefficients capturing the effect of education. In all three of the equations, education leads to greater approval of political compromise and of "compromisers." Of the demographic controls, age is the only variable that reaches significance in all three equations, and older respondents, as expected, are more compromising than younger respondents. Nonwhite respondents are less likely to accept compromise than white respondents in all three equations, a relationship that reaches statistical significance in two of the three surveys. The effect of being a woman versus a man is inconsistent across the three surveys.

In a second iteration of our analysis, we layer in an additional variable to test whether education matters to conservatives as it does to everybody else in accepting compromise. This variable is an interaction term combining ideology and education and allows us to capture the difference that education makes in accepting compromise, but only for conservatives. A statistically significant interaction term indicates that the effect of education for conservatives is different from the effect of education for everyone else, and a negative coefficient indicates that that effect is smaller, which is what we hypothesize based upon the relationships we have observed in figure 4.2.

In fact, the coefficients of interest are all sizable and significant in all three equations. As in the first equation, the difference of education is meaningful, with better-educated people being more accepting of compromise. And ideology matters, too, with nonconservatives being more willing to accept compromise than conservatives. Most important to our hypothesis, the interaction term is negative and statistically significant in all three surveys. This finding confirms that education contributes less to the acceptance of compromise for conservatives than it does for others, all else being the same.

But this exercise is not over. What we aim to do in the third iteration of our analysis is to introduce variables into the equations to explain *why* education matters less for conservatives. If we are right, then the additional variables will take the interaction term coefficient out of statistical significance. Our hypothesis is that there are other attitudes that well-educated conservatives hold that make them less disposed to accept compromise, which helps to explain why they are distinctive in their relative rejection of compromise.

The explanatory variables we focus on represent disdain for government and a preference for smaller, less-intrusive, less-powerful government.

Such ideas, of course, permeate conservative thought. The concept behind our hypothesis is that compromise, a necessary ingredient for governance, may be less valued when government itself is less valued. This view is often apparent and even explicit in Washington politics. As one ultraconservative representative put it, compromise to keep the government going in a showdown with Democrats was the equivalent to "infinitesimal incrementalism."[45] Said another, "We shouldn't fear a government shutdown. Most of what we do up here is bad anyway."[46]

Our explanation for the relationship of education to compromise among conservatives is not that education does not matter to conservatives but rather that it does. Education leads well-educated conservatives to support compromise for the same reasons that it leads other people to support it. But education *also* leads to exposure to and acceptance of other attitudes about government that countervail the acceptance of compromise.

In the third iteration of our analysis, we introduce variables capturing those attitudes into the equations. Just as with compromise, where different surveys use different question wording and response categories to measure the attitude of interest, we have identified different questions capturing how people think and feel about big, more assertive government. The questions vary quite a bit, as there is more dimensionality to attitudes about the size and scope of government. In the CES survey there are two questions that test our hypothesis, one concerning trust in small governments versus large governments, the other a one-hundred-point scale asking respondents how to balance spending and taxes to address a budget deficit.[47] We introduce three variables into the ANES equation. One measures a general attitude toward more or less government activity. The second is more specific, asking about government's role in reducing income inequality. A third measures attitudes toward more or less government regulation. In the Pew equation we utilize two controls, one offering a choice between a bigger government providing more services and a smaller, less expensive government offering fewer services, the second asking whether government does "better than people give it credit for" or is "wasteful and inefficient." For ease of interpretation, all of these variables are coded so that support for activist government is associated with smaller values and more limited government alternatives are associated with larger values, thus leading to an expectation of negative logistic regression coefficients: As the preference for smaller government increases, support for compromise should decrease.

The results of this last iteration of our analysis are found in the third column of table 4.5, allowing readers to scan across the equations and see what happens to the ideology, education, and interaction term coefficients once we introduce these attitudinal controls into the mix. To start, in interpreting

TABLE 4.5. Effects of education on orientation toward compromise for liberals and conservatives

| | Model 1 | Model 2 | Model 3 |
|---|---|---|---|
| **A. CCES 2020 (dependent variable: Compromise)** | | | |
| Conservative dummy | −1.19*** | −0.86*** | −1.00*** |
| | (0.15) | (0.23) | (0.30) |
| Education | 0.40*** | 0.52*** | 0.38*** |
| | (0.09) | (0.11) | (0.13) |
| Education × Conservative | | −0.33* | −0.13 |
| | | (0.18) | (0.21) |
| Age (continuous) | 0.01*** | 0.01*** | 0.02*** |
| | (0.00) | (0.00) | (0.00) |
| Female | 0.10 | 0.09 | −0.01 |
| | (0.14) | (0.14) | (0.17) |
| Nonwhite | −0.22 | −0.20 | −0.27 |
| | (0.16) | (0.16) | (0.20) |
| Taxes vs. spending (100 pts.) | | | −0.01* |
| | | | (0.00) |
| Trust small government | | | −0.04 |
| | | | (0.09) |
| Constant | −0.27 | −0.37* | 0.18 |
| | (0.19) | (0.20) | (0.36) |
| N | 937 | 937 | 706 |
| **B. ANES 2020 (dependent variable: Compromise)** | | | |
| Conservative dummy | −0.64*** | −0.49*** | −0.44*** |
| | (0.06) | (0.09) | (0.10) |
| Education | 0.30*** | 0.36*** | 0.28*** |
| | (0.03) | (0.04) | (0.05) |
| Education × Conservative | | −0.14** | −0.07 |
| | | (0.07) | (0.07) |
| Age (continuous) | 0.01*** | 0.01*** | 0.01*** |
| | (0.00) | (0.00) | (0.00) |
| Female | −0.25*** | −0.26*** | −0.26*** |
| | (0.05) | (0.05) | (0.06) |
| Nonwhite | −0.34*** | −0.34*** | −0.37*** |
| | (0.06) | (0.06) | (0.06) |

*(continued)*

TABLE 4.5. *(continued)*

| | Model 1 | Model 2 | Model 3 |
|---|---|---|---|
| Less government | | | 0.05*** |
| | | | (0.02) |
| Less regulation | | | −0.09*** |
| | | | (0.02) |
| Government activism | | | −0.05*** |
| | | | (0.02) |
| Constant | 0.41*** | 0.35*** | 0.77*** |
| | (0.08) | (0.08) | (0.11) |
| N | 6,593 | 6,593 | 5,916 |
| **C. Pew 2021 (dependent variable: Compromise)** | | | |
| Conservative dummy | −1.13*** | −0.96*** | −0.75*** |
| | (0.05) | (0.07) | (0.08) |
| Education | 0.39*** | 0.49*** | 0.45*** |
| | (0.03) | (0.04) | (0.04) |
| Education × conservative | | −0.21*** | −0.10 |
| | | (0.06) | (0.06) |
| Age (4 categories) | 0.17*** | 0.17*** | 0.16*** |
| | (0.03) | (0.03) | (0.03) |
| Female | −0.04 | −0.04 | −0.08* |
| | (0.05) | (0.05) | (0.05) |
| Nonwhite | −0.16*** | −0.15*** | −0.34*** |
| | (0.05) | (0.05) | (0.06) |
| Smaller government | | | −0.31*** |
| | | | (0.06) |
| Government wasteful | | | −0.75*** |
| | | | (0.06) |
| Constant | −0.93*** | −0.85*** | 1.48*** |
| | (0.07) | (0.07) | (0.08) |
| N | 9,693 | 9,693 | 9,507 |

Notes: Question wordings for the three surveys are as follows:

**CCES (2020)**

Compromise: "Which statement comes closer to your view, even if neither is exactly right? (0) I like elected officials who stick to their positions. (1) I like elected officials who make compromises with people they disagree with."

Taxes vs. spending (100 points): "If your state were to have a budget deficit this year, it would have to raise taxes on income and sales or cut spending, such as education,

TABLE 4.5. *(continued)*

health care, welfare, and road construction. What would you prefer more, raising taxes or cutting spending? Choose a point along the scale from 100% tax increases (and no spending cuts) [1] to 100% spending cuts (and no tax increases) [100]. The point in the middle means that the budget should be balanced with equal amounts of spending cuts and tax increases. If you are not sure, or don't know, please check the 'not sure' box."

Trust small government: "I trust smaller governments more than larger governments." Recoded disagree strongly (0) to agree strongly (4).

**ANES (2020)**

Compromise: "Would you prefer a government official who (1) compromises to get things done, or (0) who sticks to their principles, no matter what?"

Less government: "Which of the following statements comes closer to your view? The less government the better (6) or there are more things that government should be doing (0)?"

Less regulation: "Would it be good for society to have more government regulation (6), about the same amount of regulation as there is now, or more regulation (0)?"

Government activism: "Do you favor, oppose, or neither favor nor oppose the government trying to reduce the difference in incomes between the richest and the poorest households?" Favor a great deal (0) to oppose a great deal (6).

**Pew (2021)**

Compromise: "Please choose the statement that comes closer to your own views, even if neither is exactly right. (0) Compromise in politics is really just selling out on what you believe in. (1) Compromise is how things get done in politics, even if it sometimes means sacrificing your beliefs."

Smaller government: "If you had to choose, would you rather have (0) A bigger government providing more services. (1) A smaller government providing fewer services."

Government wasteful: "Please choose the statement that comes closer to your own views, even if neither is exactly right. (0) Government often does a better job than people give it credit for. (1) Government is almost always wasteful and inefficient."

Standard errors in parentheses.

$*p < .10; **p < .05; ***p < .01.$

this third set of equations, all seven of these small-government attitudinal variables yield negative coefficients, confirming our expectations, and six of the seven reach statistical significance. If people lack trust in government, believe government is wasteful and inefficient, want a smaller, less-intrusive or -activist government, and/or believe in cutting spending before cutting taxes, they are less likely to approve of compromise as a value. Note that this effect is independent of a conservative orientation.

More important for our purposes is what the addition of these attitudinal variables into the equation does to the coefficients associated with the interaction terms. Our expectation is that these controls should absorb some of the explanatory power of the interaction coefficient. Conservatives are more likely to hold and articulate concerns about government, and well-educated conservatives are the most likely of conservatives to hold attitudes that are consistent with the actual premises of the ideology. On all seven of the attitudinal controls, highly educated conservatives are more likely than less-educated conservatives to take the small, less-intrusive government position, the differences ranging between 10 and 20 percentage points.[48] Controlling for these attitudes should reduce the negative drag on the impact of education on compromise, and indeed, it does. When we include these variables in the equations, the coefficients associated with the interaction term are cut in half and move out of statistical significance. Accounting for these attitudes toward government explains most, but not all, of the reduced impact of education on compromise among conservatives.

Our argument is that disdain for government, or at least "big government," is key to understanding why conservatives, and particularly well-educated ones, are less friendly toward political compromise. It also could be that negotiation and compromise represent the kind of "sausage-making" that reinforces what many people do not like about politics and policymaking. Of course, that would affect everybody, not just well-educated conservatives, and indeed, not just conservatives. It also could be that educated conservatives are more likely to believe that compromise threatens their belief system, though this too should not be the case just with conservatives. What truly distinguishes well-educated conservatives is their general orientation toward government, and this explains why they are less likely to embrace compromise.

## Conclusion

Conservatives are consistently more skeptical of and less accepting of compromise than liberals. This everyday predisposition has real implications for politics, setting the boundaries and creating opportunities for democratic leaders charged with solving the problems of the day. In this chapter we have attempted to offer some explanations why ideologues think so differently. To tie these two explanations—loss aversion and antipathy to activist government—together, we note that the growth of government, in general, is cumulative. Even if a Republican administration regulates less, even if some of what they accomplish is deregulatory, the administrative edifice continues to grow. The rules published annually pile up and the size of the *Code of Federal Regulations* continues to expand.[49] Even if the federal deficit varies from year to year or from administration to administration, it is nonetheless almost always a deficit, and the federal debt keeps growing. Indeed, it has tripled over the last twenty years.[50] As a general proposition, then, the very passage of time leads to "bigger government," which naturally puts conservatives concerned about the size and scope of government in a position of loss aversion. This is a stance, as we have shown, that affects how they would generally view processes such as political negotiation and compromise and explains their consistent differentiation from liberals and moderates.

Whatever its sources, the stance toward compromise has implications for politics in city councils, state legislatures, and Congress. Public opinion on various issues does not often constrain the behavior of legislators. In part, this is because most members of the mass public do not have meaningful and detailed opinions on many, indeed most, of the issues that legislatures confront. Most citizens pay only fleeting attention to politics and are not likely to follow negotiations closely. But when constituents have a strong attachment to core principles, and preferences about process (in this case, the choice between engaging with others or rejecting cooperation), that broader orientation is more likely to constrain representatives as they engage in the work of legislating. When that process orientation is created and amplified by a network of media outlets and figures, as we discussed in the last chapter, it makes the influence of mass attitudes even more powerful. As Jeffrey Berry and Sarah Sobieraj argue, "outrage" media is not just a problem of the Right, but it is a problem that leans right.[51] The point, of course, is that what rank-and-file conservatives think and how they differ from other ideologues (and nonideologues) matters to governance, and not just between political parties but within them. How orthodox must our side be? How much can we tolerate a diversity of ideas? Can we find positions that bridge a span of opinions? How much agreement do we have on the question of ends and means (a question that we explore further in the next chapter)?

What ideologues think about political process goes beyond how it influences elected officials. Political culture extends to all the everyday ways—within institutions and outside them—in which we create rules, allocate things of value, resolve conflicts, and advance causes. Citizens must rely on compromise in their daily lives as they navigate relationships, conduct business, and plan for the future. The fact that there is a reservoir of support for it among everyday democrats—liberals, moderates, and conservatives alike—and that this inclination shows up as a majority stance in most of our surveys and analyses is meaningful for a pluralistic, heterogeneous American society. That this reservoir is at risk of losing some of its volume is a challenge for our times.

## CHAPTER FIVE

# Support for Federalism

## A Test of Consistency

The question of how consistently people rely upon ideological principles, or any political principles for that matter, as they navigate the real
world is one that has long called to social scientists. They have shown that
it is often quite difficult to apply ideals to specific situations. They have
explored the contours of "the paradox of tolerance," the imperative in a
democratic society to occasionally be tolerant of intolerance, and written
about the "principle-implementation gap," the difference between embracing civil liberties and applying those liberties to unpopular groups
of people.[1] They have discussed the disjunction between the ethos of
equality in American political culture and the persistence of racial and
economic inequality in this country (and the individual-level attitudes
that support that inequality).[2] It is actually quite difficult to connect principles to real-world situations, to first recognize that these principles are
relevant to a particular situation and then have those principles transcend
immediate political interests. But the ability to apply abstract principles
to circumstances, especially when one's specific preferences are compromised, is, we argue, a good thing in a democracy, and we are not the only
ones to do so. In each of the examples above, the underlying scholarly
assumption is that consistency is a virtue; we argue that it is a component of everyday democracy. Now, one might argue that we just spent a
chapter arguing that a flexible mindset is also an everyday-democratic
virtue. Acceptance of compromise, however, is a principle, a recognition
that give-and-take is required for a democracy to work, even if some of
the "give" includes some of one's own interests. What we look at in this
chapter is a different instance of applying principle. Here we look at how
everyday democrats—liberal and conservative—faithfully apply a general
principle to individual policy circumstances, even when their own interests might be harmed.

This general principle is the concept of federalism and the concentration or dispersal of political power.[3] It is a topic that is well suited to this question of consistency. As is well documented, political attitudes are not wholly informed by political philosophies,[4] and there are certain circumstances in which the big ideas about federal power might be short-circuited by shorter-term interests in their application, where conservative enthusiasm for federalism might wane while liberal support would wax in order to pursue other political or policy goals. Where conservative values and policies can be achieved by the federal government and thus be applied to all (for example, a federal abortion ban), those values and policies could well trump the idealized notion that states or localities should be the locus of power. And if liberals can achieve their goals at the state or local level when Washington is controlled by conservative Republicans or even when liberal policies are stymied by the filibuster, that should logically lead to more support for the devolution of power to states and localities. Consider situations where states pass environmental regulations that are more stringent than federal regulations, assure access to abortion in wake of the *Dobbs* decision, or make it easier to vote.

In pursuing these questions, we make the argument, developed in the pages to follow, that conservatives are significantly more attached to the broad principle of federalism than liberals are to the general idea of national supremacy and are more consistent in their preference for where power should lie. And we contend that the conservative attachment to the devolution of power is genuine, and that it often survives, albeit with some erosion, when policy preferences are at stake. For liberals, attitudes toward federalism are more instrumental and situational, and they are more likely to be a by-product of their policy goals.

Underlying this argument are two foundational points. First, the concept of power devolution is neatly articulated in conservative thought. Of course, the devolution of power has been instrumental in allowing conservatives to dominate the politics of the South, to maintain slavery before the Civil War and Jim Crow after Reconstruction, and to vigorously resist civil rights throughout much of the twentieth century. Indeed, "states' rights" became shorthand for resistance to civil rights. Yet conservatism also encompasses libertarian notions that government is intrinsically oppressive and, importantly, that the devolution of power to smaller units, units closer to the individual, is the ideal. As the *New York Times* columnist Ross Douthat argues, conservatism stands for "local community and local knowledge, against expert certainty and bureaucratic centralization."[5] Moreover, dual sovereignty, the foundation of federalism, is an important innovation enshrined in the US Constitution. In the views of the founders, it is what made democracy possible across a large country with very different regional interests. Conservatism venerates and promotes principled fidelity to the founding document, and federalism fits nicely into the constellation of ideas that constitute a conservative viewpoint. One need only look to the arguments behind originalism that have defined conservative jurisprudence to tie fidelity to the Constitution to a conservative preference for the decentralization of power.

Of course, liberalism does embrace stronger, more assertive government, and the devolution of governmental responsibility to the constituent units can erode the ability of the central government to accomplish things. Liberalism puts more emphasis on egalitarianism, a value that more often than not is enhanced by uniform laws and policies that apply to all. Moreover, robust federal government power may sit in the liberal constellation of principles because of the success of the New Deal and the Great Society or because the notion of federalism, in Martha Derthick's turn of phrase, "suffered fatally from the burden of the South's deviant social system."[6] The devolution of power, however, does not necessarily equate to weak or aloof government. Richard Nathan argues persuasively that federalism is naturally progressive, pro-government, and "a fuel and force for building up governmental activities."[7] It is a principle that some legal scholars and politicians on the left have pragmatically discovered as the stigma of Jim Crow states' rights has dissolved,[8] but *discovered* is the operative word. Federalism has not historically or naturally fit into the liberal constellation of ideas.

The second foundation for our argument comes from recent work in political science that suggests that the Right and the Left differ in fundamental ways that would lead the former to be less pragmatic and more ideologically consistent in their approach to policymaking than the latter. Matt Grossmann and David Hopkins argue that Republicans are generally more unified than Democrats, and more supportive of a party that is ideologically pure at the expense of shaping policy. Democrats, on the other hand, comprise diverse interest groups, are more tolerant of ideological and positional diversity, and are motivated by continual, modest policy progress. These differing orientations lead to fundamentally different views of political purpose and the parties' general misunderstanding of each other.[9] They write, "Republicans claim that they are the party of principles, where the Democrats are the party of giveaways. Democrats view themselves as the party of productivity and problem solving, while criticizing Republicans as the party of extremism and obstruction."[10] If this characterization holds, then we would expect Republicans—and the conservatives who make up the core of the party—to show more fidelity to their principles about the structure of government and less concern for modest policy gains than Democrats and their liberals, who tend to have a more incremental approach to politics and take their policy wins when and where they can get them.

In this chapter, we will argue, as have others, that conservatives are more attached to the federalist principle than liberals, showing that the difference is among the most dramatic in the whole panoply of ideas that differentiate those on the right and those on the left. We then test what we call the "genuineness hypothesis" and look at a variety of issues where policy and principle come into conflict to see how liberals and conservatives respond. There is, as would be expected, some alignment between attitudes about where that policy should be made and policy preferences. That said, we show that conservatives are more likely to stick with their principles than liberals, even in a dramatic situation like the COVID pandemic, when the executive branch is controlled by a conservative administration. Finally, we probe what it is about the decentralization of power that resonates more with conservatives than liberals with a battery of statements about federalism. A couple of very simple ideas—one about states' rights and the other a preference for small rather than large governmental units—differentiate those on the right from those on the left.

## How Genuine Is the Commitment?

The foundation of this chapter is the finding that contemporary liberals and conservatives have markedly different attitudes toward federalism in its broadest articulation. In a 2010 survey from the Pew Research Center, 39 percent of liberals and 73 percent of conservatives responded affirmatively to the prompt that "the federal government is interfering too much in state and local matters."[11] That is certainly a large gap, but this particular Pew survey gives us a sense of just how large by allowing us to compare responses to that question with responses to twenty-three others tapping attitudes toward politics and governance. This assortment of questions, shown in figure 5.1, covers everything from how much the government should regulate business to whether the government threatens personal rights and freedoms, and much else. What is notable is that the liberal-conservative difference that emerges on the federalism question is larger than all but one of the other twenty-three items. In an environment where liberals and conservatives seem so opposed in so many ways, the fact that one of the biggest differences between them is about governance and not policy is notable.

Is that substantial liberal-conservative difference intact in more recent surveys? We replicated the question in a module that appeared on our 2020 CES survey. The gap between the two sets of ideologues is still very large,

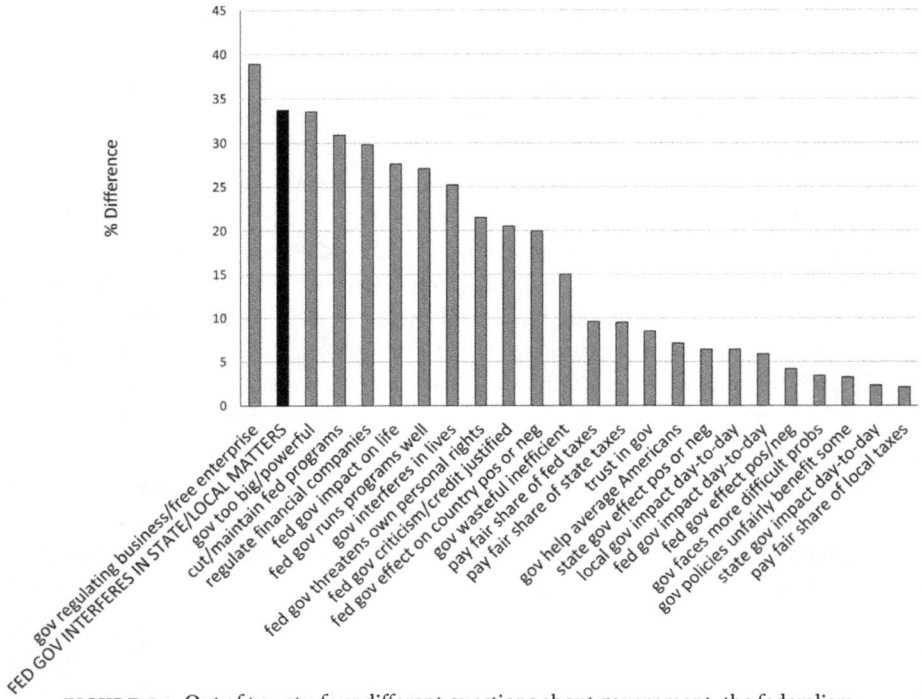

FIGURE 5.1. Out of twenty-four different questions about government, the federalism question evokes the second largest liberal-conservative difference

with 32 percent of liberals and 59 percent of conservatives responding in the affirmative. For additional confirmation, we added a second question to capture yet another dimension of federalism and again find a very sizable difference. When asked whether "the federal government should run only those things that cannot be run at the local level," 43 percent of liberals and 79 percent of conservatives agreed.[12]

Before we accept the conclusion that conservatives are more supportive of federalism or policy devolution than liberals, we want to further probe the general finding to see whether it holds in practice as well as in principle. As with many things, the commitment to the principle of devolution of power is easier in the absence of details. Of course, in some instances, when the federal government is run by Republicans and is implementing conservative policies, federalism may not be such a great thing for conservatives. Likewise, liberals should be more open to the concept of devolution when their state government is promulgating policies more to their liking.[13] Such circumstances are the true test of the conservative attachment to the idea that power should lie more in state and local hands or, for that matter, the liberal attachment to a strong central government.

Pollsters only occasionally ask about federalism in the context of various issues, but we have collected some of these questions here, and they allow us to test how solid the commitment to the principle of devolution is. Take, for instance, the issue of abortion and where decisions about it should be made. Should there be a blanket policy across the country, or should states and localities be able to apply the morals and beliefs of the majority of their own citizens in determining access to abortion? We studied the question before the Supreme Court's *Dobbs* decision, with the starting point being that a modest majority of Americans overall are pro-choice,[14] while in some states pro-life sentiment is dominant. Given that *Roe v. Wade*, in a broad sense, established a national policy that some states, over decades, attempted to modify on the margins, it is not surprising that conservatives are much more likely than liberals to believe that abortion policy should be made at the state level (table 5.1). But there is an analytical opportunity here. What of liberals who are pro-life or conservatives who are pro-choice? In such instances, an individual's policy preference and their ideological principle would not lead to the same answer. What is striking is that pro-choice conservatives align perfectly with pro-life conservatives on this question.[15] There are not large numbers of pro-choice conservatives—just seventy-two in the sample—but it is enough to give some sense that conservatives are genuinely federalist in their orientation on this issue. There are only twenty-seven pro-life liberals in the sample, but packaging liberals and moderates together, being pro-life instead of pro-choice does lead to instrumental support for state-based abortion policies, in remarkable contrast to conservatives.

Another issue—that of school prayer—also offers a simple test of whether ideologues are principled or pragmatic when it comes to federalism (see again table 5.1). Over recent decades, the General Social Survey (GSS) has regularly asked a question about support for a Supreme Court decision that prevents states or localities from requiring the reading of the Lord's Prayer or the Bible in their public schools. Pooling responses from surveys in the 2000s gives us a very large number of cases to work with and provides us the opportunity to introduce an important control into the relationship of ideology and attitude.[16] Conservatives are much more likely to disagree with the court's decision and instead to support the ability of states and localities to require a statement of religiosity in their public schools.[17] Almost two-thirds of conservatives believe this, but only 41 percent of liberals do.

However, this pattern could in fact be explained by the fact that conservatives are much more religious on the whole than liberals. Taking that simple fact into account could diminish the ideological difference on this

TABLE 5.1. Liberal and conservative attitudes toward federal versus state/local balance on various policies

| | Liberals (%) | Moderates (%) | Conservatives (%) |
|---|---|---|---|
| **A. Associated Press/NORC Center for Public Affairs Research (2021)** | | | |
| "Regardless of your opinion about abortion, which do you think should have a larger responsibility for making laws related to abortion: each state government or the federal government?" | | | |
| Each state government | 29 | 46 | 62 |
| | (245) | (532) | (297) |
| Pro-choice | 26 | 40 | 61 |
| | (218) | (322) | (72) |
| Pro-life | 52 | 54 | 62 |
| | (27) | (208) | (224) |
| **B. General Social Survey (2000–2018 pooled)** | | | |
| "The United States Supreme Court has ruled that no state or local government may require the reading of the Lord's Prayer or Bible verses in public schools. What are your views on this? Do you approve or disapprove [of the decision]?" (disapprove is federalist position) | | | |
| Disapprove | 41 | 60 | 67 |
| | (3,693) | (5,175) | (4,771) |
| Attend weekly | 59 | 74 | 73 |
| | (711) | (1,439) | (1,978) |
| Attend less frequently | 41 | 59 | 63 |
| | (1,811) | (2,472) | (2,039) |
| Don't attend | 31 | 46 | 59 |
| | (1,145) | (1,229) | (747) |
| **C. Kaiser Health Tracking Poll (2015)** | | | |
| "Which level of government should be primarily responsible for creating and implementing policies to reduce the number of people abusing prescription painkillers? The federal government, state government or local government?" | | | |
| State/local government | 51 | 59 | 69 |
| | (1,068) | (1,486) | (1,578) |
| **D. National Survey on Energy and Environment (2017)** | | | |
| "For the last 50 years, a federal law has given California the ability to set stricter standards for vehicle emissions than those set in Washington, DC. This has regularly resulted in California's standard becoming the national one over time. Would you say you strongly support, somewhat support, somewhat oppose, or strongly oppose the policy that allows California to set stricter standards for vehicles?" | | | |
| California should be allowed (removing NA/refused) | 72 | 68 | 55 |
| | (183) | (244) | (220) |

TABLE 5.1. *(continued)*

| | Liberals (%) | Moderates (%) | Conservatives (%) |
|---|---|---|---|
| **E. National Survey on Energy and Environment (2018)** | | | |
| "For the last 50 years, a federal law has given California the ability to set stricter standards for vehicle emissions than those set in Washington, DC. If the federal government were to lower the fuel efficiency requirement for automakers, California has stated that it will seek to maintain its existing vehicle emissions standards for new cars and trucks sold in the state. Do you think California should or should not be allowed to maintain this standard if the federal government lowers the national standard?" | | | |
| California should be allowed (removing NA/refused) | 83 (172) | 75 (212) | 58 (190) |

Note: Sample size in parentheses.

question. Looking at the religious, measured by self-reported attendance at services, separately from the less religious and the nonreligious, does indeed show a conditional relationship. Among conservatives, the more religious are more supportive of state/local control over school prayer than the less religious. But even among nonreligious conservatives, a significant majority—59 percent—support devolution on the issue. It is liberals whose response to the issue swings much more by religiosity. For liberals, one's position on the question of which level of government should control school prayer is heavily determined by their religiosity. While a substantial majority of religious liberals believe that school prayer should be determined by state and local governments, a substantial majority of nonreligious liberals believe that this should be a national policy. These findings provide some evidence that most conservatives are more genuinely dedicated to the concept of state and local control, and that liberals approach the question more instrumentally.

We also offer an issue where there is no obvious reason that either conservatives or liberals should favor state and local control other than the application of the federalism principle to the question (see again table 5.1). In 2015, a Kaiser Family Foundation survey asked respondents, "Which level of government should be primarily responsible for creating and implementing policies to reduce the number of people abusing prescription painkillers? The federal government, state government or local government?" Here again we observe a substantial gap between liberals and conservatives, with roughly half of liberals believing that the responsibility rests with states and localities but 69 percent of conservatives taking that position, even though there is no apparent conservative policy advantage at the state and local level. It seems a pure test of the idea that conservatives more naturally apply the devolution of power principle to issues, and the results align with those above.

Finally, we probe the genuineness hypothesis by identifying an issue where conservatives, by right of their policy preferences, should desire federal control over an issue, while liberals should support state and/or local control (see again table 5.1). The issue is environmental regulation, specifically the right of a state such as California to adopt greenhouse gas standards and vehicle emission controls that are stricter than the federal ones. Conservatives are notably less sympathetic to environmental regulation, at any level of government, so this issue does allow us to test, for both liberals and conservatives, whether the ideological principle of policy devolution eclipses a policy preference. Interestingly, the conflict between policy and principle was not lost on the Republican administration or on the Democrats in California defending their standards. Said the Environmental Protection Agency administrator Andrew Wheeler about the issue, "We embrace federalism and the role of the states, but federalism does not mean that one state can dictate the standards for the nation." On the other side, California Attorney General Xavier Becerra highlighted Republican hypocrisy in his commentary on the situation: "Our message to those who claim to support states' rights is 'Don't trample on ours.' We cannot afford to backslide in our battle against climate change."[18]

The National Survey on Energy and the Environment (NSEE) annually captures attitudes on these issues, and in several years the survey has included questions about whether a state should have the right to set stricter standards than the federal government. In the 2017 NSEE survey, the question is informed by the speculation—which turned out to be correct—that the Trump administration would overturn California's ability to set higher standards. The 2018 survey captures the administration's assertion of national policy supremacy on this issue. These questions allow us to see what happens when preference collides with principle from yet another angle.[19]

Responses to both survey questions show quite similar results. Liberals are considerably more likely than conservatives to believe that California should have the ability to set its own policies on emissions. The gaps between liberals and conservatives range from 17 percentage points in 2017 to 25 percentage points in 2018. Is it liberals or conservatives who are driving this anomalous result? We argue that it is the former. On both questions, majorities of conservatives still give the pro-federalism response. On the 2018 survey, for instance, 58 percent of conservatives—and *52 percent of those conservatives who do not believe in climate change* (not shown in the table)—express a view that California law should prevail. It is liberals who fully embrace policy devolution here, with more than 80 percent agreeing that California rules should prevail over the federal government's rules on this issue. Their preference on the policy overwhelms any sort of notion of a unified national standard. Now it is true that over the past fifty years, the national standard has continually adjusted to the California one—and the 2017 question acknowledges as much—but that is still a devolution argument that liberals are embracing.

By looking at how liberals and conservatives respond to the question of the devolution of power on these various issues, we conclude that conservatives have a more principled attachment to the idea that policies are best made by states and localities. Like John Dinan and Jac Heckelman, we find that liberals do not seem as guided by the principle of federal control or national law.[20] Instead, their responses to these questions are more situational; even though they tend to prefer more centralized policymaking, when their policy preferences are best served by the states, they are more likely to favor state control.

## COVID and the Devolution of Responsibility

Another extraordinary opportunity to test the genuineness of the conservative commitment to federalism—as well as the commitment of liberals to a dominant national government—came with the government's response to the emerging COVID-19 pandemic. The question of which level of government has primary responsibility for dealing with a pandemic was omnipresent through the early months of the crisis. The urgency of the situation made this more than just a theoretical concern: decisions had to be made, and authority had to be asserted; people's lives and the economy were at stake. In this context, even President Trump found himself in a quandary. On the one hand, the perceived conservative preference for state and local authority and long-held expectations that public health decisions belonged to states and localities appeared to be on his mind. On the other hand, he clearly desired to project strong leadership from the White House. Deferring to governors was not the way to do that. The result was an absolute muddle, with Trump toggling between taking command and eschewing responsibility. Of course, Trump has never been a paragon of consistency, seeing unpredictability as a virtue and regularly dodging responsibility by casually changing his positions.[21] But in this instance he would change his position even as he was talking, as in a statement made at a briefing early in the crisis: "I like to allow governors to make decisions without overruling them, because from a constitutional standpoint, that's the way it should be done. If I disagreed, I would overrule a governor, and I have that right to do it. But I'd rather have them—you can call it 'federalist,' you can call it 'the Constitution,' but I call it 'the Constitution'—I would rather have them make their decisions." His famous tweets were likewise gesturing in different directions. On a Sunday, he tweeted, "Get your states [*sic*] testing programs & apparatus perfected. Be ready, big things are happening. No excuses!" The very next day, he emphasized his own authority: "For the purpose of creating conflict and confusion, some in the Fake News Media are saying that it is the Governors [*sic*] decision to open up the states, not that of the President of the United States & the Federal Government. Let it be fully understood that this is incorrect."[22] One can hardly blame Trump for struggling with the question of where the federal government has control and where it does not. It was a profoundly difficult question, given the mix of political and policy considerations. Not just policy was at stake, but also government performance and accountability. While the pandemic did require governments to promulgate policies, the additional question here is which level of government was best equipped to provide access to services and needed resources in the context of a crisis. The extraordinary situation offers yet another way to explore how people think about federalism, this time about the devolution of responsibility as much as the devolution of power.

To test our ideas, we placed questions on our 2020 CES module to examine attitudes toward the devolution of responsibility in the early months of the crisis (table 5.2). We asked survey respondents which level of government—the federal government or "your state government"—should be handling the pandemic. Our goal was to establish the natural predilection of conservatives and liberals when assigning responsibility for the pandemic. Much in line with what we have shown above, liberals are much more likely than conservatives to say that the federal government should have that responsibility: While 76 percent of liberals take this position, only 43 percent of conservatives do so.

We also asked respondents which level of government they trusted to take the lead role in the pandemic. In other words, in addition to where pandemic responsibility should lie, we asked where that responsibility would most likely be met. Here, as before, it is liberals who are more situational than conservatives. Even with a conservative Republican president leading the executive branch, only 49 percent of conservatives trust the federal government to lead the effort. For liberals, with Donald Trump as president, only 24 percent of them trust the federal government to lead, despite the fact that they overwhelmingly think that the federal government should do so.

TABLE 5.2. Responses to federalism in the context of the COVID pandemic

| | Liberals (%) | Moderates (%) | Conservatives (%) |
|---|---|---|---|
| Which level of government do you think should be handling the coronavirus pandemic, your state government or the federal government? | | | |
| Federal government | 76 | 57 | 43 |
| | (331) | (257) | (336) |
| Which level of government do you trust more to handle the coronavirus pandemic, your state government or the federal government? | | | |
| Federal government | 24 | 35 | 49 |
| | (331) | (257) | (336) |

Source: 2020 CES.

Note: Sample size in parentheses.

In this case, undoubtedly, liberals are responding to a conservative president, a reality that dominates their federalist principles. What is notable is that conservatives do not offer a mirror image. Their federalist principles more faithfully guide their opinion on which level of government should assume responsibility and lead through the pandemic. Thankfully, pandemics are not everyday events, but the everyday predilections of liberals and conservatives did inform their thinking about the crisis, about whom to look to for leadership, and about whom to trust to handle it as it unfolded.

## Explanations

Up to now our focus has been on simply documenting a basic difference between liberals and conservatives. From here we seek to explain this difference. First, we note that we are not the first to make the argument that conservatives are more federalist than liberals in their orientation and more consistent in that orientation, nor are we the first to try to explain why this is the case. Hunter Rendleman and Jon Rogowski analyze a series of questions capturing various dimensions of federalism, aggregated into a scale. They find that ideology has a significant relationship with that scale. Notably, they do not find a relationship of partisanship to federalist attitude but do conclude that attitudes toward the balance of power between state and national governments "are rooted in more deeply-seated political values" that accompany ideology.[23] Wolak, too, finds that conservatives are more likely than liberals to support the devolution of power. In what she calls a "thermostatic model of responsiveness," the relationship is especially

pronounced when the size of the national government grows larger relative to state and local governments.[24] As that happens, both conservatives
and liberals respond, widening the ideological gap. David Konisky and Paul
Nolette argue that this difference we see in the conservative and liberal
orientation toward federalism may be less a function of the application of
ideological principles and due more to the fact that Republicans control
more state governments at the same time that conservative jurisprudence
is restricting policymaking by federal agencies.[25] In this view, conservatives
may be more federalist than liberals, but this is a response to the structural
advantages held by Republicans in our federalist system. While the explanations for the ideological difference are many, they all start with the basic
liberal-conservative difference that we do. We explore our own explanations in the pages to follow.

## INTERACTIONS WITH GOVERNMENT

We start with a hypothesis that hinges on interactions or perceived interactions with the different levels of government. Could it be that liberals
and conservatives have different stances with respect to policy and responsibility devolution because they have different encounters with state and
local governments? Perhaps conservatives engage more with state and local governments and thus see those governments as more benign. Perhaps
the liberal mistrust of states and localities is also rooted in experience. The
question of how Americans engage with state and local governments and
how they view their encounters with state and local officials is of course en-
meshed with the question of race. Black Americans and liberals may not be
as friendly toward the notion of state or local power, given that public safety
and legal officials—generally state and local officials—have generally treated
Black citizens more harshly than white citizens and have worked within
systems of institutional racism. These "government encounters" could also
shape Black and white liberal responses to the questions of federalism.

The only problem with the government-encounters hypothesis is that
it fails to gain traction from the start, for there is no apparent difference in
how liberals and conservatives engage with the various levels of government. Surveys that allow us to test this idea come from the early 2000s,
but there is little reason to believe that these findings should be different
twenty years later. The differences between liberals and conservatives in
their engagement with various levels of government are slender and inconsistent. For instance, when asked in a Pew Internet and American Life Poll
from 2009, "Just in general, which level of government would you say you
deal with most often?," 50 percent of liberals say their local government and

TABLE 5.3. Liberal and conservative attitudes toward interaction with and trust of local government

| | Liberals (%) | Moderates (%) | Conservatives (%) |
|---|---|---|---|
| **A. Pew Internet & American Life Poll (2009)** | | | |
| "Just in general, which level of government would you say you deal with most often, local government, state government or the federal government?" | | | |
| Local | 50 | 56 | 54 |
| State | 23 | 23 | 23 |
| Federal | 20 | 15 | 14 |
| | (463) | (762) | (794) |
| "Now I'm going to ask you about various organizations and types of organizations. How much of the time do you think you can trust your local government?" | | | |
| Just about always | 8 | 8 | 10 |
| Most of the time | 34 | 38 | 31 |
| Some of the time | 44 | 43 | 47 |
| Never | 13 | 11 | 13 |
| | (471) | (766) | (798) |
| **B. John F. Kennedy School of Government Social Capital Community Survey (2006)** | | | |
| "From what level of government do you feel you get the most for your money?" | | | |
| Local | 44 | 34 | 37 |
| State | 30 | 30 | 28 |
| Federal | 26 | 36 | 35 |
| | (573) | (682) | (1,094) |

Note: Sample size in parentheses.

20 percent say the federal government (table 5.3). For conservatives, those percentages are 54 percent and 14 percent. In that same survey, 42 percent of liberals and 41 percent of conservatives respond "just about always" or "most of the time" when asked about their trust of local government.

The largest difference to emerge in these comparisons is from a 2006 survey that asks, "From what level of government do you feel you get the most for your money?"[26] Here, surprisingly, it is conservatives who are more likely than liberals to name the federal government as providing value, 35 percent to 26 percent (and modestly less likely to name local government as providing value, 37 percent to 44 percent). It would be a mistake to overinterpret this difference, as these questions do not capture assessments of the quality of government interactions, but we do come away from these analyses with modest confidence that the liberal-conservative gap in federalist attitudes does not spring from differential levels of engagement with different levels of government. And while there is an ideological difference in trust in the federal government (discussed below), there is no difference in trust of local governments.

## OTHER EXPLANATIONS

What if the ideological differences we have observed have little to do with ideology? What if they are simply a function of other ways in which liberals and conservatives differ from each other? To further explore the distinctive thinking of conservatives—and liberals—we undertake a multivariate analysis. The idea here is to see whether the liberal-conservative difference holds even after we control for various correlates of ideology.

In table 5.4, we offer a series of multivariate regressions that build successively upon each other. Using data from the 2010 Pew survey, we started with the one general question on federalism as our dependent variable. The statement "The federal government is interfering too much in state and local matters" evokes one of the largest differences between liberals and conservatives in the Pew survey (see again fig. 5.1). Our analytical strategy is to compare liberals and conservatives on this question not to each other, but to those people who are neither liberal nor conservative. This approach allows us to look at what makes both liberals and conservatives distinctive. We thus create two dummy variables—one for liberals and one for conservatives— with moderates and nonideologues (people who do not identify themselves as being at any point on the scale) serving as the base category.

We start by regressing the belief that the federal government interferes too much on the liberal and conservative dummy variables. We then layer on other variables in a series of analyses to test whether these controls explain the distinctive positions of liberals and conservatives. If these controls are explanatory, then the coefficients associated with the ideology variables in the original equation should move out of statistical significance. If the controls do not reduce the significance of the ideology variables, that means that some other factor explains the distinctly different attitudes of liberals and conservatives on the question of federalism.

The first regression shows, unsurprisingly, that being a liberal or a conservative, as opposed to a moderate, is powerfully important (table 5.4). In this equation, liberals are less likely and conservatives more likely than those in the base category to believe that the federal government interferes too much in state and local affairs. The coefficients associated with the two dummies are large and statistically significant and provide the basis for comparison as we add controls into the equation.

TABLE 5.4. Liberal and conservative attitudes toward federalism (logistic regression)

| | Model 1 | Model 2 | Model 3 |
|---|---|---|---|
| Liberal | −1.01** | −0.84** | −0.28 |
| | (0.12) | (0.12) | (0.16) |
| Conservative | 0.51** | 0.65** | 0.48** |
| | (0.12) | (0.12) | (0.16) |
| Age | | 0.03 | 0.02 |
| | | (0.02) | (0.02) |
| Education | | −0.17** | −0.13** |
| | | (0.03) | (0.04) |
| Black | | −0.22* | 0.39** |
| | | (0.09) | (0.11) |
| Rights/freedoms | | | 0.58** |
| | | | (0.05) |
| Trust in government | | | 0.38** |
| | | | (0.07) |
| Effective | | | 0.17** |
| | | | (0.06) |
| Regulations | | | 1.11** |
| | | | (0.05) |
| Constant | 0.62** | 0.87** | −4.96** |
| | (0.11) | (0.15) | (0.29) |
| $N$ | 1,576 | 1,546 | 1,458 |

Source: Pew Research Center Poll on Government Trust (2010).

Notes:

Federalism (dependent variable): "The federal government is interfering too much in state and local matters. Do you completely agree, mostly agree, mostly disagree, completely disagree?" (recoded to 0 disagree and 1 agree)

Liberal: Liberals vs. base category (moderates and respondents who don't place on scale)

Conservative: Conservatives vs. base category (same)

Black: Black vs. non-Black, inclusive of Asians and non-Black Latinos. Base category is non-Black.

Rights/freedoms: "Do you think the federal government threatens your own personal rights and freedoms, or not? [If yes] Is this a major threat or a minor threat?" (1 No threat; 2 Yes, minor threat; 3 Yes, major threat)

*(continued)*

TABLE 5.4. *(continued)*

Trust in government: "How much of the time do you think you can trust the government in Washington to do what is right? Just about always, most of the time, or only some of the time?"

Effective: "All in all, how good a job does the federal government do running its programs? An excellent job, a good job, only a fair job, or a poor job?"

Regulations: "The government has gone too far in regulating business and interfering with the free enterprise system. Do you completely disagree (1), mostly disagree, mostly agree, or completely agree (4)?"

*$p$ .05; **$p < .01$.

The first controls we introduce into the equation are demographic: education, age, and race. Could the fact that ideologues are better educated than nonideologues help explain the difference between liberals and conservatives? Perhaps the fact that conservatives are more likely to be white and older and liberals to be Black and younger is shaping the effect of ideology on attitudes toward the federal government. Indeed, two of the three demographic control variables (education and race) achieve statistical significance in the multivariate analysis displayed in the second column in table 5.4. Older people are not statistically different from young people, a surprising finding given that the oldest respondents might associate forceful federal action with the New Deal and its role in delivering the country out of the Great Depression. The effect of education is strong and significant: The better educated are more likely to believe that the federal government is not interfering inappropriately in state and local matters. And the effect of race is real: Black respondents are more supportive of the supremacy of the national government than are non-Black respondents. Moreover, introducing these demographic controls into the equation does affect the ideology coefficients: The impact of being liberal as opposed to moderate/nonideological decreases, and the impact of being conservative as opposed to moderate/nonideological increases. In both cases, however, the change in these coefficients is quite modest, and, notably, these coefficients retain statistical significance. All else being the same—at least, demographically—liberals and conservatives hold distinctly different views on federalism from those in the middle—and certainly from each other.

Building upon this model, we add four attitudinal variables capturing various views about the federal government to the equation. As Marc Hetherington and John Nugent argue in their study of attitudes toward devolution, "State government popularity is, in part, a function of the federal government's unpopularity."[27] If this is so, then the conservative attachment to a federalist structure could simply be a function of not liking the national government or viewing its authority as a problem. Alternatively, if liberals like and trust the national government more, then perhaps they mind less when the federal-state balance leans more toward the former. The four controls we add to the model capture different ways that people might react to and think about the federal government:

- Do you think the federal government threatens your own personal rights and freedoms, or not? [If yes] Is this a major threat or a minor threat?
- How much of the time do you think you can trust the government in Washington to do what is right? Just about always, most of the time, or only some of the time?
- All in all, how good a job does the federal government do running its programs? An excellent job, a good job, only a fair job, or a poor job?
- The government has gone too far in regulating business and interfering with the free enterprise system. Do you completely agree, mostly agree, mostly disagree, or completely disagree?

It makes sense that people who view the federal government to be personally threatening, untrustworthy, or ineffective would be loath to see the federal government involved in state and local matters. Likewise, believing that the federal government interferes too much with our economic system also could lead to a more generalized concern about federal intrusiveness. We view these relationships with interest. But we also look at them as explanations for the distinctly different perspectives on federalism of liberals and conservatives. What happens to the ideology coefficients when we account for how conservatives and liberals view the federal government?

In the third model, the four attitudinal variables all operate as expected. The more one mistrusts the federal government, finds it threatening or ineffective, and objects to its interference with private enterprise, the more likely one is to respond favorably to the federalism question.[28] What is noteworthy is how these controls affect the relationship of ideology to federalist attitude. Their effect is not symmetrical. When the attitudinal controls are introduced into the equation, the difference between being liberal and being moderate or not ideological shrinks notably and to a point that is no longer statistically significant. For liberals, their preference for national over state governance is explained by how they feel about the federal government. However, these controls do not explain the distinctly conservative belief that the federal government should stay out of state and local governmental business. The coefficient associated with being conservative loses a little of its power, but it remains strongly significant even in this third model. Negative views of the federal government do not fully explain why conservatives differ from moderates and nonideologues in their attitudes toward federal-state balance, at least with this particular measure in this particular survey.

The multivariate exercise is meaningful, to be sure, but it still leaves us without an answer as to what might best explain why conservatives, in particular, hold distinctive views on federalism. To further investigate, we crafted a variety of statements about federal versus state and local control to see which of them evokes the largest differences between liberals and conservatives. In this, we are taking a tack similar to that taken by Nicholas Jacobs, who seeks to understand why individuals "think federally" and how ideas about government might differentiate liberals from conservatives.[29] In our study, respondents are asked to agree or disagree with eight statements, each one crafted with a potential explanation for the liberal-conservative difference in mind. We placed this exercise on the 2020 CES.

Three of the eight statements in table 5.5 generate little difference between liberals and conservatives (or moderates, for that matter). One possible reason for the ideological difference is that conservatives are much more likely than liberals to live in rural places where state and local public officials are naturally more likely to be politically aligned. That may be true,[30] but it does not translate into how liberals and conservatives perceive their local and state officials. There is no difference at all in liberal and conservative responses to the statement "My state and local officials are more likely than federal officials to make decisions that I will agree with."

One of the most prominent arguments about the benefits of federalism is that it creates a "laboratory for democracy." When Justice Louis Brandeis coined this phrase back in 1932 in his decision in *New State Ice Co. v. Liebmann,* he wrote, "It is one of the happy incidents of the Federalist system that a single courageous State may, if its citizens choose, serve as a laboratory; and try novel social and economic experiments without risk to the rest of the country."[31] Brandeis wrote this in the last paragraph of the decision, without a great deal of exposition, but the metaphor and this pro-federalism argument have long resonated. We were eager to see whether the laboratory argument resonates in contemporary times, and whether it does so with some people more than others. The answer to the first question is a likely yes. A strong majority of all respondents—over 60 percent—agree that "giving power to state and local governments provides opportunities to experiment with policies." For our purposes, however, acceptance of the idea does not vary much across the ideological spectrum. Conservatives may be more enamored with federalism conceptually, but it is not because they are more likely than liberals to believe in the democratic laboratory,

TABLE 5.5. Liberal and conservative responses to some explanations for devolution (percentage who agree or strongly agree)

| | Liberals | Moderates | Conservatives | Difference between liberals and conservatives |
|---|---|---|---|---|
| "My state and local officials are more likely than federal officials to make decisions that I will agree with." | 47 | 47 | 44 | −3 |
| "It's best when decisions are made by officials who are most in touch with the people." | 89 | 77 | 84 | −5 |
| "Giving power to state and local governments provides opportunities to experiment with policies." | 57 | 55 | 64 | 7 |
| "Throughout history, the federal government has been more likely than state and local governments to infringe on the rights of individuals." | 31 | 31 | 43 | 12 |
| "It's important to have policies made by the national government so that all citizens are treated fairly and equally." | 76 | 69 | 64 | −12 |
| "Throughout history, state and local governments have been more likely than the federal government to infringe on the rights of minority groups." | 59 | 45 | 42 | −17 |
| "'States' Rights' is an important principle." | 52 | 72 | 87 | 35 |
| "I trust smaller governments more than larger governments." | 34 | 47 | 73 | 39 |
| Number of respondents in survey (weighted) | 331 | 257 | 336 | |

Source: 2020 CES.

or because liberals are more likely than conservatives to be concerned that state laboratories will be a friendly environment for democratic backsliding or under-the-radar ideological innovation.[32]

Likewise, the statement "It's best when decisions are made by officials who are most in touch with the people" does little to distinguish liberals from conservatives. In conceiving this statement, we hypothesized that perhaps conservatives might be more populist in their orientation to government or more accepting of what Greg Shaw and Stephanie Reinhart call "the old antifederalist argument that government close to the people is good government."[33] The fact is that an overwhelming percentage of all respondents—left, right, and center—want their representatives to be "close" to "the people," however that term is defined. Indeed, liberals are modestly *more* likely than conservatives to agree with the statement and moderates modestly less so. But the key to understanding the ideological difference in attitudes toward federalism clearly does not rest with a populist explanation.

Three other statements do modestly distinguish between liberals and conservatives, with the differences ranging between 10 and 20 percentage points. For instance, conservatives are more likely than liberals to agree that "throughout history, the federal government has been more likely than state and local governments to infringe on the rights of individuals," while liberals are more likely than conservatives to agree that "throughout history, state and local governments have been more likely than the federal government to infringe on the rights of minority groups" and that "it's important to have policies made by the national government so that all citizens are treated fairly and equally." These differences are meaningful, and the findings suggest that some of the difference in how liberals and conservatives think about federalism has to do with how they think about whether and how the government respects the rights of individuals versus those of groups. This reasoning would be consistent with what Grossmann and Hopkins argue is a fundamental difference between the Left and the Right,[34] with the former concerned with group interests and the latter with individual liberties.

The largest differences, however, emerge in responses to two other statements. The two statements offer the most basic of ideas, but they clearly capture fundamentally different orientations toward how power and responsibility should be divided between national and state government. The term "states' rights" has lingered for decades and over the course of the Jim Crow era came to represent the defense of segregation. The point was not that segregation was somehow right—though, of course, that was a common belief among southern whites—but that Southerners had a right to their own societal rules without interference from the federal government. The rhetorical strategy of southern politicians was to conflate federal interference in state affairs with authoritarianism or even communism. States' rights are "the only guarantee we have that a kind of Kremlin will not be established in Washington," as Strom Thurmond put it as he was campaigning for president as a Dixiecrat in 1948.[35]

Conspicuously, both liberals and conservatives respond to the term "states' rights," but they diverge a lot, with conservatives much more likely to agree that this is an "important principle." It is difficult to interpret this as anything but a profoundly different reaction to racial change and civil rights. Conservatives are much more likely than liberals to express racial resentment in the CES survey (and in most every study), and taking this into account does explain some (but not all) of the ideological difference we see on this item. On one CES question asking for a response to the statement "Irish, Italians, Jewish, and many other minorities overcame prejudice and worked their way up. Blacks should do the same without any special favors," the differences between liberals and conservatives are stark (4 percent of the former and 67 percent of the latter agree). On another, "Generations of slavery and discrimination have created conditions that make it difficult for Blacks to work their way out of the lower class," the differences are even broader, with 84 percent of liberals and 14 percent of conservatives in agreement.

To see what difference racial attitudes make to the states' rights responses, we regress the states' rights question on two dummy variables capturing liberals and conservatives (both vis-à-vis moderates and the non-ideological), as well as on some demographic controls (including a dummy variable capturing Black respondents). We then create a racial resentment scale from the two items above and add that variable to that equation.[36] As seen in table 5.6, the coefficients associated with the two ideology dummies do shrink, but they remain significant in the second equation, with the conservative coefficient at .05 rather than .01 significance. The results suggest that the conservative attachment to and liberal concern about federalism are informed by the fact that "states' rights" became code for resisting racial change, but they do not explain the entire relationship.[37]

The other question that profoundly distinguishes liberals from conservatives is one that captures a different orientation toward things big and small. Three-quarters of conservatives and just short of one-third of liberals "trust smaller governments more than larger governments." The question does not involve a sophisticated analysis on the part of the respondent but simply captures a response to size and perhaps to the complexity and bureaucracy that accompany larger units of government as well as the diversity of their

TABLE 5.6. Effect of racial attitudes on the relationship between ideology and a favorable view of states' rights (logistic regression)

|  | Model 1 | Model 2 |
|---|---|---|
| Liberal | −0.63** | −0.42** |
|  | (0.09) | (0.10) |
| Conservative | 0.34** | 0.22* |
|  | (0.08) | (0.10) |
| Age | −0.003 | −0.003 |
|  | (0.002) | (0.002) |
| Education | −0.04 | −0.04 |
|  | (0.02) | (0.02) |
| Black | 0.27** | 0.51** |
|  | (0.11) | (0.12) |
| Racial resentment |  | 0.08** |
|  |  | (0.02) |
| Constant | 9.48** | 9.31* |
|  | (3.78) | (4.34) |
| $N$ | 921 | 801 |

Source: 2020 CES.

Notes:

States' rights (dependent variable): "States' rights is an important principle."
(1 disagree strongly to 5 agree strongly)

Liberal: Liberals vs. base category (moderates and respondents who don't place on scale)

Conservative: Conservatives vs. base category (same)

Black: Black vs. non-Black, inclusive of Asians and non-Black Latinos. Base category is non-Black.

Racial resentment: "Irish, Italians, Jewish, and many other minorities overcame prejudice and worked their way up. Blacks should do the same without any special favors"; and "Generations of slavery and discrimination have created conditions that make it difficult for Blacks to work their way out of the lower class." Both variables are five-point items (agree strongly to disagree strongly). The first variable has been recoded so that disagreement is the resentful response and then aggregated with the second variable to form a nine-point scale.

$*p < .05; **p < .01.$

jurisdictions. Smaller governments, on the other hand, are more likely to preside over more homogeneous populations and tend to be less complex organizations.

This finding is certainly consistent with various psychological studies that show that liberals and conservatives respond differently to complexity, bureaucracy, and diversity. Dana Carney and colleagues, for instance, discuss how liberals are far more likely than conservatives to tolerate messiness and to be comfortable with difference.[38] Believing that power should devolve to smaller units—states or even localities—is thus consistent with the psychological predispositions that many conservatives have. While it is true that a federalist system is in some ways "messier," with policies varying across the landscape, individuals tend only to live in one state and one locality, and conservatives clearly are more comfortable with the smaller units. Liberals, on the other hand, are less likely to have a bad reaction to those things in the polity that require a stronger central government or to the various features of such a government.

Before concluding, we make one final observation. Cindy Kam and Robert Mikos show experimentally that when subjects are primed to consider the value of devolution, they respond. In their study, which looked at attitudes toward a federal ban on physician-assisted suicide, subjects were significantly influenced by elite discourse on the issue.[39] If it is Republican much more than Democratic politicians who are expounding upon the virtues of federalism—and that does appear to be the case, at least since the Reagan years—then Kam and Mikos's findings would help to explain the relatively consistent differences between liberals and conservatives that appear above. The question then goes back to why Republican and conservative politicians have absorbed the value of federalism more than Democrats and liberals. That would require a different kind of study, though certainly one worth pursuing.

## Conclusion

In this chapter, we demonstrate that conservatives are distinctive in their embrace of federalism, even in specific circumstances, and even in specific circumstances where it may not be in their political interest to do so. Liberals view the question of government power more instrumentally and are sometimes more supportive of the devolution of power to the states, sometimes less so. We interpret this difference as being due to the fact that conservatives are more likely to call upon their ideological principles and apply them to situations—a generally positive thing, in our view.

Of course, the fact that racial attitudes are contributing to the federalist commitments among conservatives both tempers and complicates any praise of consistency. Moreover, one might interpret our lauding of such consistency as an admiration for hard stances. It is not that we think that ideologues should be inflexible and unyielding all the time. As we discuss in chapter 4, reaching for and accepting compromise is also a critical democratic virtue, and compromise is easier to reach when interests rather than principles are at stake. And it is not always even desirable to be perfectly consistent. Slavish consistency is dogmatic—"the hobgoblin of little minds," in Emerson's words.[40] Nonetheless, we argue that when it comes to the day-to-day political encounters that most citizens face, a more consistent application of ideology to reality can contribute to weeding some of the expediency and cynicism out of our democratic politics. A political process that is rooted more in general principles is about more than just winning. Ideology offers clarity of purpose in the political process, and it boosts ideas above self-interest. Again, taken too far, completely ideological politics would be undesirable; but a dose of consistency, it seems to us, could have some value in how we govern ourselves and in how citizens interact with one another.

One final, more global point is that the general ability to translate a principle into an issue position or to apply a principle to a political circumstance is an everyday virtue, the kind of predisposition that gives coherence and meaning to democratic life. What we show in this chapter is but one instance of a larger idea informing particular opinions, albeit an important one. This way of thinking could manifest itself in other everyday ways, perhaps in the application of religious principles to daily life or holding ethical positions that guide daily decisions. However it might happen, we argue that connecting big ideas to small ones has real political value, and as we note above, political scientists, theorists, and empiricists have long seen this ability as a true indicator of meaningful citizenship.

## CHAPTER SIX

# Charity and Volunteerism

Writing in his 2006 book, *Who Really Cares*, the economist Arthur Brooks took up what he believed to be a libel against conservatives: that conservatives were selfish, mean-spirited, and uncaring because they rejected the welfare state. In the same vein, he said liberals were mistakenly perceived to be more generous because their professed core values stressed helping to improve the lives of those in need. In his words, "These are, perhaps, the most common stereotypes in our modern American political discourse: The political left is compassionate and charitable toward the less fortunate, but the political right is oblivious to suffering."[1]

Drawing on a number of surveys, Brooks determined that it was conservatives who were more generous in terms of both money contributed to philanthropy and time spent volunteering for charitable organizations. He identified four critical correlates that explain why conservatives are more generous. More than anything else, philanthropy is linked to religiosity, and conservatives are much more likely to belong to a congregation and attend services. The other foundational roots of charity, he argues, are skepticism about the role of government, strong family ties, and personal entrepreneurialism. Brooks says that these factors are all tied to a conservative philosophy.[2]

*Who Really Cares* received a great deal of attention, and its counterintuitive findings heartened conservatives. Liberals were chastened by the findings but also offended by the book's antagonistic tone toward them. One notable argument in the book was that it was "intact" families that nurtured charity and that "secularism and family breakdown occur less frequently among conservatives than liberals."[3] Brooks seemed to delight in making the case that there is a characterological difference between conservatives and liberals. Still, he held out hope for liberals and at the end of his book concludes, "I am asking liberals to stand up for charity."[4]

## Liberal Hypocrisy?

Brooks is a respected scholar, and *Who Really Cares* continues to be a central work in the study of philanthropy. In our initial reading of the book, we thought the evidence on conservatives was intriguing but wondered about Brooks's charged accusation of liberal hypocrisy. We had just completed research on some of the other topics in this book and had not observed broad characterological flaws among liberals.

Using Brooks's provocative findings as a portal, we move here to broaden our understanding of the differences between conservatives and liberals. Charity and voluntarism may seem outside of politics and government: The act of writing a check to the United Way or participating in a school bake sale does not conjure up images of citizens taking action to advance either their political party or specific policy goals. Yet we believe that the seemingly ordinary, everyday motivations to give to charity and to volunteer can grow out of the same sentiments that lead us to become directly involved in elections or to become active in overtly political organizations. The motivation to donate to a social services nonprofit may spring from the same place in our character that leads to supporting liberal Democrats in elections. Moreover, churches and secular nonprofits can be political—congregations mobilizing people to vote, for example. An especially important aspect of the nonprofit sector is that the United States depends on nonprofit organizations to deliver social services.[5] A significant portion of the funding for such nonprofits comes from charitable donations.

The ostensibly nonpolitical sector of churches, charities, and nonprofits is tied in multiple ways to the push and pull of the political system. These voluntary organizations exist because they aggregate many hearts encompassing habits of caring and compassion. They are essential to everyday democracy, as they bring people together to work in the spirit of cooperation on solving community problems in pragmatic ways. They have also been sources of innovation, using their small scale to their advantage in creating new ways to approach long-standing issues.

Similar to our lines of inquiry in previous chapters, we base much of our analysis on the role of ideology and values in influencing behavior and attitudes. At the same time, the research here has its roots in a variety of developments in the demographics of America, the ideological evolution of our two parties, and the changing role of churches, charities, and nonprofits. For conservatives, a historical dimension stands out as a focus on voluntarism has diminished. Accepting the Republican nomination in 1980, Ronald Reagan pledged to restore "the American spirit of voluntary service." He established an office in the White House to encourage public-private partnerships. George H. W. Bush spoke of the voluntary sector as a "thousand points of light" and created a Commission on National and Community Service. George W. Bush notably labeled himself a "compassionate conservative" and created an Office of Faith-Based and Community Initiatives in the White House.[6] In a startling contrast to these earlier Republican presidents, Donald Trump not only failed to generate any initiatives on philanthropy or voluntarism during his first term, but he went out of his way to mock them. At a campaign stop during the 2018 congressional elections, Trump gratuitously asked the crowd, "Thousand points of light? I never quite got that one. What the hell is that?"[7]

Liberalism has changed as well. Most broadly, the demographics of the liberal sector of the population have evolved dramatically, and people of color are a much larger proportion of it than they were just twenty years ago. What does this suggest about the generosity of today's generation of liberals? It is not clear. Women have swung more toward the liberal side in elections, and there is literature indicating that when women have resources, they are more generous than men.[8] But there are a lot of moving parts to conjectures on gender and charity, and recent scholarly literature does not show a consistent pattern.

The population of those who are the donors to charity may have changed in other ways. Although the total amount given to charity continues to grow, the percentage of households that contributes has contracted. Unfortunately, this decline has been substantial. A survey in 2000 showed that around two-thirds (66 percent) of American households contributed to charity.[9] In 2021 the figure had dropped to 56 percent.[10] Census data show the same trend.[11] The question then is, who is it that has moved away from giving (or who never started giving)? Additionally, does the ideological asymmetry identified by Brooks still hold?

Changes in the population of donors also may come from the downward trend in religious identity, since those who are religious are more likely to donate to a charitable cause than are nonbelievers. The declining support across American religious denominations seems likely to accelerate, for the strongest rejection of religious identity comes from young adults.[12] A 2021 Gallup Poll found that only 47 percent of Americans said they belonged to a religious congregation. In over eighty years of asking this question, this was the first time Gallup reported that fewer than half of respondents belonged to a church or other religious congregation.[13]

Another change comes from tax law, since the incentives to donate to charity were significantly reduced by President Trump's Tax Cuts and Jobs Act of 2017 (TCJA). The new law lowered marginal tax rates, and among the many other provisions, it doubled the standard deduction. The result was that the number of those itemizing deductions immediately fell from around 25 percent of taxpayers to slightly less than half of that number.[14] Only those with a lot of deductions now have reason to itemize. In the absence of the deduction, the effective cost of a charitable contribution for many middle-income taxpayers rose. In essence, the federal government significantly reduced its subsidy for charity through the tax code. In the first tax year after passage, giving by individuals fell by an estimated 3.4 percent.[15]

Other scholars have investigated Brooks's conclusion about charity and ideology with more recent data, and collectively, the results of this research are contradictory. Some determine, like Brooks, that conservatives are more generous, some find liberals are, and others find neither side is more likely to give than the other. We will not individually review each of the studies in this extensive literature but will instead try to explain why a consensus has failed to emerge.[16] To begin with, the questions asked vary: The basic line of inquiry may be whether an individual or household gave, or how much was given, or what charities received a donation. And for any one of these, the wording of a survey question can differ, and that affects responses.

We also should note that questions have been raised about the accuracy of Brooks's initial analysis. In their monumental study of religion, *American Grace*, Robert Putnam and David Campbell harshly indict Brooks's quantitative work. They conclude that Brooks misinterpreted his own data, and their reanalysis shows that charity comes from religion *independent* of ideology. In other words, giving is related to being religious; whether you are a conservative or liberal has little to do with it.[17]

Finally, our exploration of ideology in this book leads us to be cautious in any expectation that modern liberalism or conservatism is linked to greater generosity. In an earlier era of social science, the presumption might have been that charity is related to altruism, a psychological predisposition toward helping others that takes root in childhood. Another reason to be skeptical of ideology as a dominant factor in charity is that the most reliable way for a nonprofit to raise money is to ask a potential donor in a face-to-face setting. This is surely a major reason religiosity plays an oversized role: People are asked in church to give. More broadly, social networks are crucially important, since the more one interacts with others, the more likely they are to be asked to make a contribution. Still, in this day and age it seems that just about everything is politicized, and Brooks's initial premise—that ideology plays a critical role in the level of charitable donations—may still be correct despite whatever shortcomings may be present in his analysis. This is what we set out to explore.

# Ideology and Charity

After reviewing this multidisciplinary literature, we believed that we could best contribute to what has already been done by following two survey research strategies. The first was to ask not simply about whether respondents gave or whether they volunteered, but more specifically about who they gave to or what they volunteered for. Second, survey questions about charity and volunteering are often limited in number, small parts of larger surveys that are more general in nature. In contrast, we asked an entire battery of relevant questions in the extensive module we placed on the 2020 CES.

To gain insight into which charities liberals and conservatives respond to, we asked respondents whether they contributed to each of four types of organizations. Later in the survey individuals were asked whether they volunteered for these same types of charities. For the charity questions, the specific wording was, "In the past 12 months have you donated to any of the following":

- Religious congregation or other religious charities
- A charitable organization that focuses on health, disease, or disability
- Social service organizations (for example, Meals on Wheels, student mentoring organizations, antipoverty organizations)
- Other nonprofit organizations (for example, United Way, neighborhood associations, local arts organizations)

Each of these types of organizations serves different constituencies, and we designed the wording to elicit varying considerations that are likely to come into play when potential donors ponder them. Donations to religious congregations are seemingly straightforward; they offer a means of supporting one's own spiritual beliefs. Separating out this category pulls it away from charity in general so we can distinguish the strong force of religion from other motivations to donate. For most respondents, the "health, disease, and disability" category should not prompt any political or ideological sentiments, as such charities disproportionately attract those with personal, family, or a friend's experience with a particular disease or facility. The wording for "social service organizations" with the specific example of "antipoverty organizations" is intended to highlight organizations that provide charity to individuals in need. Finally, "other nonprofit organizations" was designed to evoke thoughts of community and neighborhood through the examples of "neighborhood associations" and "local arts organizations."[18]

The largest amount of charity in the United States goes to organized religion ($136 billion in 2021), and conservatives dominate religious giving.[19] About 50 percent of the conservative respondents in our survey say they donate to a religious congregation or other religious charity, while only 21 percent of liberals give to such an organization (fig. 6.1). This donation rate for conservatives is the highest positive response of any of the ideological cohorts for any of the four types of charity. This finding comes as no surprise, since conservatives are much more likely than liberals to attend church, but the differential with liberals is striking. Data from 2018–19 indicate that roughly 80 percent of Republicans identify as Christian, while only 55 percent of Democrats are self-described Christians. Among Democrats, those who do not identify with any religion—whom religious scholars call "nones"—constitute 34 percent of the party, which is a significant increase in nones from 20 percent in 2009. Nones on the Republican side increased to 16 percent from 10 percent during the same time period.[20]

Mainstream Protestant denominations have decreased precipitously in numbers, and Catholic religiosity has dropped as well. Evangelical Christians are often cited as an exception to the serious decline in religious identity in the United States. Evangelicals did increase in numbers in the 1970s and 1980s and were then stable before declining in the 1990s.[21] This decline

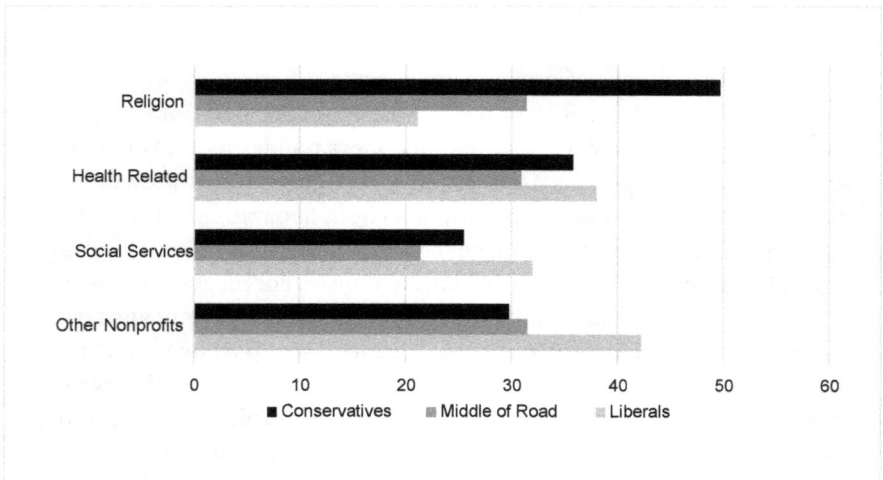

FIGURE 6.1. Ideology and charitable giving

Source: 2020 CES

Note: $N$ = 806.

in all major denominations means that fewer people will hear a spiritual message at religious services telling them that they should help those who are less fortunate. The most common topic that worshippers recall hearing at services concerns hunger and poverty. Indeed, 91 percent of those who attend services say that they have heard sermons on this topic.[22] Another serious consequence of declining religiosity is that charitable behavior can be practice driven: Learning to give takes place at church, and the habit of giving is taught there.[23]

If liberals are true to the ideal of equality, we would expect the clearest expression of support to be in the area of social services. The cues for this category were fashioned to evoke charity that reaches individuals with references to hunger, mentoring of students, and poverty. In the American nonprofit world, charitable social service organizations include those serving the homeless, victims of domestic abuse, families in crisis, the hungry and malnourished, low-income single parents, teenage runaways, and new immigrants, to name just some constituencies. While liberals may respond because of a desire to fight inequality by helping people at the bottom of the income scale, we do not dismiss the secular message that conservatives might receive. Classic conservative ideology holds that the state should be small and that welfare should come from charity and be targeted at individuals with demonstrated need. This perspective contrasts with liberals' emphasis on building a strong safety net made up of government programs.

Thus, although we expected that liberals would have a stronger response to this sector, there are reasons conservatives might find such social service nonprofits worthy of their support. In the end, our tests show that liberals are in fact more likely to contribute to social services (32 percent) than are conservatives (26 percent). Although this difference may seem modest, it is statistically significant, and across the entire American population, it constitutes a meaningful number.

Another secular category, health-related charities, provides an important point of comparison to nonprofit sectors that may be involved in efforts to reduce inequality. Decisions to donate to health organizations would seem to be independent of broad political sentiments. If someone donates to the Alzheimer's Association, the stimulus for that gift likely stems from having a family member, friend, or friend of a friend who suffers from the disease or recently died from it. A decision to respond to a solicitation from the Alzheimer's Association directly, or from a relative or a friend to make a donation on their behalf when they participate in the annual Memory Walk fundraising event, will likely be made on grounds having little to do with any political sentiments. The survey results support this thinking, with liberals being only slightly higher in terms of the percentage who contribute (38 percent) than conservatives (36 percent).

The gap between liberal (42 percent) and conservative (30 percent) donor participation is substantially wider for those contributors to the more generic "other" nonprofit category. This grouping includes a huge variety of organizations, but, as noted above, the cues in the survey question (United Way, neighborhood associations, and local arts organizations) are suggestive of community and neighborhood. Since this is a broad category that encompasses any "other" organizations that the respondent did not connect to the first three categories listed in the survey template, some caution is warranted in attributing selection to particular kinds of organizations in the donors' minds. Nevertheless, the three examples were chosen to suggest communities and neighborhoods, and it seems likely that many who say they contribute to organizations in this category have their own community or neighborhood in mind.

Overall, combining all four categories, it is liberals, not conservatives, as claimed by Brooks, who are more likely to contribute to charity. Conservatives are much more likely to give to their church, but across the other three categories, by varying margins, it is liberals who have higher participation rates. Charity, it turns out, is segmented, with liberals and conservatives valuing different sectors of the nonprofit world—a finding about a habit of the heart with implications for what is expected, and what is not expected, from government.[24]

## How Generous?

When we read about philanthropy, it is likely about staggering gifts from fabulously wealthy benefactors. Amazon's Jeff Bezos, for example, gave $10 billion to the Bezos Earth Fund. Not to be outdone, his ex-wife, MacKenzie Scott, has been rapidly giving away the fortune of Amazon stock she received in her divorce settlement. Over one four-month stretch in 2020, she gave away $1 billion per month. Fortunes often go to family foundations, and recently the Nike mogul Phil Knight and his wife, Penny, gave $900 million to the Knight Foundation.

These gifts bolster the annual amount donated to charity, and they enable important work by the nonprofits that receive the grants that are ultimately derived from these mega-gifts. Yet these large gifts may mislead us into thinking all is well in the world of philanthropy. As noted earlier, the proportion of the population that gives to charity has been shrinking, and it is the middle class that is not sharing the load. Plotting the confluence of money donated by family income reveals a U-shaped pattern: Those with the highest and the lowest incomes give more generously.[25]

The analysis so far has focused on whether people donate, not on how much they give. These are different questions, since some may give regularly to a charity or two but not give very much as a proportion of their income. Is someone who gives a small amount but has the capacity to give a large amount a charitable individual? We are not able to calculate the amount of charitable gifts against family financial capacity, but our data do show, as previous research has established, that family income and amount contributed are not significantly correlated.[26]

A question we can address is the relationship between ideology and generosity. As with the literature on propensity to donate, previous scholarship is not of one mind as to whether liberals or conservatives or more generous. Notably, though, Brooks found that "secular liberals are poor givers."[27] To gain some purchase on this question, we asked those respondents who indicated that they had given to a congregation or other religious charity, "Could you offer a rough estimate of how many dollars you have donated to religious congregations or other religious charities during the past 12 months?" A similar question was posed to those who had given to any one of the secular categories.[28] In both instances respondents entered a specific amount into a box rather than chose from a scaled set of choices. These are estimates by respondents, of course, and may exaggerate what they actually gave. The goal, however, is to determine the differences between ideological sectors, and possible exaggerations of amounts should not undermine such analysis if we assume that both sets of ideologues are equally likely to practice exaggeration.

The results from cross-tabulating average donations with ideology are revealing (table 6.1). The differences between liberals and conservatives are large and quite consistent with our data on whether respondents give and to whom they give. Although fewer people give to religious charities than secular ones, the amount contributed is impressive: close to $2,000 a year for conservatives and around $1,000 for liberals. The higher amount in

TABLE 6.1. Liberal and conservative giving trends (mean $)

|  | Liberal | Moderate | Conservative |
| --- | --- | --- | --- |
| Religious donations | 1,015 | 1,145 | 1,926 |
| Secular donations | 669 | 402 | 438 |

Source: 2020 CES.

Note: Means are calculated from donors only. $N = 274$ for religious donors; $N = 424$ for secular donors.

comparison to secular gifts surely reflects in part any yearly dues required to formally belong to a congregation.

Secular donations show an opposite trend. Liberals are much more generous, with an average annual contribution of $669, while conservatives donate $438. The nonprofits in the three secular categories span the entire breadth of civil society, and these figures aggregate into considerable amounts. In sum, we find that analysis should not focus simply on who gives more but rather on who gives to what institutions, because the recipient organizations liberals and conservatives give to have very different purposes.

## Volunteering

Volunteering may spring from some of the same motivations as donating to charity, but it is important to separate them out in terms of analysis, as they are very distinct forms of civic engagement.[29] A charitable donation can be highly impersonal—filling out a form sent in the mail or sending in a contribution online. It can also be more interactive—making phone calls or going to a reception, for example. Most volunteering, though, sits at the higher end of the engagement scale. Tutoring adult learners, leading a Boy or Girl Scout troop, manning a food bank, participating in a park or neighborhood cleanup, serving as a volunteer firefighter, teaching Sunday school, reading to the blind, coaching kids' soccer, registering voters, lobbying for a nonprofit, soliciting toys for underprivileged children, building homes for Habitat for Humanity, shelving books at a neighborhood library, participating in a Red Cross blood drive, helping residents at a homeless shelter, driving seniors to doctor's appointments, leading Alcoholics Anonymous meetings, taking a term on the board of one's church, mentoring high school students, coordinating a community garden, and delivering Meals on Wheels are just some the things that Americans are involved in as volunteers.

Volunteering is popular in America, and it is truly part of the soul of the nation, a habit not just of the heart but of the body. Tocqueville marveled at Americans' propensity to participate in an endless array of organizations dedicated to improving the community and the country. He noted that "the citizen of the United States is taught from his earliest infancy to rely upon his own exertions." As a result, America is populated by "a vast number" of associations operating outside of government.[30] Participating in civic organizations is an opportunity to give back, to do something that makes one feel like a good person. The face-to-face component of volunteering generates a sense of community, and that is an enriching reward in and of itself. A bonus beyond such satisfactions is that volunteering is good for one's health.[31]

Volunteering is not merely an important part of the social fabric but an instrumental component of the economy, for it provides labor for activities where there is insufficient financial support from government or charity. Seventy-seven million Americans volunteer in a year, providing seven billion hours in unpaid labor. The estimated annual value of that labor is $167 billion.[32] Volunteering is a form of charity, of course, but it does not require financial resources to participate, and those with little or no discretionary income can become meaningfully engaged in nonprofit work.

Volunteering is popular across the population, from high school students looking for something to put on their college applications to senior citizens who have a lot of free time on their hands. Yet it is middle-aged Americans (i.e., those aged thirty-five to fifty-four) who are the most likely to volunteer. This age cohort may be drawn to volunteering so they can work on behalf of their children's schools and sports leagues; or they may wish to join a neighborhood civic association after purchasing a home; or they recognize that they have developed skills at the workplace that are of value to community groups.[33] Volunteering is the very essence of everyday democracy, and no habit of the heart is as valuable to American society as working with other volunteers to support one's community.

## Political Profile

Although there is a vast literature on volunteering, there is little in it on the relationship of ideology or partisanship to participation rates. In line with his other findings, Brooks concluded that conservatives are more likely to volunteer than are liberals.[34] Penny Edgell Becker and Pawan Dhingra found no difference between liberals and conservatives in volunteering rates, while Steven Yen and Ernest Zampelli determined that liberals were more inclined to volunteer.[35]

Our series of questions in the CES on volunteering began simply, asking respondents, "In the past 12 months, have you engaged in any volunteer work?" The aggregate scores show that liberals are modestly more likely than conservatives to have reported volunteering in the past year, 35 percent versus 29 percent, while those who are moderate in their politics are much lower, at 19 percent.

More revealing are the patterns for volunteering when the data are disaggregated by sector (fig. 6.2). Those respondents who indicated that they had volunteered in the past twelve months were then asked which sectors

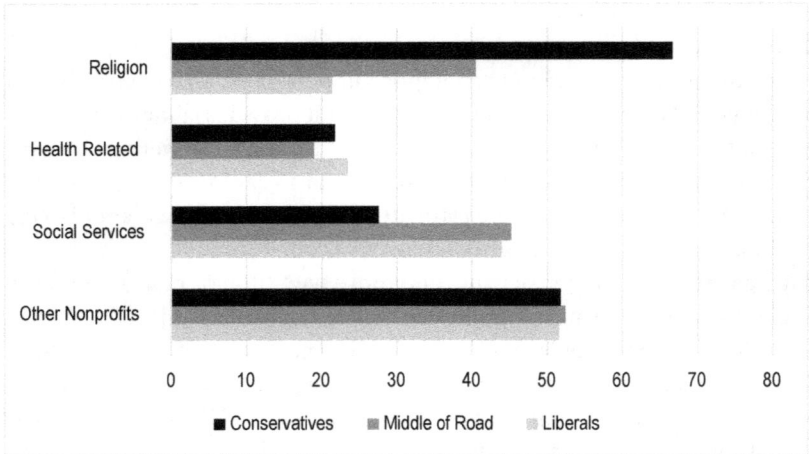

FIGURE 6.2. Ideology and volunteerism

Source: 2020 CES

Note: $N = 807$.

they volunteered for. Most striking is the participation rate for conservatives in congregations and other religious charities. Fully two-thirds of all conservatives who said they volunteered in the past year were involved with a religious organization (presumably their own congregation). This is the highest rate of participation among all volunteers across the four categories. Given that liberals have such low rates of identification with organized religion, it is not surprising that just over a fifth (21 percent) volunteer for religious organizations.

Liberals show a relatively high participation rate (44 percent) for social service organizations, higher than that for conservatives (28 percent). Clearly, social service organizations are more attractive to those who share a worldview wherein programmatic assistance should be readily available to those in need. Health care organizations draw far fewer volunteers, and there is no significant difference between liberals and conservatives in this area. One reason this sector may score lower is that there are fewer opportunities to volunteer for hospitals and other health care facilities. Hospitals ask for your money, but they do not need you to help out in the emergency room. Disease-related charities, also a part of this category, have more opportunities for participation, though most of it is related to fundraising. The Susan G. Komen charity holds annual walks and runs across the country to support breast cancer research and services, but volunteers are not a huge part of the organization outside of the walks and runs.

The "other" category shows the highest rate across the three ideological positions, above 50 percent for each (among those who volunteered anywhere). Perhaps it is relatively high because of this grouping's broad expanse, covering any organization the respondent may think of that does not seem to fit in the first three options in the survey. But this explanation does not seem to work well for the donation questions where the "other" category is not as far out of line as it is here. The cues in the question's wording—"for example, United Way, neighborhood associations, local arts organizations"—may be key. Local organizations are more easily accessible for potential volunteers. Your neighborhood association is made up of, well, your neighbors—you may be friends with some of them. Social networks are also pathways to volunteering, as one's friends and acquaintances may personally ask for help.

Since asking people whether they volunteer does not reveal the intensity of their commitment, we also asked them how much time they spend participating. Our survey asked people to place themselves on a five-point scale ranging from volunteering just once in the past year to volunteering every week. There are no meaningful differences in magnitude between liberals and conservatives by this measure. In addition, we asked subjects whether they volunteered in their "community during the coronavirus pandemic, either in person or virtually." Again, there were no significant differences between liberals and conservatives.

## Race and Gender

To complete an examination of who volunteers, we turn to measuring the impact of race and gender, and we include donation patterns here as well. Race is of note both because of the increasing diversity of the American population and because of the central role of churches in communities of color. In low-income neighborhoods, churches are not only places of worship but often provide various services to those in need. The data from our survey show more support from nonwhite respondents for donating and for volunteering to religious congregations and charities in comparison to white respondents, though the magnitudes are modest. For the other three categories of charities, there are no racial differences in donation or volunteer patterns. Thus, the growing diversity of the American population is not doing much to change civic engagement in either charity or volunteering.

One reason gender is particularly interesting in terms of volunteering is because of the role women played in American civic life prior to the women's movement. For those women who did not need or chose not to work, volunteer work was often a central activity. It was women who led the bake sales at church, devoted time to the PTA, and raised money for local community funds. As Kay Schlozman, Nancy Burns, and Sidney Verba found, the skills women picked up in such volunteer activities were critical in creating a pathway into politics for those interested. These skills (giving a talk at a meeting, working on a task force, asking for donations, and so on) compensated for not gaining equivalent experience at the workplace.[36]

Workforce participation for women has increased sharply from the 1950s, and one would expect that overall women's volunteer activism would decline after they began accepting paid employment. In their landmark citizen participation survey in 1990, Schlozman and colleagues found that this was the case, as there were no significant differences between men and women in their general rates of volunteering. The only gender differences were in the area of religion: Women went to services more often, volunteered at church more, and were more likely to donate money to their congregation.[37]

The detailed data we have from our 2020 survey allow us to look at gender and volunteering across the range of church and secular nonprofits. The aggregate scores for all volunteering do not show any statistically significant

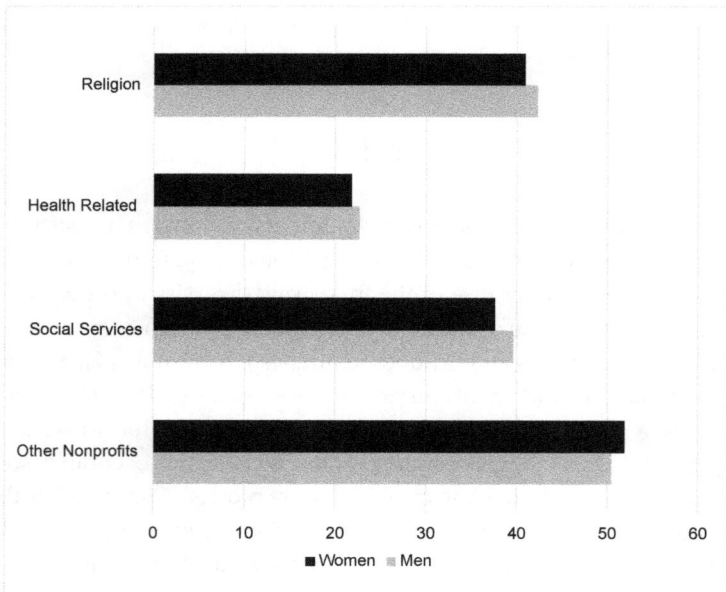

FIGURE 6.3. Gender and volunteerism

Source: 2020 CES

Note: $N$ = 807.

difference between men and women (fig. 6.3). In each of the separate categories of religion, health related, social services, and all other nonprofits, the scores for men and women are close to identical.

In contrast, contribution patterns are different for men and women. For donations to churches and religious charities, men give considerably more ($1,801 vs. $1,283 for women). For secular nonprofits, the difference is more modest, with women giving a bit more ($552 on average) than men ($505). Adding marital status to the analysis also makes a difference in these calculations. Married women give to secular charities by a greater margin than married men. For religious charities, this gap between married men and married women lessens considerably.

## Impact of Ideology

The analysis so far has examined a number of separate tests comparing liberals and conservatives. The results point in different directions across many tests. But stepping back from the discrete findings for each of these, we ask here whether this all fits together in a way that would let us conclude that behavior and attitudes are driven by ideology. We focus on donating and ask whether ideology predicts charitable giving in a manner consistent with broad political worldviews. To try to answer these questions, we used multivariate analysis to weigh relevant factors against one another. Most notably, we wanted to determine whether being a liberal or a conservative serves as a foundation of charitable behavior. Six standard demographic variables (age, gender, education, household income, church attendance, and race) were included in these calculations. Two additional independent variables, being a liberal and being a conservative (dummy variables), were added to these; being moderate served as the base category. The dependent variables were whether respondents had contributed to each of the four charitable sectors (religion, health, social services, and other) and in a separate calculation whether they had volunteered for them.

Table 6.2, which focuses on donations, shows strong associations between increasing age, education, and family income with giving to charity across all four categories of nonprofits, which surely reflects the reality of stages of life and available resources most conducive to charitable giving. In light of Brooks's argument, what is most striking in these findings is that, all else being the same, conservative ideology has no statistically significant relationship with charitable behavior. Liberal ideology is not a factor in terms of giving to secular organizations, but there is a negative association with giving to religion.[38] This finding makes sense given the lower number

TABLE 6.2. Donation behavior across nonprofit sectors (logit)

|  | Religion | Health | Social services | Other nonprofit |
|---|---|---|---|---|
| Liberal | −0.991*** | 0.120 | 0.378 | 0.343 |
|  | (0.293) | (0.218) | (0.243) | (0.215) |
| Conservative | 0.021 | −0.212 | −0.139 | −0.299 |
|  | (0.270) | (0.222) | (0.253) | (0.225) |
| Age | 0.037*** | 0.234*** | 0.004 | 0.013** |
|  | (0.007) | (0.005) | (0.006) | (0.005) |
| Male | −0.034 | −0.090 | −0.461** | −0.086 |
|  | (0.228) | (0.172) | (0.193) | (0.172) |
| Education | 0.346** | 0.360*** | 0.653*** | 0.464*** |
|  | (0.144) | (0.109) | (0.124) | (0.109) |
| Household income | 0.092*** | 0.132*** | 0.155*** | 0.157*** |
|  | (0.035) | (0.027) | (0.030) | (0.027) |
| Church attendance | 1.013*** | 0.235*** | 0.314*** | 0.092* |
|  | (0.076) | (0.052) | (0.058) | (0.052) |
| Nonwhite | 0.701*** | 0.111 | 0.113 | 0.205 |
|  | (0.251) | (0.196) | (0.213) | (0.195) |
| Constant | −6.496*** | −3.738*** | −3.894*** | −3.082*** |
|  | (0.619) | (0.428) | (0.479) | (0.414) |
| $N$ | 748 | 748 | 748 | 748 |
| $\chi^2$ | 393.11 | 96.29 | 129.38 | 100.82 |

Source: 2020 CES.

Note: Standard errors in parentheses.

*$p < .10$; **$p < .05$; ***$p < .01$.

of liberal ideologues who belong to a congregation. Finally, church attendance, a measure of religiosity, is strongly related to donating to all types of charities. For conservatives, it may be that it is their religious rather than their political identity that leads them to charitable behavior.

We will not detail the similar tests we ran on volunteering, but briefly, we found a similar negative association between liberal ideology and volunteering for religious organizations. Beyond that, there is little in our political and demographic variables that is associated with volunteering for nonprofits. Motivations would appear to come from other sources.

In designing our survey, we considered alternative overarching explanations besides ideology and included a large battery of questions on values that might motivate individuals to give. Values represent the relative weight individuals place on attitudes and behaviors and, unlike ideology, do not necessarily represent an underlying worldview that incorporates some degree of consistency in opinion about the role of government.[39] To gain some insight into the values associated with civic behavior, we posed the following question in our CES module: "Which of the following best describe the reason for your decision to donate to a charitable organization in the past 12 months? You may select up to three choices." Ten choices for donating to charities were offered, some reflecting underlying personal values and others instrumental in nature, having to do with solicitations from friends or organizations.

Four of the choices were instrumental in nature: "I receive a tax credit for charitable contributions"; "I was personally asked to by a friend, co-worker, family member, or community leader"; "I was asked by the charity itself"; and "Others close to me place a high value on donating to charities." As shown in figure 6.4, not one of these scored well. Two choices did not fall clearly into either the values or instrumental categories but may

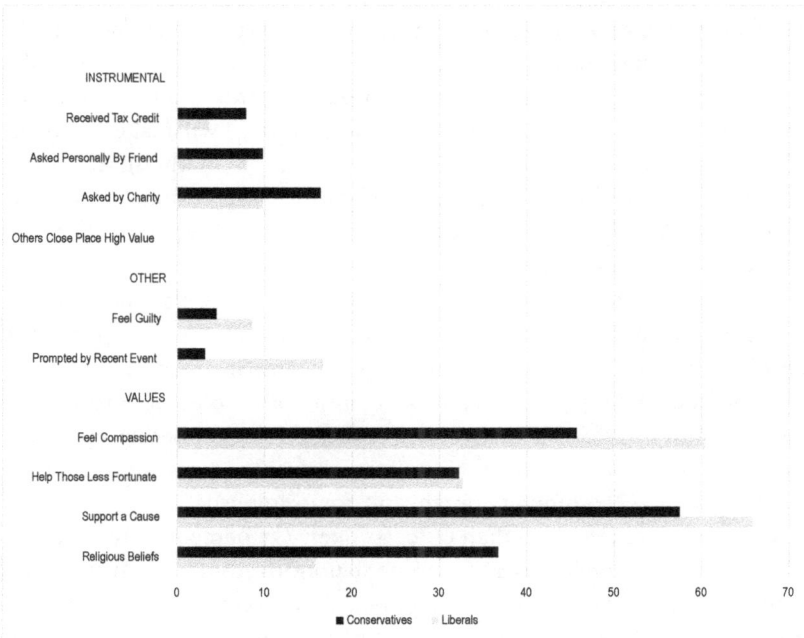

FIGURE 6.4. Ideology and motivations for charitable giving

Source: 2020 CES

Note: $N = 432$.

reflect emotional reactions: "I feel guilty that others are less fortunate than me" and "I was prompted by a recent event in the news." Neither of these showed significant support, and the same was true of an eleventh option to indicate that none of the ten rationales apply to the respondent's charity decisions.

It was the four value-laden choices that subjects tended to select for their three motivations for charity: "I feel compassion toward people in need"; "I feel better helping those less fortunate than me"; "I want to support a cause or community that is important to me"; and "My religious beliefs place a high value on donating to charity." One note of caution is that the differences in preferences between value choices and instrumental choices likely underplay the importance of instrumental reasons for giving at a particular point in time. When given the choices we offered, respondents may have been inclined to emphasize those reasons that suggest they are good people, giving from the heart rather than simply because they were asked. Still, people's perceptions of their charity choices tell us something important about the values they embrace, and the sharp differences in scores say something important about personal attitudes toward those in need.

Our analysis also examines whether these values connect in meaningful ways to liberal or conservative ideologies. We see values as potentially being specific manifestations of ideology. Our expectations were that liberals' motivations were largely compassionate in nature—a keen desire to help those in need as well as to support institutions that will make the world a kinder and more equitable place. Conservatives, we thought, should respond more to religious beliefs and obligations. The results, as detailed in figure 6.2, largely affirm these expectations. Liberals were more likely to choose compassion toward those in need than are conservatives (60 percent vs. 46 percent). There is no implied judgment in the statement of why the recipients of charity are in need; it simply asks whether compassion is a primary motivation. Liberals are moderately more inclined to respond to the rationale for supporting a cause or community (66 percent to 58 percent for conservatives). This statement comes closest to offering a political reason for charity, as some might interpret a "cause" to mean more political types of charities (community organizing, for example).

Conservatives are more than twice as likely (37 percent to 16 percent) to select religious beliefs as a core value that motivates them. At the same time, this choice was not selected by as many respondents as the compassion or cause rationales. Finally, liberals and conservatives have nearly identical response rates (around 32 percent) for giving because they feel better when they help those less fortunate. On the surface this statement may seem only subtly different from the one about giving because you feel compassion toward those in need. "Less fortunate" may evoke being unlucky in life, making them more deserving in the minds of conservatives, than poor people in general ("those in need"). This distinction is important, since research shows that conservatives are more critical of those who are poor. As Younghwa Lee and colleagues conclude, "Donors who have strong moral identity tend to avoid donating to recipients who are deemed responsible for their plight."[40] Lisa Farwell and Bernard Weiner note, "Conservatives tend to attribute poverty to causes such as self-indulgence and laziness."[41] However, conservatives had a higher positive response to compassion than to the item about the less fortunate.

This statistical analysis was rerun with the responses disaggregated by type of nonprofit. There were few anomalies from the initial analysis, and the patterns for reasons given for charitable contributions were largely consistent across categories. In the end, these data point toward a straightforward conclusion: Values matter. Liberals and conservatives are guided by different north stars in their choices as to whether and to whom they choose to give.

## Conclusion

Donating to a charitable cause or volunteering for a nonprofit that is dear to your heart may seem far removed from the highly charged, polarized atmosphere of American politics. But they are the embodiment of Tocqueville's notion of habits of the heart—ordinary things we do over time that represent our values. Although we may not think of such acts as putting twenty dollars in the collection plate at church or taking tickets at a school concert as having political implications, charitable and volunteer activity are entwined in larger political belief systems. Many see voluntary organizations as the building blocks of a less polarized, more civic-minded democracy. Philanthropic foundations as varied as the Rockefeller Brothers Fund and the Charles Koch Foundation have made major commitments to nonprofit groups working in new ways to solve community problems through collaborative and collegial means. Stephen Heintz, president of the Rockefeller Brothers Fund, says they are supporting such groups because Americans believe "that democracy is overlooking them." He adds, "These are remarkable examples of citizens just coming together and saying, 'We've got to fix something.'"[42]

We began this chapter with a question about ideology: Are conservatives, as Arthur Brooks claimed, more charitable than liberals? The question has a clear answer: Our research shows that they are not. More of those on the liberal side of American politics give to charity, and liberals are a bit more likely to volunteer as well. But digging deeper into the data reveals two more conclusions that we believe tell us more about charity in the United States. The first is that ideology—sets of attitudes that show some consistency in the political attitudes of liberals and conservatives—is not the critical explanatory variable.

Our second conclusion is that while there is substantial charitable behavior by both liberals and conservatives, they tend to engage in different spheres of the nonprofit world. Conservatives are very generous when it comes to donating to their congregations and volunteer at a high rate for those same institutions. Liberals are not as active in organized religion but donate and volunteer in significant degrees across the spectrum of secular nonprofits. Their motivations may not be spiritual in nature but may spring from an analogous core belief that they have a responsibility to do good on this earth.[43]

Although the individual activity supporting both religious and secular nonprofits is to be applauded, these institutions work to benefit different sectors of society. Thus, the everyday behavior of ordinary Americans contributing money and volunteering time has large-scale implications for understanding the role of the nonprofit sector. Americans of different political stripes work to strengthen distinctly different types of charitable institutions.

Another interesting perspective is offered by Putnam in *Bowling Alone*, where he distinguishes between *bonding* social capital and *bridging* social capital.[44] Bonding social capital reflects strengthening ties to those in our immediate communities, while bridging social capital builds ties between communities. Clearly, contributions and volunteering to religious institutions are bonding, enhancing the social capital in those communities. Contributions to secular nonprofits cannot be so easily categorized, as both types of social capital can be promoted by them. Still, secular charities are more likely to build bridging social capital, since they tend to be arrayed in a wider network of relationships with other institutions.

Given the centrality of religious identity to conservatives' charity, the continuing decline of religion in the United States has unfortunate implications for the entire nonprofit sector. Church attendance is linked not only to donations to religious charities but also to charity directed at secular institutions. It is an ominous sign that the youngest Americans are the least likely to identify with a religion, and the number of churches and other congregations seems sure to continue to decline. Fewer neighborhood churches may translate into less civic engagement in those locations.

It is more difficult to judge the direction of liberal donors and volunteers and secular nonprofits. There are about 1.5 million 501(c)(3) nonprofits registered with the IRS.[45] This number does not include those organizations that are not large enough to need to register. These secular organizations cover an enormous range of activities, and their commonality is limited though central: They all appeal to our better nature to contribute time and money to virtuous causes. Despite their embodiment of virtue, though, they may be at greater risk than churches from the recent tax changes disincentivizing giving. Churches, at least, call on a higher order when they ask for money.

[ CHAPTER SEVEN ]

# This Urgent Time

Our history is one of challenges to democratic government. Frequently these challenges come from within, from Americans who believe our government has gone off the rails and whose advocacy further threatens government stability. This kind of conflict goes back to the first days of American government, with Shays's Rebellion and the mobilization of enraged farmers armed largely with pitchforks. They failed to take down the government of Massachusetts, but the Articles of Confederation collapsed and a second constitution was then written in Philadelphia in 1787.

Challenges have continued unabated. Andrew Jackson's supporters in 1824 were outraged when he got the most electoral votes as well as the most popular votes, but John Quincy Adams was elected president. The Kansas-Nebraska Act (1854) tore at the country's foundations, and an even more traumatic rift, the nation's greatest tragedy, the Civil War, followed soon afterward. And after that came Reconstruction. The economic collapse at the end of the nineteenth century led to political instability, as did the Great Depression beginning in 1929. World War II, the Korean War, and the McCarthy era stressed our system for two painful decades. Through all of these years, state-level authoritarianism and violence continued to oppress Black Americans. The civil rights movement and the anti–Vietnam War movement ushered in further political upheaval. Divisiveness reached a fever pitch during Watergate and President Nixon was forced out of office.

When friends and acquaintances ask us whether the Trump years are the worst of times, we find it hard to offer a simple response, because we know this history of America.[1] Being asked by friends to validate how awful things are is an occupational hazard of being a political scientist. The research for this book began with questions we had about American democracy before Trump became president, but then more lines of inquiry emerged out of the antidemocratic impulses of the president and his followers. As our work continued, we became increasingly convinced that we live in an urgent time, and we wanted to capture America at this period of its history. Democracies can descend into turmoil and authoritarianism, and as the historian Jill Lepore notes, "The American experiment has not ended. A nation born in revolution will forever struggle against chaos."[2] Although we are heartened by how America has withstood the tests we have faced since Shays's Rebellion, the weapons of destabilization today are more dangerous than pitchforks, and clear thinking about what the threats are and are not is critical to protecting American democracy.

## Everyday Democracy

The notion of everyday democracy frames our inquiry into the state of American democracy. By focusing on the mundane attitudes and experiences of Americans and comparing them across ideologies, we have tried to sort out broad stereotypes that exaggerate political dysfunctionality from patterns that are truly worrisome. The abrasive rhetoric in many sectors of American politics is troubling, yet we recall the political scientist Jack Citrin warning some years ago against equating the way people talk about politics with what they actually believe. When people shout "kill the umpire" at a baseball game, they do not really believe umpires making calls against their team should be summarily executed.[3]

Throughout this book, we have provided data and analysis of everyday attitudes and behaviors such as accepting compromise, applying political principles to circumstances, engaging those with different views, volunteering with a nonprofit, and watching cable news channels. In this concluding chapter, we pull back from the trees to get a better view of the forest. Most directly, what have we learned from our research about the degree to which Americans appear to cultivate their democratic habits of the heart? We approach this important question by asking how our findings relate to five central problems commonly believed to diminish and degrade our political system. First, has political conflict eroded the government's ability to act, condemning us to inaction on our most serious policy issues? Second, have we citizens become so polarized that incivility has come to dominate the way we interact with each other? Third, has intolerance become normalized, increasingly acceptable in public discussions of politics? Fourth, have our politics become more about beating the other side—"winning so much that you will get tired of it," in Trump's words—as opposed to pursuing important ideals? Finally, are we still good neighbors in our community? These are broad problems, and the discussion here will not resolve them. We hope, however, that this synthesis of our findings will add to the ongoing debate and make that debate sharper and better informed. And while the analyses in the previous chapters focused on comparisons between liberals and conservatives, here we also describe what our data show for people who consider themselves moderate (31 percent and 28 percent, respectively, in our 2018 and 2020 CES datasets), thereby providing a fuller picture of ideology and everyday democracy.

## POLITICAL PARALYSIS

One of the most common critiques of American government is that it is so polarized that its parties and their supporters reject compromise, condemning the nation to political paralysis. In some multiparty democracies like Germany and India, voters accept the postelection wheeling and dealing of parties to form governing coalitions as part and parcel of their governmental process. In a two-party system with strong ideologues on both sides, legislative compromise can be hard. This country's electoral primary system pulls the parties toward the ideological poles. Thus, with just two parties, and those beset with gravitational pulls away from the middle, compromise is ever more difficult.

How deep, how pervasive, and how serious is this problem in the United States? Scholars are divided, and some are deeply pessimistic about the future of democracy absent a means of overcoming what they see as chronic gridlock. Lee Drutman, for example, writes that unless we restructure our government, we are doomed to "increasingly dangerous consequences for our democracy."[4]

As we distilled what our survey work tells us about whether American government is doomed because of ideological intransigence and polarization, we focused on the degree to which Americans are willing to compromise. In *The Spirit of Compromise*, Amy Gutmann and Dennis Thompson conclude that "governing a democracy without compromise is impossible."[5] They argue for a "compromising mindset"—a willingness to put aside intransigent principles and entertain solutions that fall between the demands of each side. Those who compromise also place trust in the integrity of opponents and regard them as honorable adversaries.

Compromises in government are ultimately made by leaders, not followers. Still, followers' attitudes are critical: Legislators are sensitive to constituency opinion. We will come back to the relationship of leaders and followers, but we begin here by recalling that most Americans say they support compromise on the part of political leaders. Most of the survey questions we examined in chapter 4 show compromise being the majority preference among all ideological subgroups. Notably, when asked about general support for compromise, moderates were far closer to liberals in expressing high levels of support than they were to conservatives. And in our most direct test of a compromising mindset, using experiments on the minimum wage and on tax rates, the central finding is that it is possible to move some of those who prefer principle over compromise to bargain, particularly if we pay attention to the inclination for people—liberals, moderates, and conservatives alike—to be concerned more with loss than with gain. In today's contentious Congress, successful compromises require a precise set of incentives and threats that can overcome all the obstacles that stand in the way. This finding from our research squares with what we know of contemporary American politics: that compromise does not come easy, but sometimes the two parties can reach agreement. While there are some issues, such as immigration, where movement is absent, there are others, like infrastructure and public works, that are more likely to yield bipartisanship.[6]

We also found that conservatives were significantly less supportive of compromise than liberals and moderates in general and more recalcitrant than liberals to move away from principle to a compromising mindset. Looking at coverage of politics in the news, we see evidence that supports what we found in our surveys. In Congress and in state legislatures, conservative Republicans seem far more likely to prefer sticking to principles than engaging in legislative compromise than do liberal Democrats.[7] Traditionally, this attitude toward legislating might be attributed to the nature of classic conservatism, which is built on a philosophy that extols small government. Contemporary conservatives are strong advocates of active government on issues that concern them, but we note that their advocacy often centers on *banning* particular activities, such as prohibiting the teaching of certain ideas about racism in schools or banning abortion. Such activism focuses on limits and restrictions, a complicated combination (government reach in the service of prohibitions) that in reality has often characterized conservatism beyond our current political moment. Over the years this dynamic has been manifested in support for banning interracial relationships, flag burning, the use of languages other than English in government services, support for "communist" ideas, and same-sex marriage.

The analysis in chapter 2 suggests that there may be more potential for conservative compromise than is commonly assumed. Many self-identified conservatives, as we show, respond to questions about individual policy questions such as abortion, gun control, and the Affordable Care Act in distinctly moderate terms. Such moderates in conservative clothing are more likely to have heterogeneous social networks and are less likely to clash with those on the other side of the ideological divide. When we compare rates of support for compromise among consistent and inconsistent conservatives, we find that in some years, inconsistent conservatives are more likely than consistent conservatives to offer support. So capitalizing on ideological inconsistency may provide some opportunity to increase support for compromise, but not enough to close the ideological gap entirely.

Pulling these inconsistent conservatives away from more ideological Republicans who preach the morality of political principle is no small task, and GOP legislators in Washington and in state capitals have shown great unity when it comes fighting the Democrats. Yet, we know that legislators are more extreme than their constituents and misperceive how conservative their constituents are.[8] That is, legislators do not need to be as strongly ideological as they are to win reelection. If the number of compromising mindsets is to be expanded, effective leadership promoting such is critical. The skill of leaders varies considerably. Paul Ryan was better than John Boehner at holding together the contentious GOP caucus; Boehner would make deals with Democrats only to see that his members would not go along. Kevin McCarthy was undone by his inability to keep his caucus together and did not last a year as Speaker. In contrast, Nancy Pelosi was a master of the art of compromise. Despite his dealmaking business background, Trump has been terrible at promoting bipartisanship. What is important to point out is that when there is visible and consequential compromise backed by leaders, the sky does not fall on the compromisers. When election time rolls around, an opponent's accusation that the incumbent voted for a compromise is not typically a problem for the officeholder. Of course, not many congressional incumbents lose for any reason.

Political scientists differ as to how realistic it is to hope for more bipartisanship. Using surveys and experiments, Jennifer Wolak finds that there is strong support for compromise among the public.[9] Looking at legislators rather than voters, Sarah Anderson and colleagues conclude that the fear of being primaried is a substantial barrier to compromise.[10] Given what we know about attitudes toward everyday democracy, there is more potential for support for compromise by the public, but legislators do not exploit this potential, too often opting to avoid what they see as risk. As we show, conservative constituents are harder to pull toward compromise than liberals, but some can be moved, and there are many inconsistent conservatives whose policy views are in the middle.[11]

## DEBILITATING TOXICITY

One thing that Americans of all political stripes agree upon is that there is too much disagreement in our politics. The sharp, polarizing, and poisonous rhetoric that we are exposed to makes it easy to believe that our political system is in decline. A report by the Carnegie Endowment for International Peace found that "partisan sorting and rising polarization create a pernicious logic of zero-sum politics that incentivizes behavior undermining democratic institutions and norms." It concluded that this "pernicious polarization" portends "an ominous future for American democracy."[12] As *Time* magazine warned its readers, "The truth is, for decades now, America has shown rampant spikes in political obstructionism, incivility, tribalism, distrust in one another *and* our institutions, and support for political violence."[13]

Like the history of national turmoil with which we began this chapter, today's political toxicity is nothing new. Sydnor ties these two elements together, noting that "history suggests we should not be surprised by shouting, character assassination, and other fighting words during times of political upheaval."[14] Americans have endured many periods in which its citizens spoke and acted harshly toward those on the other side of the political fence. Think of the McCarthy era, for example: Those on McCarthy's side believed that many of those on the other side were communist sympathizers who did not believe in the American way of life. This suspicion developed as something more than hostile attitudes—people lost their jobs because of accusations that they were not loyal to this country.

Americans are not historians, and the public truly does believe they are now living in the worst of times politically. When Georgetown University pollsters asked about the level of political division in this country, with the end of the scale at 100 representing the "edge of civil war," the mean response was 71. The same poll showed that 83 percent of respondents believe that behavior that was previously unacceptable is now "normal behavior."[15] More rigorously, political scientists measure affective polarization over time and show that there has indeed been a growth of uncivil attitudes.[16]

It is easy to dismiss apocalyptic rhetoric, regarding it as annoying but concluding that in the final analysis it represents inappropriate behavior by inappropriate people. When Representative Marjorie Taylor Greene (R-GA) says that "the Democrats are the party of pedophiles," should we be concerned about such a ridiculous claim? Her clownish rhetoric is legend; she once called the Capitol police "the Gazpacho," confusing a soup with Nazis.[17] But, yes, we should be concerned because cumulatively such divisive rhetoric can lead to a loss of trust in government. In Suzanne Mettler and Robert Lieberman's book on democratic backsliding, *Four Threats*, two of those threats, polarization and conflict over who belongs, are aided by divisiveness that can be fueled by incendiary rhetoric.[18] Thus, thinking back on chapter 3, can we afford to be nonchalant about Tucker Carlson saying immigrants make our cities dirtier? The Fox Cable host Laura Ingraham could not have been more direct in saying that immigrants do not belong in America, telling viewers that those who are coming into America will "swamp the voting power of all of you Americans out there who still know the country's traditions, constitution and history" and "overthrow everything we love about America."[19]

In recent years no development has consumed American political science more than polarization. We have not looked at polarization in a comprehensive manner—that would be a multivolume book. In chapter 2, however, we used tweets as a measure of the toxicity of political communication. We believed Twitter was an appropriate vehicle for examining polarization, since it is known for its freewheeling format and for the controversy that often erupts from the sharp, nasty missives that are launched back and forth among online combatants. In his first term, Trump utilized Twitter expertly to assault political opponents. Importantly, X (as Twitter is now called) is exclusively an online forum, and one never has to meet adversaries face-to-face. There is no real accountability for a user who publishes falsehoods and prejudicial content.

In light of what we believe we know about political toxicity today, the results about everyday attitudes and behavior detailed in chapter 2 may seem surprising. To summarize briefly, we measured the toxicity of tweets in the sample we acquired from Twitter by using a machine learning tool that looked for tweets on a range of political topics, tweets being defined as "a rude, disrespectful, or unreasonable comment that is likely to make you leave a discussion."[20] What we discovered was that not many tweets are in fact toxic. Using a scale that judged just how toxic a tweet was in relative terms, we concluded that the vast majority of users of Twitter were not interested in being rude or disrespectful. The same was true of both conservatives and liberals. An even more granular test that we ran identified tweets that utilized name-calling. Only a small percentage of all tweets in our sample contained name-calling, and again, there was no difference between liberals and conservatives.

Our own research contrasts sharply with documentation of the lack of civility across the body politic. If uncivil attitudes have grown, why do we not see more of it in our Twitter sample? One might have guessed that given its nature, incivility on Twitter would be strikingly *worse* than what we generally observe in the political world. What may appear to be contradictory is likely explained by the differences between attitudes and behavior. Expressing your opinion about American politics is often, in context, saying how you believe that others are behaving badly. When it comes to fashioning a tweet that calls someone a name or uses other incendiary language, the writer then has to acknowledge that he or she "is that person" who is nasty and polarizing. Again, there is a difference between saying "kill the ump" and engaging in killing the ump. This apparent disconnect is also surely magnified by media analyses of the pathologies of American politics. Polarization is compelling content, and the focus on active and loud voices typically ignores a larger segment of the population that cares little about the issues at hand.[21] Occasionally there are news stories showing that Americans of different political alignments have more in common than we may think, but these are rare.[22]

We are not arguing that we Americans do not live in a highly polarized environment. There is toxic rhetoric all around us, and it is disturbing. Indeed, in another section we discuss the implications of the racially intolerant language of Fox Cable News. But what we do offer here is a glimmer of hope about how we interact with others when it comes to politics. We are not a nation of foul-mouthed, contentious provocateurs. Even among the self-selected sector of America that tweets about politics, behavior is relatively tame. The stereotype that we cannot talk to each other without falling into a nasty argument is a destructive one, since it makes participating in politics less appealing.[23] Americans are able to talk politics with those they disagree with. Many of the self-identified liberals and conservatives in our surveys deny cutting people out of their lives on account of politics. As Matthew Levendusky reminds us, "Cross-party friendships, and political discussions, do in fact occur."[24] And when we look at the moderates in our surveys, we find that they too are unlikely to block people on social media because of politics, to report having politically homogeneous social circles, and to have ended friendships over politics. We think it is critically important for more Americans to know that most Americans, including those who consider themselves to be liberal or conservative, do not cut people out of their lives because of politics. This is especially true for in-person interactions. We did see some increase in isolating behaviors between 2018 and 2020; we hope that another outcome of our research is continued support in academia for research that allows trend data on the topics analyzed here to be collected and analyzed.

## UNPRINCIPLED POLITICS

One of the bigger challenges of the Trump years was encapsulated by the president's campaign promise that "we'll have so much winning, you'll get bored of winning" over both domestic and foreign adversaries. Winning matters in politics, to be sure, but winning without advancing principles is hollow. It may seem inconsistent to call for more principled politics at the same time as calling for more compromise in policymaking, or for a politics of civility and respect. Slavish adherence to principles can get in the way of compromise and lead to paralysis in the political system. Respect may be more difficult to muster when cherished ideas are at stake. Nonetheless, when politics loses its connection to broader ideas, when what matters above all else is getting and keeping power, when outrage drives political messaging and influential media enhance it in order to draw an audience, when politics is primarily about self- or group interest, the broader enterprise of governance suffers. This is not to say that all politics is hollow. Some political actors are guided by principles in contemporary America. We call for more balance between opportunism and principle. The current balance seems out of whack.

There are many ways to evaluate a more principled approach to politics, and we have presented only one analysis here. It is noteworthy that with regard to attitudes toward federalism, conservatives are more guided by their principles than liberals, even when their immediate political interests are not met. If liberals have recently "discovered" the promise of federalism, as some have claimed, they have done so somewhat instrumentally, and they more generally and naturally embrace a national approach to problems when they hold national power. It is not that this is malicious or cynical, but it does suggest a more instrumental ends-over-means approach to politics.

The thing about the devolution of significant power to states and localities is that it does offer some potential for a larger percentage of citizens to get what they want from the political system. Devolution of power is not an all-purpose solution to national polarization, especially when, as Daniel Hopkins argues, state and local politics have become nationalized.[25] Moreover, the record of states is decidedly mixed and includes a long history of state-based oppression of civil rights. Even now some political observers are skeptical, like the *New York Times* columnist Jamelle Bouie, who calls some of the state governments "laboratories of autocracy," and the political scientist Jacob Grumbach, who pointedly titled his recent book *Laboratories Against Democracy*.[26] Our contention is not that political actors at the state or local level will always act virtuously. Rather, it is that federalism is a sharing of power that is meaningful for the operation of the whole system. We hearken back to the work of Robert Dahl and Edward Tufte, who fifty years ago argued that the ideal democratic system is one that has several levels of collective decision-making, with the different levels defined by the different sizes of those affected. They write, "Rather than conceiving of democracy as located in a particular kind of inclusive, sovereign unit, we must learn to conceive of democracy spreading through a set of interrelated political systems, sometimes though not always arranged like Chinese boxes, the smaller nesting in the larger."[27] Aspiring to the right balance between the national, the state, and the local is not quixotic. Nor is it going to solve all that politically ails us. It can, however, maximize the possibility of translating preferences into policies.

## RACIAL INTOLERANCE

Although we find some reason for optimism in our findings both relating to compromise and to the level of toxicity in personal online communications, our optimism does not extend to the work we completed on race. The data in chapter 3 are resolutely negative and paint an ugly portrait of Fox Cable News and of its viewers.

The broader stream of recent American history on race relations is arguably not as bleak as what we have documented. In the decade between 2011 and 2020, overall attitudes on race became significantly more tolerant. When survey respondents were asked whether they agree with the statement "Over the last few years, Black people have gotten less than they deserve," the percentage of those agreeing rose during this period from 20 percent to 45 percent.[28] Also encouraging are modest policy changes at the local level that followed the horrendous police murders of George Floyd and other innocent Black Americans, including greater use of body cameras, bans on choke holds, and better training.

By examining the content of Fox Cable's prime-time programming, it may seem that we have stacked the deck to show American race relations in the worst possible light. The research we did on cable was never envisioned as work that would offer a general portrait of race in the twenty-first century. Sometimes researchers focus on the "hard case," and this was certainly our strategy. In line with our general goal of capturing America at "this time, in this place," we wanted to look at a source of the poison that is at the heart of hostile race relations, in this case the everyday shows on cable news networks. At the time we undertook our research, race relations seemed to have taken a turn for the worse, with a president who was openly hostile to African Americans and Hispanic immigrants. The nontrivial size of the audience share of Fox News along with the tendency of other media outlets to talk *about* Fox News, thereby amplifying its content, further shaped our strategy.

During his first term, President Trump used his speeches and tweets to prime underlying feelings of racial resentment at the same time Fox was featuring the same themes. In our effort to understand Fox's role in the contentious politics of race, we both watched its evening programs and utilized a detailed battery of survey questions that we designed on media consumption. Our TV viewing and coding of Fox and MSNBC programs over the course of a year revealed a distinctive pattern in stories about race on Fox. Prime-time shows on Fox and MSNBC do not report the news but offer interpretation. We coded narratives according to their story line, and what we saw on Fox was truly disturbing: Black people and Hispanic immigrants were treated as fools, criminals, and irresponsible citizens. Black women were treated with particular harshness. In a nutshell, Fox stories dehumanize people of color.

What should we make of these results? Is Fox's content consequential, or is it just pandering to a small number of ideologues who self-selected to be exposed to views that they already embraced? Assessing the impact of cable programming is a daunting methodological task, and as we discussed in chapter 3, scholars have taken a number of approaches. Part of measuring the impact of content is first calculating how many people watch and then determining the prior views of those that watch. Despite the fact that the audience for an individual episode on Fox is modest, many researchers join us in believing that the aggregate (say, monthly) audience is sizable. There is also support for our conclusion that some in this audience are persuadable, either to become hardened to views they have previously embraced or to adopt new perspectives.[29] We will not repeat the case we make in our text discussing our findings as to why we believe our particular approach is valid, but we are reassured by this growing research on Fox. In the last analysis, Fox matters, and it matters a lot.

Our research captures Fox from September 2018 to September 2019, but its odious racialized content has since continued unabated. An investigative project by *The New York Times* published in 2022 concluded that Fox's Tucker Carlson had constructed "what may be the most racist show in the history of cable news."[30] What we find of particular interest is the increasing vitriol on race that emerged in tandem with Fox's obsession with what it told viewers were the dangers of Black people in America. For all intents and purposes, Fox created the issue of critical race theory and did its best to convince viewers that our schools were being hoodwinked into offering courses where white people were demonized as racists. Attacks on DEI (diversity, equity, and inclusion) in the workplace and at schools has been a recent focus as well.

We know of no research that disentangles the impact of Donald Trump on conservative public opinion from Fox News's influence. In his first term as president, Trump slavishly watched Fox and often spoke with Sean Hannity and Tucker Carlson after their nightly broadcasts. For a time Trump spoke with the head of Fox, Rupert Murdoch, three or four times a week.[31] We can only assume that this interaction between the president and the most important people at Fox led to a common path in their discussion and promotion of developing issues. What we do know is that issues come from somewhere; or, as the late Nelson Polsby put it, issues do not "appear out of the sea like Botticelli's Venus—dimpled, rosy, and complete on a clamshell."[32] Trump and Fox pushed an agenda of issues designed to anger Americans and increase their contempt for those on the other side. Unfortunately, what Trump and Fox also did, and not accidentally, was normalize racially antagonistic discourse. Our analysis shows that among self-identified conservatives, levels of racial resentment vary based on whether they watch Fox: Conservatives who do not watch Fox exhibit less resentment. Importantly, we also find this to be the case among moderates (about 33 percent of whom reported watching Fox).

Racism is nothing new in our culture, but what is notable is that Fox has so successfully monetized white antagonism toward people of color. Ultimately, though, Fox is successful with such content because there are people who like to hear Fox hosts and their guests disparage minority groups and minority leaders. In short, there is a market for racist news commentary among conservatives and also some moderates, and Fox offers that product. Sadly, what we have confirmed in our examination of various attitudes and behaviors is that there is still a sector of American society that is fervently hostile to diversity.

## COMMUNITY: A BRIGHT SPOT

The Trump years may seem to be a terrible period for researchers to be looking into for the essential goodness of America. Yet we did find goodness in our exploration of charitable giving and volunteering, two everyday activities that contribute to a better-functioning society. Charitable participation is substantial, particularly for liberals *and* conservatives alike relative to moderates, and rates of volunteering are robust. Importantly, volunteering reflects a commitment to community. The broader context of community is that it is collective action aimed at addressing a common issue. In America, collective action has always existed in tension with individualism. Our American myths celebrate both.

For political scientists, analyzing community has always been at the heart of our discipline. For much of the post–World War II era, relevant scholarship focused on the decline of community and bemoaned trends indicating that Americans were not as integrated into the civic fabric of the country as were their parents and grandparents. At the heart of this downbeat view of America were urbanists who examined what was going on in our big cities. As white residents began to flee cities for the suburbs in the 1950s and

1960s, political science began to view cities as heading inexorably toward disaster. Edward Banfield's *The Unheavenly City*, published in 1970, was the political science equivalent of a horror movie. Cities, inhabited largely by poor African Americans, who had limited options to improve their lives, were said to be descending into physical collapse.[33] A less racialized (and ultimately more enduring) critique came from the journalist Jane Jacobs. In *The Death and Life of Great American Cities*, she concluded that American cities were inadvertently designed by planners to be soulless, lifeless entities that caused a decline in social capital, our connection to other people.[34]

Thirty years later Putnam's *Bowling Alone* delivered a more empirical analysis of community in America. Like Jacobs, he bemoaned a decline in social capital and documented in detail a decline in civic engagement across a large range of activities, including political participation. An exception in his searing indictment was voluntarism. Putnam noted that a rising number of volunteers "is the most promising sign of any that I have discovered that America might be on the cusp of a new period of civic renewal."[35] There are certainly other signs of civic renewal, and cities did not turn into the hellholes that Banfield predicted. Political participation in many forms has stabilized or increased.

Americans volunteer at rates higher than those in any other country.[36] Some nonprofit organizations engage huge numbers of people who give their time (and usually their money) to a cause or community. For example, the Susan G. Komen organization enlists hundreds of thousands of volunteers who race or walk to raise money for breast cancer research and patient support. Ten thousand participated in 2022 in Columbus, Ohio alone. That year Susan G. Komen held forty-two such walk or race events in major cities across the country.[37] Although Tocqueville writes of volunteering as if it were something peculiarly American, the roots of this behavior are more complex. Such participation in the United States cannot be explained by the simple notion that it is enriching to volunteer—it would be equally enriching in whatever country it takes place. Rather, a starting point in understanding volunteering in America is that it is something learned and practiced. As our survey reveals, people's participation springs from their values. But values do not express themselves automatically. Voluntary organizations offer channels for activity and personal fulfillment.

What is especially distinctive about America is the degree to which government depends on nonprofit organizations to administer social services. Government may pay nonprofits a portion of what those organizations spend on services, but since volunteers working for free provide some or most of the labor, this "nonprofitization" of social services is a good deal for government. Elected officials get to claim credit for services being offered but do not need to raise additional tax revenue because nonprofits enlist volunteers to work for them. Nonprofits also raise charitable donations to pay a significant part of the overall price tag. Our surveys show that ideologues are more likely to donate than moderates (with conservatives more likely to donate to religious groups and liberals more likely to donate to nonreligious groups). If we view donating to causes as an element of doing one's part for everyday democracy, it is those Americans who see themselves as being on the left or the right who appear more likely to step up to the plate.

Beyond donating, volunteering is a form of civic engagement that is widely perceived to transcend politics. We could not help but notice that it is the only behavior we measured where liberals and conservatives score identically. Although volunteerism may not have ideological roots, what is important politically about volunteering may be in its second-order consequences. The time one spends volunteering at a food bank, community board, or PTA is likely to be done in a face-to-face setting. Some activity may be remote, but most volunteering is still done the old-fashioned way, in person. Depending on the organization, one's fellow volunteers may be from different backgrounds, perhaps different in their demographics and different in their political views. To further underscore that volunteering transcends politics, in our survey, self-identified moderates are similar to ideologues in their rate of volunteering for nonprofits.

Since volunteers tend to begin with some agreement as to general goals, their organizations can be places where voices are lowered and a predilection for cooperation is high. In these face-to-face environments, one may learn that those on the other side of the political fence are neither imbeciles nor revolutionaries determined to overthrow the existing social order. We draw inspiration here from the ample research on contact theory, which shows that intergroup contact reduces outgroup prejudice, particularly when the contact situation involves shared goals, equal status, lack of competition, and sanction from authorities.[38] Volunteering in community organizations is likely to be a situation where such promising conditions are present. One meta-analysis of contact research finds that prejudice reduction occurs primarily through decreased anxiety and increased empathy and perspective-taking.[39] Although this research tends not to focus on partisan or ideological intergroup contact, reducing the emotional toll of partisan interactions and increasing people's understanding of the other side strike us as particularly important outcomes when thinking about our current political climate. The type of contact that comes with volunteering should have significant potential in this regard.

# Citizenship

With our focus on how individuals act and on what they believe, this study falls squarely in the political science subfield of political behavior. Yet, its topics relate to the study of citizenship, a subfield that stands at a juncture of normative theory and empirical behavioral research. Citizenship theory can be traced as far back as 700 BCE and the emergence in Sparta of norms of citizen involvement in government. A few hundred years later Plato wrote of citizenship, and then his student Aristotle did as well. In both Sparta and Athens, not all residents were full citizens, but those in the highest strata of society could participate as equals in governing their city-state. Both political systems required that those who wanted to be full citizens undergo training, the military for Spartans and school for Athenians.[40] In other words, good citizens were not born as such but needed to be taught.

## GOOD CITIZENS

Citizenship theory is built on a foundation of obligations. Democracies need a consensus on what is minimally required of good citizens to keep the state from devolving into anarchy or authoritarianism. Across democracies worldwide, there is strong consensus around three behaviors considered to be essential: Citizens should vote, they should pay their taxes, and they should obey the law.[41] Indeed, when asked why they vote, many will respond that they do so because it is their *duty* as a citizen. We tend to think of other political activities, such as writing a member of Congress or making a campaign contribution, not as a duty but as options we can take advantage of if we choose.

With its emphasis on obligations, citizenship theory may not seem to map well onto our own investigation. The behaviors we examined are all voluntary and are arguably not even societal obligations. As we explained at the outset, our concern is with everyday thoughts and behaviors that build and sustain a democratic mindset. Still, we have found citizenship theory useful in placing our findings within the framework of our discipline, since we are ultimately interested in how individuals' daily practices can lead to a strong and vital democracy. We believe there are ways in which everyday democracy can be strengthened and citizens' impact enhanced. And we were guided by some normative assumptions—believing, for example, that if more people had a compromising mindset, our system of government would be more likely to address problems instead of kicking the can down the road.

Our work also resonates with a second face of citizenship theory, which identifies attributes that are desirable in a democratic system but that fall short of obligations. Different scholars have different notions of the nature of these second-order characteristics. Russell Dalton, a leading analyst of citizenship, distinguishes between obligations and "social citizenship," which are those qualities that distinguish "good citizens."[42] Dalton identifies four broad categories in his conceptualization of social citizenship: *participation* (activity beyond voting), *autonomy* (understanding the reasoning of others and monitoring government), *solidarity* (helping others), and *social order* (serving government when called upon).[43]

The major themes and chapter topics of this book overlap with these categories in various ways. Participation was analyzed most directly in our treatment of online communication, donating to charity, and volunteering. Understanding the reasoning of others is at the heart of this book, especially in discussion of racial tolerance and adopting a compromising mindset. Our analysis of attitudes on federalism fits into this category as well, since federalism is a prism people look through to understand government. We also use our analysis in chapter 5 to highlight the idea that our tendency to prioritize consistency as a hallmark of citizen competence is complex; we need to recognize that consistency can take on different forms, and more Americans would do well to keep that in mind when they judge the competence of their fellow citizens. Solidarity (community) is addressed in our chapter on charity and voluntarism.[44]

Dalton's is but one approach, and there are many ways this world of social citizenship can be grouped into different sets of behaviors. But while there is diversity in the manner in which scholars define the attributes of the good citizen, such behaviors and attitudes are crucial to the maintenance of democracies. Across Western democracies, these characteristics have real-world consequences—they are not just the musings of tweedy academics pushing one more article out the door.[45] Sarah Wallace Goodman writes that across democratic countries, "citizens are increasingly divided about what it means to be a good citizen, and that this division is driven by partisanship."[46] The United States, which suffered a violent insurrection after the 2020 elections, is a painful example. The people who stormed the Capitol surely thought of themselves as patriots, believing they were heeding a call similar to that felt by the revolutionaries who rebelled against the British in the late eighteenth century. Those who are trying to make it more difficult to vote in red states presumably think they are working to make elections more honest and American democracy stronger.

## IDEOLOGY AND CITIZENSHIP

A focus on ideology may seem to pull away from citizenship theory because the very idea of good citizenship is an argument for principles that transcend partisan politics. In this view we should be committed to tolerance or a compromising mindset *before* we think about how such principles will affect our desired outcomes.

The normal conversation of Americans in everyday politics is about neither the principles of good citizenship nor ideology. Everyday political conversation is about elections and policy and how awful the partisans on the other side are. But underneath those general topics is ideology: the way people structure their view of how the political world operates and their thoughts on how it *should* operate. Just how much coherence there is in average voters' worldview is one of the most enduring debates in political science.[47] Our own inquiry asked how ideology affects the behaviors and attitudes that we examine in the empirical chapters. As we demonstrate repeatedly, ideology matters, and the magnitude is sometimes considerable. We also show that the very notion of ideological coherence is not straightforward, for it can pertain to a commitment to processes and means or it can pertain to a commitment to ends, and ideologues can differ in which type of coherence they prioritize.

The many comparisons made in this book between liberal and conservative ideologues lead inevitably to the question of who are better citizens. Although the primary goal was empirical—measuring and understanding the differences between liberals and conservatives—asking about the nature of their commitment to democratic government is also valuable. In this day and age in which some Americans believe that the other side is not the loyal opposition but the embodiment of evil, it is helpful to look at objective measures that compare the two sides.

The empirical investigations here form an imperfect vessel for a categorical assessment of how everyday democracy is practiced among liberals and conservatives. A broad range of behaviors and attitudes have been explored, but they do not make for a comprehensive evaluation of contemporary ideology. However, neither did we draw a narrow or idiosyncratic set of questions about ideology. Rather, we investigated fundamental views of the political system, online behavior, and activity in one's community, to name some. As we have said throughout, these everyday behaviors capture much of the hum of politics—the daily sort of everyday experiences we have when we do something that can be classified as political.

On most tests we have also identified what the "better" behavior is in terms of everyday democracy. We believe, for example, that a compromising mindset is more often than not better for democratic citizenship than an uncompromising mindset. If we all stand on principle, problems that need addressing will be caught in the jaws of gridlock. Even so, there are a few areas where making judgments as to what is best for cultivating a democratic mindset is not so clear. Our analysis of attitudes about federalism showed that conservatives were more consistent in sticking to principle when it came to which level of government they preferred to exert authority over policy, but this long-standing preference has its roots in the legacy of states' rights, which is often driven by racism.

We avoid constructing a scorecard of who the better everyday democrats are along the many dimensions studied here because what we have studied varies considerably in how consequential each is to the optimum functioning of a democracy. There are some areas where conservatives do better, such as in the amount of charity they donate or the willingness to talk with people who disagree with them. On the other hand, liberals are more likely to give a charitable gift of any size to a nonprofit and are more likely to favor political compromise. Some tests showed similar responses: Neither liberals nor conservatives do much name-calling online. And when we bring moderates into the picture, we find further evidence of a polity that is chugging along: Some moderates cut others out of their lives due to politics, but not many; they volunteer about as often as ideologues though donate somewhat less; they support political compromise at a very high level; and most of them avoid Fox News. These findings may strike some as a hodgepodge, with too many differences and nuances to form a coherent pattern. Our own reaction is the opposite: In a large and diverse country such as the United States, is it to be expected that we all fall neatly along a Left-Right divide? Or that our attitudes and behaviors are consistently "good" or "bad" for democracy? We think not. When it comes to the day-to-day attitudes and behaviors that help make democracy possible, many Americans, left, right, and center, could do better, but many are also doing the things scholars of democracy would want them to do.

The lack of a consistent picture across the various measures used here should not obscure the differential importance of the results. We believe, above all else, that the findings on racial intolerance in chapter 3 stand out for their disquieting implications. The racialized material on Fox News, which attracts viewers who share those attitudes, reflects a prejudicial view of people of color, especially African Americans. Although the audience for any one program is modest, as we and others have shown, the aggregate monthly audience is large. Fox's enormous influence within the Republican Party amplifies the importance of this content. Our research certainly selected out Fox viewers, who are likely more racially resentful than other sectors of America, but there is considerable evidence that racial resentment is broadly prevalent in the United States and especially within the Republican Party.[48] And recall that nearly 70 percent of conservatives in our sample reported watching Fox. We emphasize these findings because we regard tolerance as a critical foundation of democracy. History teaches us that the consequences of racial, religious, and ethnic antagonism can be catastrophic. We have demonstrated both through surveys and by analyzing Fox just how extensive racial resentment is in the United States. Beyond academic research, though, is the everyday experience of minority groups, particularly Black Americans. From daily acts of discrimination to actual violence, the consequences of racial resentment and outright racism are severe.

In terms of citizenship theory, racism is a way in which people of color are made to feel that they are outside of a system that includes all others. Those who feel excluded may not think explicitly about the academic concept of citizenship, but when they consider their experiences with voting rights, police stops, or housing discrimination, they are evaluating the integrity of the political system and of their rights within it. These racial tensions have been exacerbated by a television network that has monetized conservative resentment, though Fox is not responsible for our racialized past and what their viewers believed prior to watching their shows. Racial antagonism is not just morally repugnant; it is dangerous. As Mettler and Lieberman argue, it "makes for extremely volatile politics, and the potential expansion of democracy—or its rollback—is at stake."[49]

## Better Everyday Democrats

Writing a book about the problems in American government leads to an obvious question for the authors: Given the problems outlined, what are the solutions? Books on the democratic condition often conclude with reform plans advocating institutional change. These might include campaign finance reform, adding third parties, shortening the election cycle, curbing gerrymandering, instituting ranked-choice voting, and eliminating the Electoral College. Such broad-scale reform is difficult at any time but maybe even more so now in such a highly polarized environment. In an effort to promote change that might actually come about, we offer a list of pragmatic ideas that do not require institutional change or public assent. Rather, since this is a book about individual behavior, we have restricted ourselves to everyday things an individual can choose to do.[50] To ensure that these reforms are practical, we set forth three criteria that each had to meet:

1. Each of these is relatively easy to do. Most do not require huge investments of time. Many do not need the cooperation of others. They do not need to be part of a new political movement.
2. They do not require confrontation. In our polarized time, some people equate becoming politically active with entering a combative arena where individuals may aggressively criticize you.
3. They will not cost money. With one exception, none of our suggestions requires individuals to spend money to engage in this behavior.

Although our federal structure of governance is not without flaws, it offers great opportunities for citizens to get involved and make perceptible differences in both policies and the broader political climate. Most of our recommendations capitalize on these opportunities. We organize them into four categories: voting, participation, news and opinion, and thinking about politics.[51]

## VOTING

We begin with what is most important: voting.

*Vote in every election, not just the generals.* If you want to make your voice heard in government, vote not just in the general elections in November of even-numbered years, but also in primaries and in elections held at other times. And be sure to vote in local elections, even if they are held in odd-numbered years, when relatively few participate. Keep in mind that the people who end up in the state legislature or in Congress often get their start as members of a city council or a school board.

*Independents and reregistering.* If you are a registered independent, you may not be able to vote in party primaries. Independents should give some thought to registering as a Republican or Democrat if they live in one of the twenty-two states that either prohibit them from voting in a party primary or have some contingent restrictions. If you do not vote in primaries, you cannot influence who gets nominated.

*Preregister.* Parents should encourage their teenagers to preregister to vote in the states that allow it. Fifteen states allow sixteen-year-olds to preregister for the next election in which they will be able to vote, while four other states allow seventeen-year-olds to do so. Many states also allow those under eighteen to preregister to vote when obtaining a driver's license.

*Be a poll worker.* While this act is a bit more taxing, election infrastructure is critical to any democracy, and the strength of our elections depends on the work of everyday citizens who are able and willing to work a shift on election day checking in voters and giving them instructions. Many states also offer stipends that cover the costs of travel and other related expenses for volunteers.

*Register voters.* Election outcomes can be decided by turnout, and high turnout depends in part on high registration. In terms of cost-benefit analysis, it is surely more efficient to spend your time working to register unregistered voters who are likely to support your side than to try to convince already registered voters to move to vote in a way they were not intending to do in the first place. More simply, changing minds on who to vote for is very difficult; registering voters is less so.

## PARTICIPATION

There is a broad range of political activities beyond voting, and not all are covered below. But here are some that may not leap to mind when you think about how to become more involved in politics:

*Join your local neighborhood association.* If you were to spend a few hours a month on a political activity, what would be the most effective use of that time—where would your hours have the most chance of having an impact? That is a complicated question, and we do not know how to make the calculation. But we do have an educated guess, and that is to volunteer with your local neighborhood association. Not many people participate in them, and thus you would be one of a few. Do neighborhood associations have an impact in local politics? We know the answer to this and it is "yes." Local governments are relatively open, and neighborhood associations get their phone calls returned and are regarded as legitimate representatives of their neighborhoods.[52]

Neighborhood associations are particularly well suited to participate in zoning and licensing proposals. Cities and states commonly incorporate citizen participation requirements into their planning processes. Neighborhood groups will commonly use these processes to slow down enactment and force developers to the bargaining table, where something more acceptable to the neighborhood can be hammered out. Participating in a neighborhood association therefore offers a chance to engage deeply with local officials and fellow residents on substantive issues.

*Consider joining in boycotts.* When cable networks, talk radio, or other corporate entities act irresponsibly or promote extremism, you can boycott them and their sponsors. In the wake of calls for boycotting sponsors on Fox after incendiary comments by program hosts, well-known companies fled the network. Spotify was hurt financially when some consumers left the platform after an episode of its podcast "The Joe Rogan Experience" spread false information about vaccines. The power of boycott advocacy is also illustrated by conservative online activists who asked readers to stop buying Bud Light after Budweiser featured a transgender influencer in a TV ad. Sales for the beer dropped 29 percent and stayed down for months.[53]

In the interest of full disclosure, the three of us are ambivalent when it comes to recommending boycotts as a method of engaging in everyday democracy. We recognize the historical power of boycotts and their potential for giving individuals political agency. They allow the communication of public sentiment in a compelling manner, one that need not be vitriolic or needlessly confrontational. And despite conventional wisdom to the contrary, many Americans want business leaders to do more when it comes to advancing political causes.[54] Boycotts could play an important role in shaping corporate decision-making in this regard. On the other hand, we are not always comfortable with the manifestations of some contemporary boycotts, particularly when they focus more on firing up the outrage machine than on providing an avenue for public engagement. And boycotts can run the risk of hurting vulnerable workers associated with the targeted companies. As with all of our recommendations here, we hope you consider the ones that feel right to you and that you engage in the activity with the goal of being an everyday democrat, with all that that entails.

*Be the squeaky wheel.* Despite the bias toward the status quo in our political system, it is still the squeaky wheels that can get grease. But it can take a long time to see results. So get involved on issues you care about, at any level of government, while remembering that politics is a long game.

*Avoid hateful exchanges, but do engage in conversations across differences.* Most political conversations find agreement, not disagreement. But conversations across differences can be healthful and not always unpleasant while allowing people to identify areas of common purpose and potential compromise. They can de-demonize the other side and introduce more civility into the polity. Emerging research suggests that conversation can be a fruitful way to reduce affective polarization, and we still have much to learn about best practices in this regard.[55] There are also several organizations devoted to modeling and guiding thoughtful discussions across ideological differences that provide resources and training that people could bring into their own lives and communities. Examples of such organizations include Living Room Conversations, the Civic Health Project, Essential Partners, and the Listen First Project.

*Volunteer.* A few types of volunteer activities have already been mentioned, but let us offer a general plea to volunteer for nonprofits. Voluntary associations are the foundation of civil society. If you have time, volunteer for one more organization or increase the hours you devote to nonprofits in which you are already involved.

## ONLINE AND NEWS

At the heart of debate over polarization in America is concern about the abrasive and inaccurate nature of much of the media landscape. There is the temptation for individuals to silo, just looking at sources that agree with their own point of view. Some like inflammatory media that sticks it to the other side. Here is a commonsense guide to choosing what media to consume and suggestions about what to avoid:

*Subscribe to a local paper.* We make one exception here to our effort to promote activities that do not cost money. Supporting local newspapers is crucial as they continue to go out of business, and democracy suffers when policymakers are less accountable. In addition to legacy newspapers, new models of journalism are emerging, and some small cities and towns have new online news sites that rely on donations rather than subscriptions.

*Pause before hitting "send."* We do not want to recommend that people shun online discourse altogether. Engaging in political discussions online can provide an important form of engagement and connection as well as an opportunity to hear arguments and perspectives that one might not encounter in one's daily offline life. But if you participate in online discourse, remember the Golden Rule: treat others as you wish to be treated. It may also be good practice to craft your comments as you would if you were saying them to someone in person or as you would if any of your family members, friends, or coworkers were participating in the conversation. We all disagree with family, friends, and coworkers on occasion, and most of us try to be thoughtful in how we express such disagreement. Carry that thoughtfulness into your online interactions.

*Do not follow or "friend" unreliable ideological news and opinion sites on social media platforms, and report hateful content to the companies.* Although many social media companies provide some moderation of hateful and false postings, none do it sufficiently. Consequently, a great deal of false and bigoted content is not filtered or censored. Reporting and unfollowing those accounts help to limit exposure to such content.

*Do not watch ideological cable news networks.* The business model of outrage cable channels is to be offensive. Ask yourself, "Why do I want to support that?" If you receive cable television in your home, it's very likely you get Fox and MSNBC as part of whatever programming package you purchase. You can ask your distributor if it offers à la carte pricing, and if so, you can choose not to pay for networks you find offensive.[56]

*Learn about and consider local candidates' platforms (for school board, city council, etc.) by using nonpartisan websites.* Ballotpedia is just one example of a nonpartisan site that provides detailed platforms, issue stances, prior voting history, and general background on most local elected officials and candidates. And if you support local media, as we recommend above, you will have those media as a resource for learning about local candidates as well. There may also be podcasts in your area on which local candidates for office are interviewed.

## THINKING ABOUT POLITICS

This final set of recommendations is not a set of actions but ways of thinking about politics. The common catchphrase "Think before you act," may be a rather simple directive, but the reality is that we all take cognitive shortcuts that bring us to a decision or conclusion without doing the hard work of thinking something through.

*Purposefully think about issues from another point of view.* What are the principles that those on the other side espouse? Try to see the losses and the gains in a particular proposal, recognizing that loss can be profoundly difficult for people. Our suggestion is not to change or even adjust one's own positions, but to better understand the other side and allow that it actually may be principled.

*Disentangle principles from interests.* Compromise theory posits that it is more possible to compromise on interests than on principles. Interests are divisible in ways that principles are not, and most government compromise is interest based. In assessing the work of our representatives, citizens may be surprised how principles and interests fare; that should decrease cynicism about politics and our legislators.

*Help the children in your lives understand that democracy can be messy.* We teach children to revere our democracy and national values, but we do not do enough to help them appreciate what it actually takes to work across competing interests. Be cognizant of the language you use when talking about politics around or with children. Remind them that people with different life experiences may see the world differently. Teach them that when it comes to elections and policies, you win some and you lose some, and you need to work with people even if you do not particularly like them.

*Don't confuse media attention with magnitude.* The media will give the impression that everyone is extreme and hates the other side. That is not true. Most people are not especially involved in politics, and even those who think of themselves in ideological or partisan terms are seldom extreme or intransigent.

*Have sympathy for elected officials.* While hating politicians may be the one thing that Americans of all backgrounds have in common, we need people who are willing to take on the task of running for office and to serve. They put themselves and their families through a lot to take on a very difficult and important job. It is okay to support them and thank them.

*Remember that democracy is never "done."* Even if there is a time when things seem stable or policies seem to be favoring your preferred outcomes, democracy requires that we continue to do the everyday work. Be an everyday democrat because democracy needs us.

In these recommendations, we consciously focused on actions that people could start doing today if they so choose. We recognize that there are many players in the American political system, each with their own opportunities—and responsibilities—to act in ways that bolster American democracy, and that includes political elites. By "elite," we primarily mean elected and appointed leaders at all levels of government, though the term can also encompass leaders across institutions such as corporations and the media. For elites, a basic and pressing responsibility is to act in ways that sustain the guardrails of democracy, as laid out powerfully by Levitsky and Ziblatt in *How Democracies Die*: Engage in mutual toleration of one's opponents and practice forbearance by showing respect for norms that enable compromise and the peaceful transition of power and by protecting the institutional arrangements laid out in the Constitution, even if doing so means one's own side might not prevail in the next election.[57] Even better, elites could actively promote mutual toleration and forbearance, and they could go out of their way to draw people's attention to their importance. One effort of note is the "Disagree Better" initiative from the National Governors Association, where governors cross party lines to engage the public in thoughtful discussions about division in America. The very premise of this effort is grounded in mutual toleration, which, as Levitzky and Ziblatt argue, enhances forbearance because it reduces the temptation to break democratic norms.[58] Further, such discussions model cross-partisan dialogue for the general public.

We plead guilty to idealism. And we also recognize that we are preaching incrementalism rather than rapid change. But incremental changes aggregate, and if large numbers of Americans followed at least some of these

prescriptions, our politics could begin to shift. We have consciously fashioned these recommendations around ideas that both conservatives and
liberals should be able to embrace without thinking the other side is trying
to stack the political deck. These suggestions are aimed only at individual
behavior. We hope that our work starts an internal conversation that leads
people to ask themselves: What is it that I can do to be a better everyday
democrat?

# Acknowledgments

This project began nearly a decade ago. We have tried to keep good records of the many people who have helped us along the way in hopes that someday we'd be writing book acknowledgments in which we could thank them publicly. And here we are. First, we would not be at this point without the incredible research assistance of several students, including Bennett Fleming-Wood, Alex Landy, and Alexis Tatore. Next, we benefited greatly from ongoing discussions with our colleagues at Tufts University, including Eitan Hersh, Brian Schaffner, Peter Levine, David Garman, and Kei-Kawashima Ginsburg. Staff assistance at Tufts has also been invaluable, and for that we thank Paula Driscoll and Linsday Riordan.

Along the way we had the opportunity to get helpful feedback from colleagues elsewhere as well. We are particularly grateful for perspectives offered by Eunji Kim, Brian Hamel, John Dinan, Soren Jordan, Timothy Ryan, Ryan Enos, Dean Lacey, Dan Hopkins, Michael Martinez, Leonie Huddy, Stanley Feldman, Rob Davis, Wendy Schiller, and Eric Patashnik. Berwood Yost at the Franklin and Marshall Poll helped us design and field questions for one of our survey experiments.

Portions of analyses throughout the book can be found elsewhere:

- James M. Glaser and Jeffrey M. Berry, "Compromising Positions: Why Republican Partisans Are More Rigid Than Democrats," *Political Science Quarterly* 133, no. 1 (2018): 99–125.
- Deborah J. Schildkraut, Jeffrey M. Berry, and James M. Glaser, "Charge and Retreat: Asymmetric Patterns of Political Engagement Among Liberals and Conservatives," in *Dynamics of American Democracy: Partisan Polarization, Political Competition and Government Performance*, edited by Eric M. Patashnik and Wendy J. Schiller, 200–224. University of Kansas Press, 2020.

- Deborah J. Schildkraut, Jeffrey M. Berry, and James M. Glaser, "Ideological Bubbles and Two Types of Conservatives," *Public Opinion Quarterly* 84, no. 2 (2020): 508–22.
- Jeffrey M. Berry, James M. Glaser, and Deborah J. Schildkraut, "Race and Gender on Fox and MSNBC," *Forum* 18, no. 3 (2021): 297–317.
- James M. Glaser, Jeffrey M. Berry, and Deborah J. Schildkraut, "Education and the Curious Case of Conservative Compromise," *Political Research Quarterly* 74, no. 1 (2021): 59–75.
- James M. Glaser, Jeffrey M. Berry, and Deborah J. Schildkraut, "Ideology and Support for Federalism in Theory—and in Practice," *Publius* 53, no. 4 (2023): 511–35.

This list may strike some as long; normally only a couple of articles precede a book in our line of work. The works listed above represent our early thinking about particular facets of democratic citizenship. Synthesizing the ideas we developed in these articles as we wrote this book has given us the opportunity to bring their seemingly disparate lines of inquiry together under the theoretical umbrella of everyday democracy, which we use to develop our broad assessment of the American public. It is by considering our findings in total that we emerge with our thoughts on areas for both hope and concern. Readers who may be familiar with any of these works will find that their treatment here has been not only updated but also deepened and broadened.

We are grateful for the team at the University of Chicago Press for taking a chance on our work. Thank you to Sara Doskow for supporting this project and to Adam Berinsky for bringing it into the Chicago Studies in American Politics series. Barbara Norton did a superb job copyediting the manuscript, and we thank her.

The three of us would not be where we are without the steadfast support of our families.

Our partners, Lori, Pam, and RJ, lift us up and bring us back to earth, each at the right time.

Support for the institutions of government has long been of interest to political scientists. Generalized support of government—and indeed, support for other societal institutions—is part of everyday democracy, even if that support is sometimes hard to come by. With this in mind, the three of us wish to express our deep appreciation for an institution that has given us such a wonderful environment in which to pursue our careers as teachers, scholars, and leaders. For Debbie, it is even the institution that educated her. As Jeff enters into retirement and Jim moves to a leadership position at Santa Clara University, it seems fitting to dedicate this book to Tufts University, our academic home for a collective one hundred plus years.

# Notes

CHAPTER ONE

1. Brendan Hartnett and Alexandra Haver, "Unconditional Support for Trump's Resistance Prior to Election Day," *PS: Political Science & Politics*, July 18, 2022, 1–7, https://doi.org/10.1017/S1049096522000695.

2. John Sides et al., *Identity Crisis: The 2016 Presidential Campaign and the Battle for the Meaning of America* (Princeton University Press, 2018); Thomas E. Mann and Norman J. Ornstein, *It's Even Worse Than It Looks: How the American Constitutional System Collided with the New Politics of Extremism* (Basic Books, 2016); Suzanne Mettler and Robert C. Lieberman, *Four Threats: The Recurring Crises of American Democracy* (St. Martin's Publishing Group, 2020); Sara Wallace Goodman, *Citizenship in Hard Times: How Ordinary People Respond to Democratic Threat* (Cambridge University Press, 2022).

3. Sean M. Theriault, *The Gingrich Senators: The Roots of Partisan Warfare in Congress* (Oxford University Press, 2013); Frances E. Lee, *Insecure Majorities: Congress and the Perpetual Campaign* (University of Chicago Press, 2016); Lee Drutman, *Breaking the Two-Party Doom Loop: The Case for Multiparty Democracy in America* (Oxford University Press, 2020); Lawrence R. Jacobs, *Democracy Under Fire: Donald Trump and the Breaking of American History* (Oxford University Press, 2022); Steven Levitsky and Daniel Ziblatt, *Tyranny of the Minority: Why American Democracy Reached the Breaking Point* (Penguin Random House, 2023).

4. Goodman, *Citizenship in Hard Times*; Nathan P. Kalmoe and Lilliana Mason, *Radical American Partisanship: Mapping Violent Hostility, Its Causes, and the Consequences for Democracy* (University of Chicago Press, 2022); Herbert McClosky, "Consensus and Ideology in American Politics," *American Political Science Review* 58, no. 2 (1964): 361–82; Philip Converse, "The Nature of Belief Systems in Mass Publics," in *Ideology and Discontent*, ed. David Apter (Free Press, 1964), 206–61; Gabriel Almond and Sidney Verba, *The Civic Culture: Political Attitudes and Democracy in Five Nations* (Princeton University Press, 1963).

5. Robert A. Dahl, *A Preface to Democratic Theory* (University of Chicago Press, 1956); Robert A. Dahl, *On Democracy* (Yale University Press, 1998); Arend Lijphart, *Patterns of Democracy* (Yale University Press, 1999), https://yalebooks.yale.edu/book/9780300172027/patterns-democracy; Steven Levitsky and Daniel Ziblatt, *How Democracies Die* (Crown, 2018); Mettler and Lieberman, *Four Threats*; Charles Tilly, *Democracy* (Cambridge University Press, 2007).

6. Kalmoe and Mason, *Radical American Partisanship*; John Sides et al., *The Bitter End: The 2020 Presidential Campaign and the Challenge to American Democracy* (Princeton University Press, 2022).

7. Shanto Iyengar and Sean J. Westwood, "Fear and Loathing Across Party Lines: New Evidence on Group Polarization," *American Journal of Political Science* 59, no. 3 (2015): 690–707; Alan I. Abramowitz, "The New American Electorate: Partisan, Sorted, and Polarized," in *American Gridlock: The Sources, Character, and Impact of Political Polarization*, ed. James A. Thurber and Antoine Yoshinaka (Cambridge University Press, 2015), 19–44; Matthew S. Levendusky, "Americans, Not Partisans: Can Priming American National Identity Reduce Affective Polarization?," *Journal of Politics* 80, no. 1 (2018): 59–70; Shanto Iyengar et al., "The Origins and Consequences of Affective Polarization in the United States," *Annual Review of Political Science* 22 (May 2019): 129–46, https://doi.org/10.1146/annurev-polisci-051117-073034; Lilliana Mason, "Ideologues Without Issues: The Polarizing Consequences of Ideological Identities," *Public Opinion Quarterly* 82, no. S1 (April 11, 2018): 866–87, https://doi.org/10.1093/poq/nfy005; Christopher Ellis and James A. Stimson, *Ideology in America* (Cambridge University Press, 2012); Donald R. Kinder and Nathan P. Kalmoe, *Neither Liberal nor Conservative* (University of Chicago Press, 2017).

8. Nicholas T. Davis, Keith Gaddie, and Kirby Goidel, *Democracy's Meanings: How the Public Understands Democracy and Why It Matters* (University of Michigan Press, 2022).

9. Adam Przeworski, *Democracy and the Market: Political and Economic Reforms in Eastern Europe and Latin America* (Cambridge University Press, 1991), 10, https://doi.org/10.1017/CBO9781139172493.

10. Levitsky and Ziblatt, *How Democracies Die*.

11. Robert A. Dahl, *Polyarchy: Participation and Opposition* (Yale University Press, 1971).

12. Alexis de Tocqueville and Isaac Kramnick, *Democracy in America: An Annotated Text, Backgrounds, Interpretations*, Norton critical ed. (W. W. Norton, 2007), 203, https://books.google.com/books?id=DBokAQAAIAAJ; Alexis de Tocqueville, *Democracy in America* (Vintage Books, 1835); Robert D. Putnam, *Bowling Alone: The Collapse and Revival of American Community* (Simon & Schuster, 2000); Robert A. Dahl, *Dilemmas of Pluralist Democracy: Autonomy vs. Control* (Yale University Press, 1983); Robert Neelly Bellah et al., *Habits of the Heart: Individualism and Commitment in American Life* (University of California Press, 2008); Philip Converse, "The Nature of Belief Systems in Mass Publics"; Benjamin Barber, *Strong Democracy: Participatory Politics for a New Age* (University of California Press, 2003); Dahl, *Polyarchy*; Russell J. Dalton, *The Good Citizen*, 3rd ed. (CQ Press, 2021).

13. Tocqueville and Kramnick, *Democracy in America: An Annotated Text*, 203.

14. Tocqueville, *Democracy in America*, 262–63.

15. Bellah et al., *Habits of the Heart*, 37.

16. Alexander Hamilton et al., *The Federalist Papers* (Dover Publications, 2014), 41–47.

17. Bellah et al., *Habits of the Heart*, 38.

18. Tocqueville, *Democracy in America*, 155.

19. Tocqueville, *Democracy in America*, 155.

20. Putnam, *Bowling Alone*, 122.

21. Putnam, *Bowling Alone*, 292.

22. Putnam, *Bowling Alone*, 19.

23. Levitsky and Ziblatt, *Tyranny of the Minority*.

24. Dahl, *Polyarchy*.

25. For more discussion on when to extend or withdraw such "civic respect," see Jeff Spinner-Halev and Elizabeth Theiss-Morse, *Respect and Loathing in American Democracy: Polarization, Moralization, and the Undermining of Equality* (University of Chicago Press, 2024).

26. Kalmoe and Mason, *Radical American Partisanship*, 10.

27. Masket, "We Freaking Warned You," *Mischiefs of Faction* (blog), January 9, 2021, https://www.mischiefsoffaction.com/post/we-freaking-warned-you.

28. Levitsky and Ziblatt, *How Democracies Die*.

29. Mettler and Lieberman, *Four Threats*.

30. Theriault, *The Gingrich Senators*.

31. Angus Campbell et al., *The American Voter* (University of Chicago Press, 1960); Ellis and Stimson, *Ideology in America*.

32. Matthew Levendusky, *The Partisan Sort: How Liberals Became Democrats and Conservatives Became Republicans* (University of Chicago Press, 2009); Mason, "Ideologues Without Issues"; Alan I. Abramowitz, "Peak Polarization? The Rise of Partisan-Ideological Consistency and Its Consequences" (Ray Bliss Institute, University of Akron, 2021).

33. Christopher M. Federico, "Ideology and Public Opinion," in *New Directions in Public Opinion*, 3rd ed., ed. Adam J. Berinsky (Routledge, 2020), 76.

34. Jacob S. Hacker and Paul Pierson, "Confronting Asymmetric Polarization," in *Solutions to Political Polarization in America*, ed. Nathaniel Persily (Cambridge University Press, 2015), 59–71; Mann and Ornstein, *It's Even Worse Than It Looks*; Drew Desilver, "The Polarization in Today's Congress Has Roots That Go Back Decades," Pew Research Center, March 10, 2022, https://www.pewresearch.org/fact-tank/2022/03/10/the-polarization-in-todays-congress-has-roots-that-go-back-decades/.

35. See also Ellis and Stimson, *Ideology in America*.

36. Lisa L. Miller, "Up from Federalism," *Boston Review*, July 18, 2022, https://bostonreview.net/articles/up-from-federalism/.

37. Spinner-Halev and Theiss-Morse, *Respect and Loathing in American Democracy*; James N. Druckman et al., *Partisan Hostility and American Democracy: Explaining Political Divisions and When They Matter* (University of Chicago Press, 2024).

38. Yanna Krupnikov and John Barry Ryan, *The Other Divide: Polarization and Disengagement in American Politics* (Cambridge University Press, 2022); James N. Druckman et al., "(Mis)Estimating Affective Polarization," *Journal of Politics* 84, no. 2 (April 2022): 1106–17, https://doi.org/10.1086/715603; "National Politics on Twitter: Small Share of U.S. Adults Produce Majority of Tweets," Pew Research Center—U.S. Politics & Policy, October 23, 2019, https://www.pewresearch.org/politics/2019/10/23/national-politics-on-twitter-small-share-of-u-s-adults-produce-majority-of-tweets/; Douglas J. Ahler, "Self-Fulfilling Misperceptions of Public Polarization," *Journal of Politics* 76, no. 3 (July 2014): 607–20, https://doi.org/10.1017/S0022381614000085.

39. Kinder and Kalmoe, *Neither Liberal nor Conservative*.

40. Tasha S. Philpot, *Conservative but Not Republican: The Paradox of Party Identification and Ideology Among African Americans* (Cambridge University Press, 2017); Hakeem Jefferson, "The Curious Case of Black 'Conservatives': Assessing the

Validity of the Liberal–Conservative Scale Among Black Americans," *Public Opinion Quarterly* 88, no. 3 (2024): 909–32; Michael C. Dawson, *Black Visions: The Roots of Contemporary African-American Political Ideologies* (University of Chicago Press, 2001).

41. Kevin Phillips, *The Emerging Republican Majority* (Arlington House, 1969).

42. Mettler and Lieberman, *Four Threats*, 3.

43. Emmanuel Felton, "Baltimore Mayor Weathers Racist Attacks After Bridge Collapse," *Washington Post*, March 31, 2024, https://www.washingtonpost.com /nation/2024/03/31/baltimore-bridge-collapse-mayor/.

44. For more on emotions and political discussion, see Taylor N. Carlson and Jamie E. Settle, *What Goes Without Saying: Navigating Political Discussion in America* (Cambridge University Press, 2022).

45. Jonathan M. Ladd, *Why Americans Hate the Media and How It Matters* (Princeton University Press, 2012); Devin J. Christensen et al., "Mainstream Media Recirculation of Trust-Reducing Social Media Messages," *American Politics Research* 50, no. 2 (March 1, 2022): 213–26, https://doi.org/10.1177/1532673X211023931; Paul R. Ward et al., "Predictors and Extent of Institutional Trust in Government, Banks, the Media and Religious Organisations: Evidence from Cross-Sectional Surveys in Six Asia-Pacific Countries," *PLOS One* 11, no. 10 (October 4, 2016), https://doi.org/10.1371/journal .pone.0164096.

46. Emily Pears, *Cords of Affection: Constructing Constitutional Union in Early American History* (University Press of Kansas, 2021).

47. Drutman, *Breaking the Two-Party Doom Loop*.

48. Steven Levitsky and Daniel Ziblatt, "End Minority Rule," *New York Times*, October 23, 2020, https://www.nytimes.com/2020/10/23/opinion/sunday/ disenfranchisement-democracy-minority-rule.html.

CHAPTER TWO

1. Emily Cochrane, "Sarah Huckabee Sanders Was Asked to Leave Restaurant over White House Work," *New York Times*, June 23, 2018, https://www.nytimes .com/2018/06/23/us/politics/sarah-huckabee-sanders-restaurant.html; Avi Selk and Sarah Murray, "The Owner of the Red Hen Explains Why She Asked Sarah Huckabee Sanders to Leave," *Washington Post*, October 23, 2021, https://www.washingtonpost .com/news/local/wp/2018/06/23/why-a-small-town-restaurant-owner-asked-sarah -huckabee-sanders-to-leave-and-would-do-it-again/.

2. Emily Stewart, "The Past 72 Hours in Sarah Sanders's Dinner and the Civility Debate, Explained," *Vox*, June 25, 2018, https://www.vox.com/policy-and-politics/ 2018/6/25/17500988/sarah-sanders-red-hen-civility; Michael A. Cohen, "Thanks, Red Hen, for Kicking Out Sarah Huckabee Sanders," *Boston Globe*, June 25, 2018, https:// www.bostonglobe.com/opinion/2018/06/25/thanks-red-hen-for-kicking-out-sarah -huckabee-sanders/LrZ8CyqZvwtXkV6K7Cp3HN/story.html.

3. Mattie Kahn, "No, Sarah Huckabee Sanders Shouldn't Be Able to Eat Dinner in Public," *Glamour*, June 26, 2018, https://www.glamour.com/story/sarah-huckabee -sanders-civility-politics.

4. "Let the Trump Team Eat in Peace," Editorial Board, *Washington Post*, June 25, 2018, https://www.washingtonpost.com/opinions/let-the-trump-team-eat-in-peace/ 2018/06/24/46882e16-779a-11e8-80be-6d32e182a3bc_story.html.

5. Selk and Murray, "The Owner of the Red Hen Explains Why She Asked Sarah Huckabee Sanders to Leave."

6. Aja Romano, "'OK Boomer' Isn't Just About the Past: It's About Our Apocalyptic Future," *Vox*, November 19, 2019, https://www.vox.com/2019/11/19/20963757/what-is-ok-boomer-meme-about-meaning-gen-z-millennials.

7. Nicole Spector, "'OK Boomer' Is Dividing Generations: What Does It Mean?," *NBC News*, November 6, 2019, https://www.nbcnews.com/better/lifestyle/ok-boomer-dividing-generation-what-does-it-mean-ncna1077261.

8. Derek Robertson, "How 'Owning the Libs' Became the GOP's Core Belief," *Politico*, March 21, 2021, https://www.politico.com/news/magazine/2021/03/21/owning-the-libs-history-trump-politics-pop-culture-477203.

9. Gregory Krieg, "Keurig Roasted? The Latest Effort to 'Own the Libs,'" CNN, November 14, 2017, https://www.cnn.com/2017/11/14/politics/keurig-protest-owning-the-libs-meme/index.html.

10. Sonny Bunch, "Conservatives Are Dying to Own the Libs: Can Anyone Use That Logic to Get Them Vaccinated?," *Washington Post*, September 21, 2021, https://www.washingtonpost.com/opinions/2021/09/21/conservatives-are-dying-own-libs-can-anyone-use-that-logic-get-them-vaccinated/.

11. A previous iteration of this analysis was published in Deborah J. Schildkraut et al., "Charge and Retreat: Asymmetric Patterns of Political Engagement Among Liberals and Conservatives," in *Dynamics of American Democracy: Partisan Polarization, Political Competition and Government Performance*, ed. Eric M. Patashnik and Wendy J. Schiller (University Press of Kansas, 2020), 200–224.

12. Tocqueville, *Democracy in America*.

13. Nina Eliasoph, *Avoiding Politics: How Americans Produce Apathy in Everyday Life* (Cambridge University Press, 1998); Diana C. Mutz, *Hearing the Other Side: Deliberative Versus Participatory Democracy* (Cambridge University Press, 2006); Nicole Curato et al., "Twelve Key Findings in Deliberative Democracy Research," *Daedalus* 146, no. 3 (2017): 28–38; James S. Fishkin and Jane Mansbridge, "Introduction," *Daedalus* 146, no. 3 (2017): 6–13.

14. Bernard Manin, "Political Deliberation and the Adversarial Principle," *Daedalus* 146, no. 3 (2017): 39–50; Krupnikov and Ryan, *The Other Divide*; Carlson and Settle, *What Goes Without Saying*.

15. Throughout this chapter, we refer to this platform as Twitter, since that is what it was called when we collected our data and conducted our analyses.

16. See Carlson and Settle, *What Goes Without Saying*.

17. See Emily Sydnor, *Disrespectful Democracy: The Psychology of Incivility* (Columbia University Press, 2019), for an examination of conflict avoidance.

18. Lynn M. Sanders, "Against Deliberation," *Political Theory* 25, no. 3 (1997): 347–76; Manin, "Political Deliberation and the Adversarial Principle."

19. Fishkin and Mansbridge, "Introduction"; Carlson and Settle, *What Goes Without Saying*.

20. Peter Levine, *We Are the Ones We Have Been Waiting For* (Oxford University Press, 2013), 162.

21. Curato et al., "Twelve Key Findings in Deliberative Democracy Research," 32.

22. See also Spinner-Halev and Theiss-Morse, *Respect and Loathing in American Democracy*, for discussion of the importance of granting civic respect to one's political

opponents, which involves listening to the other side and trying to understand opposing perspectives.

23. Mutz, *Hearing the Other Side*; Manin, "Political Deliberation and the Adversarial Principle."

24. Robert Huckfeldt and John Sprague, "Networks in Context: The Social Flow of Political Information," *American Political Science Review* 81, no. 4 (1987): 1197–1216.

25. Sydnor, *Disrespectful Democracy*.

26. Eliasoph, *Avoiding Politics*.

27. Huckfeldt and Sprague, "Networks in Context"; Charles A. Dorison et al., "Selective Exposure Partly Relies on Faulty Affective Forecasts," *Cognition* 188 (2019): 98–107.

28. Matthew Levendusky, *Our Common Bonds* (University of Chicago Press, 2023).

29. Sanders, "Against Deliberation."

30. Arthur Lupia and Anne Norton, "Inequality Is Always in the Room: Language and Power in Deliberative Democracy," *Daedalus* 146, no. 3 (2017): 64–76.

31. Mark Jurkowitz et al., "Americans Are Divided by Party in the Sources They Turn to for Political News," Pew Research Center's Journalism Project, January 24, 2020, https://www.pewresearch.org/journalism/2020/01/24/americans-are-divided -by-party-in-the-sources-they-turn-to-for-political-news/.

32. Jeffrey M. Berry and Sarah Sobieraj, *The Outrage Industry: Political Opinion Media and the New Incivility* (Oxford University Press, 2014); Nicholas A. Valentino et al., "The Changing Norms of Racial Political Rhetoric and the End of Racial Priming," *Journal of Politics* 80, no. 3 (July 2018): 757–71, https://doi.org/10.1086/694845.

33. Davin Phoenix, *The Anger Gap: How Race Shapes Emotion in Politics* (Cambridge University Press, 2019), 33.

34. Antoine J. Banks et al., "Black Politics: How Anger Influences the Political Actions Blacks Pursue to Reduce Racial Inequality," *Political Behavior* 41, no. 4 (2019): 917–43.

35. Christopher Parker and Matt Barreto, *Change They Can't Believe In: The Tea Party and Reactionary Politics in America* (Princeton University Press, 2013); Bryan T. Gervais and Irwin L. Morris, *Reactionary Republicanism: How the Tea Party in the House Paved the Way for Trump's Victory* (Oxford University Press, 2018); Rachel Blum, *How the Tea Party Captured the GOP: Insurgent Factions in American Politics* (University of Chicago Press, 2020).

36. Dannagal G. Young, *Irony and Outrage: The Polarized Landscape of Rage, Fear, and Laughter in the United States* (Oxford University Press, 2020).

37. Mark S. Granovetter, "The Strength of Weak Ties," *American Journal of Sociology* 78, no. 6 (May 15, 1973): 1360–80, https://doi.org/10.1086/225469.

38. Albert O. Hirschman, *Exit, Voice, and Loyalty: Responses to Decline in Firms, Organizations, and States* (Harvard University Press, 1970).

39. Meredith Ringel Morris et al., "Tweeting Is Believing? Understanding Microblog Credibility Perceptions," in *Proceedings of the ACM 2012 Conference on Computer Supported Cooperative Work—CSCW '12* (ACM Press, 2012), 441, https://doi.org/10 .1145/2145204.2145274.

40. "Wave 19 of the American Trends Panel Survey, Conducted July 12–August 8, 2016," Pew Research Center, 2016, http://www.people-press.org/dataset/american -trends-panel-wave-19/.

41. "Most Democrats, Republicans Have 'Just a Few' or No Friends in Opposing Party," Pew Research Center, October 4, 2017, http://www.people-press.org/2017/10/05/8-partisan-animosity-personal-politics-views-of-trump/8_02/.

42. Amy Mitchell et al., "Political Polarization and Media Habits," Pew Research Center, October 21, 2014, https://www.pewresearch.org/journalism/2014/10/21/political-polarization-media-habits/.

43. Daniel Cox and Robert P. Jones, "'Merry Christmas' vs. 'Happy Holidays': Republicans and Democrats Are Polar Opposites," PRRI (blog), December 19, 2016, https://www.prri.org/research/poll-post-election-holiday-war-christmas/.

44. Spinner-Halev and Theiss-Morse, *Respect and Loathing in American Democracy.*

45. Leticia Bode, "Pruning the News Feed: Unfriending and Unfollowing Political Content on Social Media," *Research & Politics* 3, no. 3 (August 12, 2016): 205316801666187, https://doi.org/10.1177/2053168016661873; see also Dannagal G. Young and Katherine Anderson, "Media Diet Homogeneity in a Fragmented Media Landscape," *Atlantic Journal of Communication* 25, no. 1 (January 31, 2017): 33–47, https://doi.org/10.1080/15456870.2017.1251434.

46. The Cooperative Congressional Election Survey (CCES) became the Cooperative Election Study (CES) between 2018 and 2020.

47. Throughout all of our analyses, "liberal" combines respondents who say they are liberal and very liberal; "conservative" combines respondents who are conservative or very conservative. Only respondents who said they use social media platforms were asked subsequent questions about social media.

48. Gregory Eady et al., "How Many People Live in Political Bubbles on Social Media? Evidence from Linked Survey and Twitter Data," *Sage Open* 9, no. 1 (February 28, 2019), https://doi.org/10.1177/2158244019832705.

49. The actors were Joe Biden, Hillary Clinton, Kirsten Gillibrand, Chris Hayes, Van Jones, Rachel Maddow, Bill Maher, Joe Manchin, Barack Obama, Lawrence O'Donnell, Nancy Pelosi, Bernie Sanders, and Chuck Schumer; and Susan Collins, Ted Cruz, Lindsey Graham, Sean Hannity, Hugh Hewitt, Laura Ingraham, John McCain, Mitch McConnell, Bill O'Reilly, Mike Pence, Paul Ryan, Ben Shapiro, and Donald Trump.

50. The tool is available at https://github.com/pablobarbera/twitter_ideology?fbclid=IwAR3BdRPALjLfF5jtm3h3T8kdFoUBMYG50f3-rrmkdiECPAPgzRKeYdNxjrA.

51. Users whose ideology could not be estimated because they do not follow at least two of the more than one thousand elite accounts in the ideology estimator tool were dropped from our sample.

52. Eady et al., "How Many People Live in Political Bubbles on Social Media?"

53. Nicholas A. Valentino et al., "Election Night's Alright for Fighting: The Role of Emotions in Political Participation," *Journal of Politics* 73, no. 1 (January 1, 2011): 156–70, https://doi.org/10.1017/S0022381610000939; Banks et al., "Black Politics"; George E. Marcus and Michael B. MacKuen, "Anxiety, Enthusiasm, and the Vote: The Emotional Underpinnings of Learning and Involvement During Presidential Campaigns," *American Political Science Review* 87, no. 3 (1993): 672–85; Carlson and Settle, *What Goes Without Saying.*

54. Dorison et al., "Selective Exposure Partly Relies on Faulty Affective Forecasts."

55. Berry and Sobieraj, *The Outrage Industry*; Gervais and Morris, *Reactionary Republicanism.*

56. For the purposes of this study, our control on race distinguishes white from nonwhite respondents.

57. Leticia Bode, "Closing the Gap: Gender Parity in Political Engagement on Social Media," *Information, Communication & Society* 20, no. 4 (June 28, 2016): 587–603.

58. Bode, "Pruning the News Feed."

59. Berry and Sobieraj, *The Outrage Industry*.

60. Berry and Sobieraj, *The Outrage Industry*; Jeffrey M. Berry et al., "Race and Gender on Fox and MSNBC," *Forum* 18, no. 3 (2020): 297–317, https://doi.org/10.1515/for-2020-2011.

61. We also ran our models using a measure of trust in conservative media instead of consumption. The correlation between the trust and consumption scales is .60. Our substantive results are unchanged with this alternative specification. We also ran our models omitting media variables altogether. All substantive results in table 2.2 are unchanged.

62. Carlson and Settle, *What Goes Without Saying*.

63. Among the other variables in our model, not much matters. Older respondents are less likely to report changing their social media settings, and people with higher levels of education are more likely to say they have blocked someone and that most of their friends share their political views. Conservative media consumption is insignificant in every model.

64. Sydnor, *Disrespectful Democracy*.

65. Our 2020 CES module did not contain the same measure of conservative media consumption as our 2018 module; the models in tables 4.2 and 4.3 use the same controls otherwise. The results indicate that older respondents are less likely to report changing their social media settings than younger people and more likely to report having politically homogeneous social networks. They also show that people with higher levels of education are more likely to report three of the four bubble-sustaining behaviors than people with lower levels of education.

66. Ellis and Stimson, *Ideology in America*.

67. Ariel Malka and Yphtach Lelkes, "More Than Ideology: Conservative–Liberal Identity and Receptivity to Political Cues," *Social Justice Research* 23, nos. 2–3 (September 22, 2010): 156–88, https://doi.org/10.1007/s11211-010-0114-3; Christopher J. Devine, "Ideological Social Identity: Psychological Attachment to Ideological In-Groups as a Political Phenomenon and a Behavioral Influence," *Political Behavior* 37, no. 3 (September 17, 2015): 509–35, https://doi.org/10.1007/s11109-014-9280-6; Mason, "Ideologues Without Issues."

68. Matt Grossmann and David A. Hopkins, *Asymmetric Politics: Ideological Republicans and Group Interest Democrats* (Oxford University Press, 2016).

69. For all ten questions in our operational ideology score, the liberal response was coded −1 and the conservative response was coded +1. The responses were then added together, for a scale ranging from −10 (most operationally liberal) to +10 (most operationally conservative). The items measured support or opposition to: banning assault rifles; allowing a woman to obtain an abortion as a matter of choice; prohibiting the expenditure of funds authorized or appropriated by federal law for any abortion; increasing spending on border security by $25 billion, including building a wall between the United States and Mexico; providing legal status to children of immigrants who are already in the United States and were brought to the United States by their parents and providing these children the option of citizenship in ten years if they meet

citizenship requirements and commit no crimes; cutting the corporate income tax rate from 39 percent to 21 percent; repealing the Affordable Care Act; raising the state minimum wage to $12 an hour; increasing taxes on incomes that exceed $1 million by 4 percent to pay for schools and roads; and strengthening the Environmental Protection Agency enforcement of the Clean Air Act and Clean Water Act even if it costs US jobs.

70. As in 2018, for all ten questions in our operational ideology score, the liberal response was coded −1 and the conservative response was coded +1. The responses were then added together, for a scale ranging from −10 (most operationally liberal) to +10 (most operationally conservative). The items measured support or opposition to: banning assault rifles; allowing a woman to obtain an abortion as a matter of choice; prohibiting the expenditure of funds authorized or appropriated by federal law for any abortion; increasing spending on border security by $25 billion, including building a wall between the United States and Mexico; granting legal status to all illegal immigrants who have held jobs and paid taxes for at least three years and not been convicted of any felony crimes; repealing the Affordable Care Act; raising the minimum wage to $15 an hour; strengthening the Environmental Protection Agency enforcement of the Clean Air Act and Clean Water Act even if it costs US jobs; increasing the number of police on the street by 10 percent, even if it means fewer funds for other public services; and amending federal laws to prohibit discrimination on the basis of gender identity and sexual orientation.

71. We also ran the 2018 models without the media consumption variable. In that specification, the results in table 2.4 became substantively identical to the results in table 2.5. Specifically, the coefficient on "consistent conservative" in the model for whether people have blocked someone else goes from $p = .07$ to $p = .15$. The rest of the substantive results in table 2.4 were unchanged.

72. Most of our control variables are insignificant in all models in both years. In 2018 we find that conservatives who consume conservative media were more likely to report having a homogeneous social network, while nonwhite conservatives were less likely. In 2020 we find that women were less likely to report ending friendships due to politics than men.

73. Diana C. Mutz and Byron Reeves, "The New Videomalaise: Effects of Televised Incivility on Political Trust," *American Political Science Review* 99, no. 1 (February 2005): 1–15; Deana A. Rohlinger, "American Media and Deliberative Democratic Processes," *Sociological Theory* 25, no. 2 (June 24, 2007): 122–48, https://doi.org/10.1111/j.1467-9558.2007.00301.x; Sydnor, *Disrespectful Democracy*; Robert G. Boatright et al., eds., *A Crisis of Civility? Political Discourse and Its Discontents* (Routledge, 2019).

74. Gervais and Morris, *Reactionary Republicanism*.

75. Berry and Sobieraj, *The Outrage Industry*, 246.

76. The specific search terms are the following: *health care*: Obamacare, Affordable Care Act, American Health Care Act, Trumpcare, Ryancare, repeal and replace; *gun violence*: school shooting, Sandy Hook, Parkland, Marjory Stoneman Douglas, gun rights, gun control, NRA, Second Amendment, 2nd Amendment; *environment*: the environment, climate change, global warming, carbon emissions, sustainability, fossil fuels; *fiscal*: government deficit, national debt, budget deficit, entitlements, welfare, social security, Medicare, minimum wage, unemployment, tax reform, tax plan, Tax Cuts and Jobs Act, economic inequality, income inequality; *immigration*: DACA, Deferred Action for Childhood Arrivals, DREAMers, Muslim ban, illegal immigrants, illegal immigration, border security, southern border, border wall; *discrimination*:

marriage equality, same-sex marriage, homophobia, black lives matter, police brutality, racism, discrimination, sexism, feminism; *government*: Congress, SCOTUS, Supreme Court, House of Representatives, Senate, Executive Branch, Presidency, POTUS, President of the United States, Trump, Obama, State of the Union, SOTU.

77. We ran our web scraping tool for more than twelve hours. With a longer time frame, this research could be replicated with a larger sample size.

78. This tool is available at https://www.perspectiveapi.com/#/.

79. List of name-calling search terms: SJW, social justice warrior, snowflake, bigot, hack, troll, idiot, moron, loon, elitist, extremist, shill, radical, fool, stupid, ignorant, ideologue, nut, lunatic, zealot, hippie, ass, dumbass, and bitch.

80. Personal Twitter handles tagged in these tweets have been deleted.

81. Kalev Leetaru, "Twitter Users Mostly Retweet Politicians and Celebrities: That's a Big Change," *Washington Post*, March 8, 2019, https://www.washingtonpost.com /politics/2019/03/08/twitter-users-mostly-retweet-politicians-celebrities-thats-big -change/?utm_term=.5affoboeaco5.

82. Our search originally yielded a higher number of name-calling tweets, but many were false positives that were manually discarded. For example, tweets that had "ass" in some form, such as in the word "embarrassed," were designated false positives.

83. Krupnikov and Ryan, *The Other Divide*.

84. Krupnikov and Ryan, *The Other Divide*.

CHAPTER THREE

1. Mehrsa Baradaran, *The Color of Money* (Harvard University Press, 2017); Richard Rothstein, *The Color of Law* (Liveright, 2017).

2. Jeremy Barr, "Critical Race Theory Is the Hottest Topic on Fox," *Washington Post*, June 24, 2021, https://www.washingtonpost.com/media/2021/06/24/critical-race -theory-fox-news/.

3. Oliver Darcy, "How Fox News Is Making a Network out of Race Baiting," *CNN Business*, July 23, 2021, https://www.cnn.com/2021/07/23/media/fox-news-race -baiting/index.html.

4. Berry and Sobieraj, *The Outrage Industry*, 13.

5. Young, *Irony and Outrage*, 5.

6. Berry and Sobieraj, *The Outrage Industry*. Note the contrast between the business model of trying to anger the audience with our findings in chapter 2 showing that conservatives did not report feeling more anger than liberals when asked about political discussion. The anger induced in real time by the incendiary content of a Fox News segment is surely different than the emotions one feels when talking politics with friends and family (and which might be face-to-face).

7. James T. Hamilton, *All the News That's Fit to Sell* (Princeton University Press, 2004).

8. Mettler and Lieberman, *Four Threats*, 218.

9. "'How Democracies Die' Authors Say Trump Is a Symptom of 'Deeper Problems,'" *Fresh Air* (National Public Radio, January 22, 2018), https://www.npr.org/ 2018/01/22/579670528/how-democracies-die-authors-say-trump-is-a-symptom-of -deeper-problems.

10. R. Lance Holbert et al., "The Electorates' Communication Dynamics," in *Democracy amid Crises: Polarization, Pandemic, Protests, and Persuasion*, ed. Kathleen

Hall Jamieson et al. (Oxford University Press, 2023), 85–86, https://doi.org/10.1093/oso/9780197644690.003.0004.

11. Mark Mwachiro, "Wednesday, April 10, 2024," TV Newser, April 12, 2024, https://www.adweek.com/tvnewser/wednesday-april-10-scoreboard-the-five-and-gutfeld-were-the-most-watched/.

12. Mark Mwachiro, "Week of April 8 Evening News Ratings," TV Newser, April 16, 2024, https://www.adweek.com/tvnewser/week-of-april-8-evening-news-ratings-world-news-tonight-leads-newscasts/?ver=1713360959826.

13. David E. Broockman and Joshua L. Kalla, "Selective Exposure and Partisan Echo Chambers in Television News Consumption: Evidence from Linked Viewership, Administrative, and Survey Data," January 8, 2024, https://doi.org/10.31219/osf.io/b54sx.

14. Andrew M. Guess, "(Almost) Everything in Moderation: New Evidence on Americans' Online Media Diets," *American Journal of Political Science* 65, no. 2 (February 19, 2021): 1017, https://doi.org/10.1111/ajps.12589; Sandra González-Bailón et al., "Asymmetric Ideological Segregation in Exposure to Political News on Facebook," *Science* 381, no. 6656 (2023): 392–98, https://doi.org/10.1126/science.ade7138.

15. Ladd, *Why Americans Hate the Media.*

16. Megan Brenan, "Americans' Trust in Media Dips to Second Lowest on Record," Gallup, October 7, 2021, https://news.gallup.com/poll/355526/americans-trust-media-dips-second-lowest-record.aspx.

17. Isabella Simonetti and Joe Flint, "TV Networks Embrace Their Aging Audience with a New Mantra: Age Doesn't Matter," *Wall Street Journal,* May 22, 2024, https://www.wsj.com/business/media/tv-networks-embrace-their-aging-audience-with-a-new-mantra-age-doesnt-matter-63badbd1.

18. The business side of cable news networks is explore in greater detail in Berry et al., "Race and Gender on Fox and MSNBC"; Berry et al., "Ideology, Racial Resentment, and the Mass Media" (paper presented at the Annual Conference of the American Political Science Association, Washington, DC, September 2019).

19. If there was more than one story between commercial blocks, we coded the one that consumed the most time. Segments were also defined as being at least three minutes in length. This was stipulated to exclude very short stories that were placed primarily as a bit of content to bridge two blocks of commercial time.

20. Mark K. McBeth et al., "Media Narratives Versus Evidence in Economic Policy Making: The 2008–2009 Financial Crisis," *Social Science Quarterly* 99, no. 2 (August 22, 2017): 791–806, https://doi.org/10.1111/ssqu.12456. See also Elisabeth Anker, "Villains, Victims, and Heroes: Melodrama, Media, and September 11," *Journal of Communication* 55, no. 1 (January 10, 2006): 22–37, https://doi.org/10.1111/j.1460-2466.2005.tb02656.x.

21. Iyengar et al., "The Origins and Consequences of Affective Polarization," 129.

22. Lilliana Mason, *Uncivil Agreement: How Politics Became Our Identity* (University of Chicago Press, 2018).

23. Ashley Jardina, *White Identity Politics* (Cambridge University Press, 2019).

24. Courtney Hagle, "Six Weeks of Fox's Alexandria Ocasio-Cortez Obsession: 'Totalitarian,' 'Ignorant,' 'Scary,' and Waging a 'War on Cows,'" Media Matters for America, April 12, 2019, https://www.mediamatters.org/fox-news/six-weeks-foxs-alexandria-ocasio-cortez-obsession-totalitarian-ignorant-scary-and-waging.

25. *The Ingraham Angle* (Fox News, August 1, 2019).

26. Gregg Price, "Fox News's Audience Almost Exclusively White as Network Faces Backlash over Immigration," *Newsweek*, August 10, 2018, https://www.newsweek.com/fox-news-white-audience-immigration-1067807.

27. A more complete analysis of gender can be found in Berry et al., "Race and Gender on Fox and MSNBC."

28. Margaret Sullivan, "Tucker Carlson's Attacks on Sen. Tammy Duckworth Are as Disgusting as They Are Predictable," *Washington Post*, July 8, 2020, https://www.washingtonpost.com/lifestyle/media/tucker-carlsons-attacks-on-sen-tammy-duckworth-are-as-disgusting-as-they-are-predictable/2020/07/08/5c9fd6fa-c12a-11ea-b4f6-cb39cd8940fb_story.html.

29. Michael M. Grynbaum and Tiffany Hsu, "Advertisers Are Fleeing Tucker Carlson. Fox News Viewers Have Stayed," *New York Times*, June 18, 2020, https://www.nytimes.com/2020/06/18/business/media/tucker-carlson-advertisers-ratings.html?searchResultPosition=1; Nicholas Confessore, "How Tucker Carlson Reshaped Fox News—and Became Trump's Heir," *New York Times*, April 30, 2022, https://www.nytimes.com/2022/04/30/us/tucker-carlson-fox-news.html.

30. Berry and Sobieraj, *The Outrage Industry*.

31. "Cable News Fact Sheet," Pew Research Center, September 14, 2023, https://www.pewresearch.org/journalism/fact-sheet/cable-news/.

32. Brian Stelter, "Lachlan Murdoch Finally Says It Aloud: Fox Is the 'Loyal Opposition,'" *CNN Business*, March 5, 2021, https://www.cnn.com/2021/03/04/media/lachlan-murdoch-fox-reliable-sources/index.html.

33. Brian Steinberg, "TV Networks Put Harder Sell Behind Hard News as 2020 Election Draws Closer," *Variety*, January 7, 2020, https://variety.com/2020/tv/news/tv-news-hard-sell-advertising-fox-news-msnbc-1203458945/.

34. "Cable News Fact Sheet."

35. Valentino et al., "The Changing Norms of Racial Political Rhetoric."

36. Brian F. Schaffner et al., "Understanding White Polarization in the 2016 Vote for President: The Sobering Role of Racism and Sexism," *Political Science Quarterly* 133, no. 1 (Spring 2018): 9–34, https://doi.org/10.1002/polq.12737.

37. Natalie Jomini Stroud, *Niche News* (Oxford University Press, 2011); Kevin Arceneaux et al., "Polarized Political Communication, Oppositional Media Hostility, and Selective Exposure," *Journal of Politics* 74, no. 1 (January 2012): 174–86, https://doi.org/10.1017/s002238161100123x.

38. Berry and Sobieraj, *The Outrage Industry*, 133.

39. Steven W. Webster, *American Rage: How Anger Shapes Our Politics* (Cambridge University Press, 2020), 3.

40. Kevin Arceneaux and Martin Johnson, *Changing Minds or Changing Channels? Partisan News in an Age of Choice* (University of Chicago Press, 2013).

41. Matthew Levendusky, *How Partisan Media Polarize America* (University of Chicago Press, 2013).

42. See Brian J. Gaines and James H. Kuklinski, "Experimental Estimation of Heterogeneous Treatment Effects Related to Self-Selection," *American Journal of Political Science* 55, no. 3 (July 2011): 724–36, https://doi.org/10.1111/j.1540-5907.2011.00518.x.

43. Josh Pasek and Kathleen Hall Jamieson, "Law and Order vs. Law and Order with Racial Justice: Debating How to Understand the Summer's Protests," in *Democracy amid Crises: Polarization, Pandemic, Protests, and Persuasion*, ed. Kathleen Hall

Jamieson et al. (Oxford University Press, 2023), 220, https://doi.org/10.1093/oso /9780197644690.003.0009.

44. Arceneaux and Johnson, *Changing Minds or Changing Channels?*; Chloe Wittenberg et al., "Media Measurement Matters: Estimating the Persuasive Effects of Partisan Media with Survey and Behavioral Data," *Journal of Politics* 85, no. 4 (2023): 1275–90, https://www.journals.uchicago.edu/doi/10.1086/724960.

45. David E. Broockman and Joshua L. Kalla, "Consuming Cross-Cutting Media Causes Learning and Moderates Attitudes: A Field Experiment with Fox News Viewers," working paper, April 2023, https://doi.org/10.31219/osf.io/jrw26.

46. Erik Wemple, "Tucker Carlson Said Immigration Makes America 'Dirtier,'" *Washington Post*, December 15, 2018, https://www.washingtonpost.com/opinions /2018/12/15/tucker-carlson-said-immigration-makes-america-dirtier-so-an-advertiser -took-action/; Confessore, "How Tucker Carlson Reshaped Fox News."

47. Berry and Sobieraj, *The Outrage Industry*.

48. Fred Dews, "Fox News' Incomparable Role on the Political Right," Brookings Institution, June 12, 2014, https://www.brookings.edu/articles/fox-news-incomparable -role-on-the-political-right/.

49. Sydnor, *Disrespectful Democracy*, 4.

50. Paul Lazarsfeld et al., *The People's Choice: How the Voter Makes Up His Mind in a Presidential Campaign* (Duell, Sloan & Pearce, 1944).

51. Mediaite, https://www.mediaite.com/; Media Matters for America, https:// www.mediamatters.org/.

52. Amy Mitchell et al., "How Americans Navigated the News in 2020: A Tumultuous Year in Review," Pew Research Center, February 22, 2021, https://www .pewresearch.org/journalism/2021/02/22/how-americans-navigated-the-news-in -2020-a-tumultuous-year-in-review/.

53. "Distribution of X (Formerly Twitter) Users Worldwide as of April 2024, by Age Group," Statista, April 2024, https://www.statista.com/statistics/283119/age -distribution-of-global-twitter-users.

CHAPTER FOUR

1. Mychael Schnell and Emily Brooks, "5 Takeaways: Biden, McCarthy Strike Deal to Raise Debt Limit," *Hill*, May 28, 2023, https://thehill.com/homenews/house/ 4024521-5-takeaways-biden-mccarthy-strike-deal-to-raise-debt-limit/.

2. Jennifer Wolak, *Compromise in an Age of Party Polarization* (Oxford University Press, 2020).

3. John R. Hibbing and Elizabeth Theiss-Morse, "Process Preferences and American Politics: What the People Want Government to Be," *American Political Science Review* 95, no. 1 (March 2001): 145–53, https://doi.org/10.1177/1065912918819860.

4. Cathy Jo Martin, "Negotiating Political Agreements," in *Political Negotiation: A Handbook*, ed. Jane Mansbridge and Cathie Jo Martin (Brookings Institution, 2016), 7–33.

5. Wolak, *Compromise in an Age of Party Polarization*.

6. Alan I. Abramowitz et al., "Incumbency, Redistricting, and the Decline of Competition in US House Elections," *Journal of Politics* 68, no. 1 (2006): 75–88, https://doi.org/10.1111/j.1468-2508.2006.00371.x.

7. Jonathan Woon, "Primaries and Candidate Polarization: Behavioral Theory and Experimental Evidence," *American Political Science Review* 112, no. 4 (2018): 826–43.

8. Roper Center for Public Opinion Research, https://ropercenter.cornell.edu/.

9. See also Druckman et al., *Partisan Hostility and American Democracy*.

10. Editorial, *Los Angeles Times*, November 15, 2007.

11. Nicholas T. Davis, "Identity Sorting and Political Compromise," *American Politics Research*, September 17, 2018, 391–414, http://journals.sagepub.com/doi/10.1177/1532673X18799273.

12. Mann and Ornstein, *It's Even Worse Than It Looks*, 24.

13. E. J. Dionne et al., *One Nation After Trump: A Guide for the Perplexed, the Disillusioned, the Desperate, and the Not-Yet-Deported* (St. Martin's Press, 2017).

14. Laurel Harbridge et al., "Public Preferences for Bipartisanship in the Policymaking Process," *Legislative Studies Quarterly* 39, no. 3 (2014): 327–55.

15. For our analysis of partisan differences in attitudes toward compromise, see James M. Glaser and Jeffrey M. Berry, "Compromising Positions: Why Republican Partisans Are More Rigid Than Democrats," *Political Science Quarterly* 133, no. 1 (March 2018): 99–125, https://doi.org/10.1002/polq.12735.

16. There are only seventeen data points in the figure, but in some months, more than one YouGov survey uses the question. In these cases, we present a weighted average of the liberal-conservative difference from the multiple surveys in the graph.

17. Daniel Kahneman and Amos Tversky, "Choices, Values, and Frames," *American Psychologist* 39, no. 4 (1984): 341–50, https://doi.org/10.1037/0003-066X.39.4.341.

18. Amos Tversky and Daniel Kahneman, "Loss Aversion in Riskless Choice: A Reference-Dependent Model," *Quarterly Journal of Economics* 106, no. 4 (November 1991): 1056.

19. Jonathan Mercer, "Prospect Theory and Political Science," *Annual Review of Political Science* 8 (June 2005): 1–21, 3, https://doi.org/10.1146/annurev.polisci.8.082103.104911.

20. "Royal Swedish Academy of Sciences," press release, October 9, 2002, https://www.nobelprize.org/prizes/economic-sciences/2002/press-release/.

21. This number represents citations of their five most frequently cited collaborative articles indexed through June 2023.

22. John R. Hibbing et al., "Differences in Negativity Bias Underlie Variations in Political Ideology," *Behavioral and Brain Sciences* 37 (June 27, 2014): 297–307, 299, https://doi.org/doi:10.1017/S0140525X13001192.

23. Luciana Carraro et al., "The Automatic Conservative: Ideology-Based Attentional Asymmetries in the Processing of Valenced Information," *PLOS One* 6, no. 11 (2011): e26456, https://doi.org/10.1371/journal.pone.0026456.

24. Jacob M. Vigil, "Political Leanings Vary with Facial Expression Processing and Psychosocial Functioning," *Group Processes and Intergroup Relations* 13 (September 2010): 547–58, https://doi.org/10.1017/pls.2019.18.

25. Natalie J. Shook and Russell H. Fazio, "Political Ideology, Exploration of Novel Stimuli, and Attitude Formation," *Journal of Experimental Social Psychology* 45 (July 2009): 995–98, https://doi.org/10.1016/j.jesp.2009.04.003.

26. Dan McLaughlin, "The Minnesota Democrats' Culture War," *National Review*, February 2, 2023.

27. Robert A. Dahl, "Myth of the Presidential Mandate," *Political Science Quarterly* 105, no. 3 (1990): 355–72.

28. Julian Borger, "'I Have Political Capital: I Intend to Spend It,'" *Guardian*, November 4, 2004, https://www.theguardian.com/world/2004/nov/05/uselections2004.usa5.

29. "State Minimum Wages," National Conference of State Legislatures, n.d., http://www.ncsl.org/research/labor-and-employment/state-minimum-wage-chart.aspx, accessed March 28, 2017.

30. The very small numbers of conservative Democrats and liberal Republicans are not presented here.

31. A previous version of this analysis was published as James M. Glaser et al., "Education and the Curious Case of Conservative Compromise," *Political Research Quarterly* 74, no. 1 (2021): 59–75.

32. It is important to note that the impact of education on political engagement can mask the underlying importance of preadult characteristics and a related selection bias in terms of the choice to attend college. The benefit to analysts is that as a proxy, a higher level of education captures a great deal that is important to political behavior, including a greater awareness of the content of different political ideologies, which is important to the phenomenon under investigation here. See also Cindy D. Kam and Carl L. Palmer, "Reconsidering the Effects of Education on Political Participation," *Journal of Politics* 70, no. 3 (July 2008): 612–31.

33. Michael Delli Carpini and Scott Keeter, *What Americans Know About Politics and Why It Matters* (Yale University Press, 1996), 6.

34. Philip Converse, "Change in the American Electorate," in *The Human Meaning of Social Change*, ed. Angus Campbell (Russell Sage Foundation, 1972), 324.

35. Mikael Persson, "Review Article: Education and Political Participation," *British Journal of Political Science* 45, no. 3 (July 2015): 689–703.

36. Thomas B. Ksiazek et al., "News-Seekers and Avoiders: Exploring Patterns of Total News Consumption Across Media and the Relationship to Civic Participation," *Journal of Broadcasting & Electronic Media* 54, no. 4 (November 30, 2010): 551–68, https://doi.org/10.1080/08838151.2010.519808.

37. Hibbing and Theiss-Morse, "Process Preferences and American Politics."

38. John Zaller, *The Nature and Origins of Mass Opinion* (Cambridge University Press, 1992); Converse, "The Nature of Belief Systems in Mass Publics"; Christopher M. Federico, "Race, Education, and Individualism Revisited," *Journal of Politics* 68, no. 3 (August 2006): 600–610, https://doi.org/10.1111/j.1468-2508.2006.00448.x; Christopher M. Federico et al., "Expertise and the Ideological Consequences of the Authoritarian Predisposition," *Public Opinion Quarterly* 75, no. 4 (2011): 686–708, https://doi.org/10.1093/poq/nfr026.

39. Education also may contribute to acceptance of particular compromises because better-educated people tend to have more resources and options than less-educated people and can simply afford to compromise more. Here, however, we are looking at a more general attitude toward compromise.

40. We use this conservative dummy variable to reflect our hypothesis that it is conservatives who are distinctive here. We are less interested in the differences we see between liberals and moderates.

41. J. B. Rosener, "Ways Women Lead," *Harvard Business Review* 68, no. 6 (1990): 119–25; Alice H. Eagly et al., "Transformational, Transactional, and Laissez-Faire Leadership Styles: A Meta-Analysis Comparing Women and Men," *Psychological Bulletin* 129, no. 4 (2003): 569–91, https://doi.org/10.1037/0033-2909.129.4.569.

42. Steven Rosenstone and John Mark Hansen, *Mobilization, Participation, and Democracy in America* (Macmillan, 1993).

43. Alfred Demaris and Renxin Yang, "Race, Alienation, and Interpersonal Mistrust," *Sociological Spectrum* 14, no. 4 (1994): 327–49, https://doi.org/10.1080 /02732173.1994.9982075; Alberto Alesina and Eliana La Ferrara, "Who Trusts Others?," *Journal of Public Economics* 85, no. 2 (2002): 207–34, https://doi.org/10.1016/S0047 -2727(01)00084-6.

44. Donald Musa et al., "Trust in the Health Care System and the Use of Preventive Health Services by Older Black and White Adults," *American Journal of Public Health* 99, no. 7 (2009): 1293–99, https://doi.org/10.2105/AJPH.2007.123927; Maurice Mangum, "Explaining Political Trust Among African Americans," *Journal of Public Management and Social Policy* 23, no. 2 (2016): 84–100.

45. Olivia Beavers, "House Freedom Caucus Faces an Internal Purge Push," *Politico*, June 23, 2023, https://www.politico.com/news/2023/06/23/house-freedom-caucus -members-00103296.

46. Annie Karni et al., "As Spending Fights Loom, Freedom Caucus Is at a Crossroads," *New York Times*, July 25, 2023.

47. See table 4.5 for the exact wordings of the questions on the 2020 CES, 2020 ANES, and 2021 Pew surveys.

48. The question on taxes versus spending on the CES 2020 survey is a 100-point scale. There, the difference in the less-educated mean and the most-educated mean is in the expected direction, though a relatively modest five points.

49. The number of rules published annually very consistently exceeds three thousand. In only one year (2019) was that not the case. Clyde Wayne Crews, "Tens of Thousands of Pages and Rules in the Federal Register," Ten Thousand Commandments 2021 (Competitive Enterprise Institute, June 30, 2021), https://cei.org/publication/ tens-of-thousands-of-pages-and-rules-in-the-federal-register-2/.

50. "What Is the National Debt?," US Treasury Department, n.d., https://fiscaldata .treasury.gov/americas-finance-guide/national-debt/, accessed July 22, 2023.

51. Berry and Sobieraj, *The Outrage Industry*.

## CHAPTER FIVE

1. Karl R. Popper, *The Open Society and Its Enemies*, new vol. ed. (Princeton University Press, 2013); John L. Sullivan, James Piereson, and George E. Marcus, *Political Tolerance and American Democracy* (University of Chicago Press, 1982); Paul M. Sniderman et al., "Principled Tolerance and the American Mass Public," *British Journal of Political Science* 19, no. 1 (January 1989): 25–45.

2. Gunnar Myrdal, *An American Dilemma* (McGraw-Hill, 1944); Philip A. Klinkner and Rogers M. Smith, *The Unsteady March: The Rise and Decline of Racial Equality in America* (University of Chicago Press, 1999).

3. James M. Glaser et al., "Ideology and Support for Federalism in Theory—and in Practice," *Publius* 53, no. 4 (2023): 511–35, https://doi.org/10.1093/publius/pjad003.

4. Kinder and Kalmoe, *Neither Liberal nor Conservative*.

5. Ross Douthat, "The Two Crises of Conservatism," *New York Times*, April 24, 2021, https://www.nytimes.com/2021/04/24/opinion/sunday/republicans-conservatism .html.

6. Martha Derthick, "American Federalism: Madison's Middle Ground in the 1980s," *Public Administration Review* 47, no. 1 (1987): 66–74, 72.

7. Richard P. Nathan, "There Will Always Be a New Federalism," *Journal of Public Administration Research and Theory* 16, no. 4 (2006): 499–510, 508.

8. Ernest A. Young, "Welcome to the Dark Side: Liberals Rediscover Federalism in the Wake of the War on Terror," *Brooklyn Law Review* 69, no. 4 (2004): 1277–1311; Kathleen Sullivan, "From States' Rights Blues to Blue States' Rights: Federalism After the Rehnquist Court," *Fordham Law Review* 75 (2006): 799–813.

9. Grossmann and Hopkins, *Asymmetric Politics*.

10. Grossmann and Hopkins, *Asymmetric Politics*, 13.

11. Here and throughout we include results for moderates as a comparison point. In our multivariate analysis, moderates become the base category. But we generally do not discuss these results, given the goals of this project.

12. There are 331 liberals and 336 conservatives in the CES survey.

13. This is not an unusual circumstance. Ann Bowman and George Krause, "Power Shift: Measuring Policy Centralization in U.S. Intergovernmental Relations, 1947–1998," *American Politics Research* 31, no. 3 (2003): 301–25, show that the amount of policy decentralization does not vary significantly across the time period. Politicians in both parties, they conclude, are instrumental in their use of federalism, pursuing their preferred policies with the power that they have, whether it be national or state and local. See also Tim Conlan and John Dinan, "Federalism, the Bush Administration, and the Transformation of American Conservatism," *Publius* 27, no. 3 (2007): 279–303.

14. Hannah Hartig, "About Six-in-Ten Americans Say Abortion Should Be Legal in All or Most Cases," Pew Research Center, June 13, 2021, https://www.pewresearch.org/fact-tank/2022/06/13/about-six-in-ten-americans-say-abortion-should-be-legal-in-all-or-most-cases-2/.

15. The AP/NORC poll question is "Which comes closest to your opinion on abortion?" and has four response categories (legal in all or most cases; illegal in all or most cases). We consider the first two responses to be "pro-choice," the latter "pro-life."

16. The wording of the GSS school prayer question is completely consistent over this period of time.

17. While "disagreeing" with "disallowing" creates a double negative in the question, which is not ideal in survey research, there is little reason to believe that this construction should affect one set of respondents more than another.

18. Both quotes in Coral Davenport, "Trump Defends Plan to Kill California's Auto-Emissions Authority," *New York Times*, September 18, 2019.

19. We should note that in general, even when Democrats have controlled the federal government, most citizens, including conservatives, recognize that federal supremacy on environmental issues does make some sense. After all, pollution, climate change, and environmental degradation do not recognize state boundaries. See Nicholas Jacobs, "Federalism, Polarization, and Policy Responsibility During COVID-19: Experimental and Observational Evidence from the United States," *Publius* 51, no. 4 (2021): 693–719; Saundra K. Schneider et al., "Public Opinion Toward Intergovernmental Policy Responsibilities," *Publius* 41, no. 1 (2011): 1–30, https://doi.org/10.1093/publius/pjq036; David Konisky, "Public Preferences for Environmental Policy Responsibility," *Publius* 41, no. 1 (2011): 76–100.

20. John Dinan and Jac C. Heckelman, "Stability and Contingency in Federalism Preferences," *Public Administration Review* 80, no. 4 (2020): 234–43.

21. Kathleen Hall Jamieson and Doron Taussig, "Disruption, Demonization, Deliverance, and Norm Destruction: The Rhetorical Signature of Donald J. Trump," *Political Science Quarterly* 132, no. 4 (Winter 2017): 619–50.

22. All quotes from Quint Forgey and Josh Gerstein, "Trump: It's My Decision, Not Governors', to Reopen Country," *Politico*, April 13, 2020, https://www.politico.com/news/2020/04/13/trump-governors-decision-reopen-183405.

23. Hunter Rendelman and Jon C. Rogowski, "Americans' Attitudes Toward Federalism," *Political Behavior* 46, no. 1 (2024): 126, https://doi.org/10.1007/s11109-022-09820-3.

24. Jennifer Wolak, "Core Values and Partisan Thinking About Devolution," *Publius* 46, no. 4 (2016): 463–85, https://doi.org/10.1093/publius/pjw021. See also Dinan and Heckelman, "Stability and Contingency in Federalism Preferences." They find that the ideological difference we observe exists no matter which party controls government.

25. David Konisky and Paul Nolette, "The State of American Federalism 2021–2022: Federal Courts, State Legislatures, and the Conservative Turn in the Law," *Publius* 52, no. 3 (2022): 353–81.

26. John F. Kennedy School of Government Social Capital Community Survey.

27. Marc J. Hetherington and John D. Nugent, "Explaining Public Support for Devolution: The Role of Political Trust," in *What Is It About Government That Americans Dislike?*, ed. John R. Hibbing and Elizabeth Theiss-Morse (Cambridge University Press, 2001), 138.

28. Some of the variables have been recoded so that the direction of the coefficients can be interpreted similarly.

29. Nicholas Jacobs, "An Experimental Test of How Americans Think About Federalism," *Publius* 47, no. 4 (2017): 572–98.

30. John J. Beggs et al., "Revisiting the Rural-Urban Contrast: Personal Networks in Nonmetropolitan and Metropolitan Settings," *Rural Sociology* 61, no. 2 (1996): 306–25.

31. New State Ice Co. v. Liebmann, 285 U.S. 262 (1932).

32. See Jacob M. Grumbach, *Laboratories Against Democracy: How National Parties Transformed State Politics* (Princeton University Press, 2022).

33. Greg M. Shaw and Stephanie L. Reinhart, "Trends: Devolution and Confidence in Government," *Public Opinion Quarterly* 65, no. 3 (2001): 369–88, 370, https://doi.org/10.1086/322849.

34. Grossmann and Hopkins, *Asymmetric Politics*.

35. "Thurmond Says States' Rights Is Only Bar to Establishment of 'Kremlin' in Washington," *New York Times*, October 27, 1948.

36. To enhance the intuition of the results, we have recoded the states' rights variable so that higher values equate to support for states' rights. The resentment scale is coded so that higher values represent higher levels of resentment.

37. The negative (and significant) coefficient associated with Black people (versus non-Black people) is a surprise in this equation, suggesting that perhaps the term "states' rights" no longer is associated with Jim Crow politics for this population.

38. Dana R. Carney et al., "The Secret Lives of Liberals and Conservatives: Personality Profiles, Interaction Styles, and the Things They Leave Behind," *Political Psychology* 29, no. 6 (October 23, 2008): 807–40, https://doi.org/10.1111/j.1467-9221.2008.00668.x.

39. Cindy D. Kam and Robert A. Mikos, "Do Citizens Care About Federalism? An Experimental Test," *Journal of Empirical Legal Studies* 4, no. 3 (2007): 589–624.

40. Ralph Waldo Emerson, *Self-Reliance* (Peter Pauper Press, 1967).

CHAPTER SIX

1. Arthur C. Brooks, *Who Really Cares* (Basic Books, 2006), 17.

2. Brooks, *Who Really Cares*, 11.

3. Brooks, *Who Really Cares*, 178.

4. Brooks, *Who Really Cares*, 182.

5. Jeffrey M. Berry with David F. Arons, *A Voice for Nonprofits* (Brookings Institution Press, 2003).

6. Benjamin Soskis, "Republicans Used to Celebrate Voluntarism and Service: What Happened?," *Washington Post*, August 3, 2018, https://www.washingtonpost.com /outlook/republicans-used-to-celebrate-volunteerism-and-service-what-happened /2018/08/03/7544bfe4-95bd-11e8-a679-b09212fb69c2_story.html.

7. Soskis, "Republicans Used to Celebrate Voluntarism and Service."

8. Karen Page Winterich et al., "Donation Behavior Toward In-Groups and Out-Groups: The Role of Gender and Moral Identity," *Journal of Consumer Research* 36, no. 2 (August 2009): 199–214, https://doi.org/10.1086/596720.

9. "The Giving Environment: Understanding Pre-Pandemic Trends in Charitable Giving" (Indiana University Lilly Family School of Philanthropy, 2021), https:// scholarworks.iupui.edu/bitstream/handle/1805/26290/giving-environment210727 .pdf; Alex Daniels, "As Charitable Giving Rates Sag, Foundations Back Ambitious New Effort to Ignite Generosity by All Americans," *Chronicle of Philanthropy*, October 12, 2021, https://www.philanthropy.com/article/as-charitable-giving-rates-sag -foundations-back-ambitious-new-effort-to-ignite-generosity-by-all-americans.

10. Dawn Papandrea, "56% of Americans Donated to Charity in 2021, at Average of $574," LendingTree, November 29, 2021, https://www.lendingtree.com/debt -consolidation/charitable-donations-survey-study.

11. "The Next Generation of American Giving" (Blackbaud Institute, 2018), https:// cdn.fedweb.org/fed-115/2/2018-Next-Generation-of-Giving.pdf.

12. Robert D. Putnam and David E. Campbell, *American Grace: How Religion Divides and Unites Us* (Simon & Schuster, 2010), 100–133.

13. Scott Neuman, "Fewer Than Half of U.S. Adults Belong to a Religious Congregation, New Poll Shows," National Public Radio, March 30, 2021, https://www .npr.org/2021/03/30/982671783/fewer-than-half-of-u-s-adults-belong-to-a-religious -congregation-new-poll-shows.

14. Jonathan Meer and Benjamin A. Priday, *Tax Prices and Charitable Giving: Projected Changes in Donations Under the 2017 TCJA*, NBER Working Paper Series, no. 26452 (National Bureau of Economic Research, 2019).

15. Meer and Priday, *Tax Prices and Charitable Giving*, 1.

16. To cite just some of the major scholarly studies, see Brandon Vaidyanathan et al., "Religion and Charitable Financial Giving to Religious and Secular Causes: Does Political Ideology Matter?," *Journal for the Scientific Study of Religion* 50, no. 3 (September 2011): 450–69, https://doi.org/10.1111/j.1468-5906.2011.01584 .x; Karen Page Winterich et al., "How Political Identity and Charity Positioning

Increase Donations," *International Journal of Research in Marketing* 29, no. 4 (2012): 346–54; Kevin F. Forbes and Ernest M. Zampelli, "The Impacts of Religion, Political Ideology, and Social Capital on Religious and Secular Giving: Evidence from the 2006 Social Capital Community Survey," *Applied Economics* 45, no. 17 (June 1, 2013): 2481–90, https://doi.org/10.1080/00036846.2012.667555; Laurie E. Paarlberg et al., "The Politics of Donations: Are Red Counties More Donative Than Blue Counties?," *Nonprofit and Voluntary Sector Quarterly* 48, no. 2 (2019): 283–308, https://doi.org/10.1177/0899764018804088. A meta-analysis by Yang and Liu came to the same conclusion as did we from our less formal review of the literature: more studies conclude that conservatives are more likely to give to charity. Yet, there are some individual studies that did not reach that conclusion. See Yongzheng Yang and Peixu Liu, "Are Conservatives More Charitable Than Liberals in the U.S.? A Meta-Analysis of Political Ideology and Charitable Giving," *Social Science Research* 99 (2021), https://doi.org/10.1016/j.ssresearch.2021.102598.

17. Putnam and Campbell, *American Grace*, 662–63.

18. All four categories designate nonprofits that can qualify for tax deductibility for donations, which is what we usually mean when we use the specific term "nonprofit." There are twenty-seven different types of nonprofit organizations defined under section 501(c) of the Internal Revenue Code, but only 501(c)(3) nonprofits, which are those organized for charitable purposes, qualify for tax deductibility for donations.

19. "Giving USA: Total U.S. Charitable Giving Remained Strong in 2021, Reaching $484.85 Billion," Lilly Family School of Philanthropy, June 21, 2022, https://philanthropy.iupui.edu/news-events/news-item/giving-usa:--total-u.s.-charitable-giving-remained-strong-in-2021,-reaching-$484.85-billion.html?id=392.

20. "In U.S., Decline of Christianity Continues at Rapid Pace," Pew Research Center, October 27, 2019, https://www.pewresearch.org/religion/2019/10/17/in-u-s-decline-of-christianity-continues-at-rapid-pace/; David E. Campbell et al., *Secular Surge: A New Fault Line in American Politics* (Cambridge University Press, 2021).

21. Putnam and Campbell, *American Grace*, 91–133; Aaron Blake, "The Rapid Decline of White Evangelical America," *Washington Post*, July 8, 2021, https://www.washingtonpost.com/politics/2021/07/08/rapid-decline-white-evangelical-america/.

22. Putnam and Campbell, *American Grace*, 432.

23. Vaidyanathan et al., "Religion and Charitable Financial Giving to Religious and Secular Causes," 467.

24. Although no one sector receives more than 50 percent of either liberals or conservatives, 52 percent of our respondents donate to at least one sector. These results roughly align to the 56 percent figure in the Papandrea study cited in note 10.

25. Russell N. James III and Deanna L. Sharpe, "The Nature and Causes of the U-Shaped Charitable Giving Profile," *Nonprofit and Voluntary Sector Quarterly* 36, no. 2 (June 2007): 218–38, https://doi.org/10.1177/0899764006295993.

26. The correlation between family income and religious donations is .10, and the correlation between family income and secular donations is .01. Neither relationship is statistically significant.

27. Brooks, *Who Really Cares*, 49.

28. To keep this line of inquiry straightforward and unconfusing, respondents were asked how much they gave for all secular charities combined (health related, social service, and other).

29. Keely S. Jones, "Giving and Volunteering as Distinct Forms of Civic Engagement," *Nonprofit and Voluntary Sector Quarterly* 35, no. 2 (June 2006): 249–66, https://doi.org/10.1177/0899764006287464.

30. Tocqueville and Kramnick, *Democracy in America: An Annotated Text*, 155; Putnam, *Bowling Alone*; Dahl, *Dilemmas of Pluralist Democracy*; Bellah et al., *Habits of the Heart*; Converse, "The Nature of Belief Systems in Mass Publics"; Barber, *Strong Democracy*; Dahl, *Polyarchy*; Dalton, *The Good Citizen*.

31. Jane Allyn Piliavin and Erica Siegl, "Health Benefits of Volunteering in the Wisconsin Longitudinal Study," *Journal of Health and Social Behavior* 48, no. 4 (December 2007): 450–64, https://doi.org/10.1177/002214650704800408.

32. United States Census Bureau, "National Volunteer Week," December 2, 2018, https://www.thenonprofittimes.com/npt_articles/volunteer-hours-now-worth-167-billion-annually/.

33. Bureau of Labor Statistics, "Volunteering in the United States—2015," February 25, 2016, https://www.bls.gov/news.release/pdf/volun.pdf.

34. Brooks, *Who Really Cares*, 24.

35. Penny Edgell Becker and Pawan Dhingra, "Religious Involvement in Volunteering: Implications for Civil Society," *Sociology of Religion* 62, no. 3 (Autumn 2001): 315–35, https://doi.org/10.2307/3712353; Steven T. Yen and Ernest M. Zampelli, "What Drives Charitable Donations of Time and Money? The Roles of Political Ideology, Religiosity, and Involvement," *Journal of Behavioral and Experimental Economics* 50 (June 2014): 58–67, https://doi.org/10.1016/j.socec.2014.01.002.

36. Kay Lehman Schlozman et al., "Gender and the Pathways to Participation: The Role of Resources," *Journal of Politics* 56, no. 4 (November 1994): 963–90, https://doi.org/10.2307/2132069.

37. Schlozman et al., "Gender and the Pathways to Participation," 971.

38. In these tests the responses of both liberals and conservatives were compared to those of moderates.

39. Hans Noel, *Political Ideologies and Political Parties in America* (Cambridge University Press, 2014).

40. Younghwa Lee et al., "How Liberals and Conservatives Respond to Equality-Based and Proportionality-Based Rewards in Charity Advertising," *Journal of Public Policy & Marketing* 37, no. 1 (April 1, 2018): 109, https://doi.org/10.1509/jppm.16.180.

41. Lisa Farwell and Bernard Weiner, "Bleeding Hearts and the Heartless," *Personality and Social Psychology Bulletin* 26, no. 7 (September 2000): 845, https://doi.org/10.1177/0146167200269009.

42. Drew Lindsay, "Major Funders Bet Big on Rural America and 'Everyday Democracy,'" *Chronicle of Philanthropy*, June 17, 2024, https://www.philanthropy.com/commons/major-funders-bet-big-on-rural-america-and-everyday-democracy.

43. Campbell et al., *Secular Surge*, 69–82.

44. Putnam, *Bowling Alone*, 22–24.

45. "Number of Nonprofit Organizations in the United States in 2021, by Subsector," Statista, n.d., https://www.statista.com/statistics/1373603/number-nonprofit-organizations-irs-subsection-us/.

CHAPTER SEVEN

1. It is common for each generation to believe that things are getting worse. Sigal Samuel, "Why Every Generation Thinks People Were Nicer in the Past," *Vox*, June 19, 2023, https://www.vox.com/future-perfect/23762261/moral-decline-philosophy-ethics -religion-spirituality.

2. Jill Lepore, *These Truths* (Norton, 2018), 786.

3. Jack Citrin, "Comment: The Political Relevance of Trust in Government," *American Political Science Review* 68, no. 3 (September 1974): 978.

4. Lee Drutman, "How Much Longer Can This Era of Political Gridlock Last," FiveThirtyEight, March 4, 2021, https://fivethirtyeight.com/features/how-much -longer-can-this-era-of-political-gridlock-last/; Drutman, *Breaking the Two-Party Doom Loop*.

5. Amy Gutmann and Dennis Thompson, *The Spirit of Compromise: Why Governing Demands It and Campaigning Undermines It* (Princeton University Press, 2014), 1.

6. Sahil Kapur and Scott Wong, "Congress Is Passing a Wave of Bipartisan Bills as Biden's Big Plans Stall," NBC News, February 11, 2022, https://www.nbcnews.com /politics/congress-passing-wave-bipartisan-bills-bidens-big-plans-stall-rcna15798; Jim Saksa, "What If Congress Isn't Hopelessly Locked in Partisan Gridlock? What If It's Getting a Lot Done?," Roll Call, March 3, 2022, https://www.rollcall.com/2022 /03/03/congress-gridlock-getting-stuff-done/; Li Zhou, "Why There's Been a Surge of Bipartisan Activity in Congress," *Vox*, February 15, 2022, https://www.vox.com/2022 /2/15/22927345/congress-bipartisan-bills-forced-arbitration-postal-reform.

7. Mann and Ornstein, *It's Even Worse Than It Looks*.

8. Joseph Bafumi and Michael C. Herron, "Leapfrog Representation and Extremism: A Study of American Voters and Their Members of Congress," *American Political Science Review* 104, no. 3 (August 2010): 519–42, https://doi.org/10.1017/ s0003055410000316; David E. Broockman and Christopher Skovron, "Bias in Perceptions of Public Opinion Among Political Elites," *American Political Science Review* 112, no. 3 (August 2018): 542–63, https://doi.org/10.1017/S0003055418000011.

9. Wolak, *Compromise in an Age of Party Polarization*.

10. Sarah E. Anderson et al., *Rejecting Compromise: Legislators' Fear of Primary Voters* (Cambridge University Press, 2020).

11. Curry and Lee show convincingly that despite the increasing cohesion of today's two parties, it is bipartisanship that continues to be the key to passing legislation. James M. Curry and Francis E. Lee, *The Limits of Party: Congress and Lawmaking in a Polarized Era* (University of Chicago Press, 2020).

12. Jennifer McCoy and Benjamin Press, "What Happens When Democracies Become Perniciously Polarized," Carnegie Endowment for International Peace, January 18, 2022, https://carnegieendowment.org/2022/01/18/what-happens-when -democracies-become-perniciously-polarized-pub-86190.

13. Peter T. Coleman and Pearce Godwin, "Americans Are Tired of Political Division," *Time*, March 30, 2023, https://time.com/6266873/american-political -division-courage-challenge/.

14. Sydnor, *Disrespectful Democracy*, 17.

15. "Overwhelming Number of Americans Frustrated with Incivility in Politics," Institute of Politics and Public Service, Georgetown University, April 24, 2019, https://politics.georgetown.edu/2019/04/24/new-survey-overwhelming-number

-of-americans-frustrated-by-incivility-in-politics-but-conflicted-on-desire-for
-compromise-and-common-ground/.

16. For an excellent short summary of polarization trend lines, see Iyengar et al.,
"The Origins and Consequences of Affective Polarization"; Bill McInturff, "Polarization
and a Deep Dive on Issues by Party" (Public Opinion Strategies, n.d.), https://pos.org/
wp-content/uploads/2023/06/Deep-Dive-on-Issues-Short-Deck-dig.pdf, accessed
May 19, 2025.

17. Trudy Ring, "11 Times Marjorie Taylor Greene Was the Worst," *Advocate*, August
12, 2022, https://www.advocate.com/politics/2022/8/12/11-times-marjorie-taylor
-green-was-worst.

18. Mettler and Lieberman, *Four Threats*.

19. Dan Froomkin, "Fox News Is Stoking Anti-Immigration Hysteria Again. Are We
Ready to Defeat It This Time?," *Salon*, February 26, 2021, https://www.salon.com/
2021/02/26/fox-news-is-stoking-anti-immigration-hysteria-again-are-we-ready-to
-defeat-it-this-time/.

20. See the discussion of Perspective API in chapter 2.

21. Krupnikov and Ryan, *The Other Divide*; Druckman et al., *Partisan Hostility and
American Democracy*.

22. David Byler, "5 Myths About Politics, Busted by Data," *Washington Post*, July 17,
2023, https://www.washingtonpost.com/opinions/2023/07/17/political-myths-pew
-research-center/.

23. Carlson and Settle, *What Goes Without Saying*.

24. Levendusky, *Our Common Bonds*, 19.

25. Daniel J. Hopkins, *The Increasingly United States: How and Why American
Political Behavior Nationalized* (University of Chicago Press, 2018), https://www.press
.uchicago.edu/ucp/books/book/chicago/I/bo27596045.html.

26. Jamelle Bouie, "A Breathtaking Contempt for the People of Wisconsin," *New York
Times*, September 8, 2023, https://www.nytimes.com/2023/09/08/opinion/wisconsin
-judge-impeachment-democracy.html; Grumbach, *Laboratories Against Democracy*.

27. Robert A. Dahl and Edward R. Tufte, *Size and Democracy* (Stanford University
Press, 1974), 135.

28. Sides, Tausanovitch, and Vavreck, *The Bitter End*, 175; Andrew M. Engelhardt,
"Observational Equivalence in Explaining Attitude Change: Have White Racial
Attitudes Genuinely Changed?," *American Journal of Political Science* 67, no. 2 (2023):
411–25, https://doi.org/10.1111/ajps.12665.

29. Among the studies concluding that Fox's audience is of significant size and/
or is persuadable are Levendusky, *How Partisan Media Polarize America*; Berry and
Sobieraj, *The Outrage Industry*; Justin de Benedictis-Kessner et al., "Persuading the
Enemy: Estimating the Persuasive Effects of Partisan Media with the Preference-
Incorporating Choice and Assignment Design," *American Political Science Review* 113,
no. 4 (2019): 902–16; Broockman and Kalla, "Consuming Cross-Cutting Media Causes
Learning and Moderates Attitudes." Studies that take a skeptical view of audience
size or persuadability include Arceneaux and Johnson, *Changing Minds or Changing
Channels?*; Eunji Kim and Taylor Carlson, "An Era of Not-So-Minimal Effects? The
Case of Fox News" (2023 MIT American Politics Conference, Cambridge, MA, 2023);
Daniel J. Hopkins et al., "Increased Fox News Viewership Is Not Associated with
Heightened Anti-Black Prejudice," *SSRN*, April 17, 2023, https://papers.ssrn.com/sol3
/papers.cfm?abstract_id=4420947.

30. Nicholas Confessore, "What to Know About Tucker Carlson's Rise," *New York Times*, April 30, 2022, https://www.nytimes.com/2022/04/30/business/media/tucker-carlson-fox-news-takeaways.html.

31. Maggie Haberman, *Confidence Man* (Penguin Random House, 2022), 327.

32. Nelson Polsby, *Political Innovation in America* (Yale University Press, 1984), 5.

33. Edward C. Banfield, *The Unheavenly City* (Little, Brown, 1970).

34. Jane Jacobs, *The Death and Life of Great American Cities* (Random House, 1961).

35. Putnam, *Bowling Alone*, 133.

36. "Countries with Highest Numbers of Volunteers," Volunteer FDIP, January 1, 2023, https://www.volunteerfdip.org/countries-with-highest-numbers-of-volunteers-usa-canada-australia-uk-france#.

37. Mark Williams, "Pink Back in Style as Komen Race for the Cure Returns to Downtown Columbus After COVID-19," *Columbus Dispatch*, May 14, 2022, https://www.dispatch.com/story/news/2022/05/14/columbus-komen-race-cure-raises-1-m-draws-7-k-participants/9708422002/; Susan G. Komen, "Susan G. Komen® Announces the Return of MORE THAN PINK Walk, Race for the Cure," June 11, 2022, https://www.komen.org/news/2022-race-walk-announcement/.

38. Gordon W. Allport, *The Nature of Prejudice* (Addison-Wesley, 1954); Thomas F. Pettigrew et al., "Recent Advances in Intergroup Contact Theory," *International Journal of Intercultural Relations* 35, no. 3 (May 2011): 271–80.

39. Thomas F. Pettigrew and Linda R. Tropp, "How Does Intergroup Contact Reduce Prejudice? Meta-Analytic Tests of Three Mediators," *European Journal of Social Psychology* 38, no. 6 (2008): 922–34, https://doi.org/10.1002/ejsp.504.

40. Derek Heater, *A Brief History of Citizenship* (New York University Press, 2004), 6–29.

41. Catherine Bolzendahl and Hilde Coffe, "Are 'Good' Citizens 'Good' Participants? Testing Citizenship Norms and Political Participation Across 25 Nations," *Political Studies* 61, no. 1 (April 2013): 45–65, https://doi.org/10.1111/1467-9248.12010.

42. Dalton, *The Good Citizen*, 22.

43. Dalton, *The Good Citizen*, 23.

44. Dalton's fourth category, social order, which refers to willingness to serve in the military and on jury duty, is not an area we cover.

45. Citizens have distinctly different views from academics about good citizenship. A survey by Pew, for example, found that after voting, respondents cited reducing the effects of global climate change as the most critical attribute of good citizenship. Richard Wike et al., "What Makes Someone a Good Member of Society," Pew Research Center, November 16, 2022, https://www.pewresearch.org/global/2022/11/16/what-makes-someone-a-good-member-of-society/.

46. Sara Wallace Goodman, "'Good Citizens' in Democratic Hard Times," *Annals of the American Academy of Political and Social Science* 699, no. 1 (January 2022): 69, https://doi.org/10.1177/00027162211069729.

47. Elizabeth N. Simas, *In Defense of Ideology* (Cambridge University Press, 2023).

48. We will not review this literature here, but a quick overview can be found in Alex Samuels and Neil Lewis, Jr., "How White Victimhood Fuels Republican Politics," FiveThirtyEight, March 21, 2022, https://fivethirtyeight.com/features/how-white-victimhood-fuels-republican-politics/.

49. Mettler and Lieberman, *Four Threats*, 22.

50. A recent report from a group of political scientists likewise recommends more feasible individual-level and institutional-level actions to shore up American democracy. See the What's Next Project, "What's Next for American Democracy?," *Democracy Journal*, 2023, https://democracyjournal.org/magazine/whats-next-for -american-democracy/.

51. We are pleased to see that many of our recommendations align well with those offered in Spinner-Halev and Theiss-Morse, *Respect and Loathing in American Democracy*.

52. For more on benefits of engaging in politics with local organizations, see Eitan Hersh, *Politics Is for Power: How to Move Beyond Political Hobbyism, Take Action, and Make Real Change* (Simon & Schuster, 2020); Jeffrey Berry and Kent Portney, "The Group Basis of City Politics," in *Nonprofits and Advocacy*, ed. Robert J. Peakkanen, Steven Rathgeb Smith, and Yutaka Tsujinaka (Johns Hopkins University Press. 2014), 21–46.

53. Julie Creswell, "Cheaper Than Water: Retailers Try to Unload Bud Light," *New York Times*, June 29, 2023, https://www.nytimes.com/2023/06/29/business/bud-light -sales.html?searchResultPosition=1.

54. Eitan Hersh, "The Political Role of Business Leaders," *Annual Review of Political Science* 26 (2023): 97–115.

55. Erin L. Rossiter and Taylor N. Carlson, "Cross-Partisan Conversation Reduced Affective Polarization for Republicans and Democrats Even After the Contentious 2020 Election," *Journal of Politics* 86, no. 4 (October 2024): 1608–12, https://doi.org /10.1086/729931; Joshua L. Kalla and David E. Broockman, "Voter Outreach Campaigns Can Reduce Affective Polarization Among Implementing Political Activists: Evidence from Inside Three Campaigns," *American Political Science Review* 116, no. 4 (November 2022): 1516–22, https://doi.org/10.1017/S0003055422000132; Erik Santoro and David E. Broockman, "The Promise and Pitfalls of Cross-Partisan Conversations for Reducing Affective Polarization: Evidence from Randomized Experiments," *Science Advances* 8, no. 25 (2022): eabn5515, https://doi.org/10.1126/sciadv.abn5515; Matthew S. Levendusky and Dominik A. Stecula, *We Need to Talk: How Cross-Party Dialogue Reduces Affective Polarization*, Elements in Experimental Political Science (Cambridge University Press, 2021), https://doi.org/10.1017/9781009042192.

56. Some may wonder why we include MSNBC here, since our criticism of cable has focused on Fox. Although MSNBC does not utilize racist tropes, its overall programming strategy is to polarize its viewers, hardening their attitudes, which are antagonistic to conservatives. See Berry and Sobieraj, *The Outrage Industry*.

57. Levitsky and Ziblatt, *How Democracies Die*.

58. Levitsky and Ziblatt, *How Democracies Die*, 111.

# Bibliography

Abramowitz, Alan I. "The New American Electorate: Partisan, Sorted, and Polarized." In *American Gridlock: The Sources, Character, and Impact of Political Polarization*, edited by James A. Thurber and Antoine Yoshinaka, 19–44. Cambridge University Press, 2015.

Abramowitz, Alan I. "Peak Polarization? The Rise of Partisan-Ideological Consistency and Its Consequences." Ray Bliss Institute, University of Akron, 2021.

Abramowitz, Alan I., Brad Alexander, and Matthew Gunning. "Incumbency, Redistricting, and the Decline of Competition in US House Elections." *Journal of Politics* 68, no. 1 (2006): 75–88. https://doi.org/10.1111/j.1468-2508.2006.00371.x.

Ahler, Douglas J. "Self-Fulfilling Misperceptions of Public Polarization." *Journal of Politics* 76, no. 3 (July 2014): 607–20. https://doi.org/10.1017/S0022381614000085.

Alesina, Alberto, and Eliana La Ferrara. "Who Trusts Others?" *Journal of Public Economics* 85, no. 2 (2002): 207–34. https://doi.org/10.1016/S0047-2727(01)00084-6.

Allport, Gordon W. *The Nature of Prejudice*. Addison-Wesley, 1954.

Almond, Gabriel, and Sidney Verba. *The Civic Culture: Political Attitudes and Democracy in Five Nations*. Princeton University Press, 1963.

Anderson, Sarah E., Daniel M. Butler, and Laurel Harbridge-Yong. *Rejecting Compromise: Legislators' Fear of Primary Voters*. Cambridge University Press, 2020.

Anker, Elisabeth. "Villains, Victims, and Heroes: Melodrama, Media, and September 11." *Journal of Communication* 55, no. 1 (January 10, 2006): 22–37. https://doi.org/10.1111/j.1460-2466.2005.tb02656.x.

Arceneaux, Kevin, and Martin Johnson. *Changing Minds or Changing Channels? Partisan News in an Age of Choice*. University of Chicago Press, 2013.

Arceneaux, Kevin, Martin Johnson, and Chad Murphy. "Polarized Political Communication, Oppositional Media Hostility, and Selective Exposure." *Journal of Politics* 74, no. 1 (January 2012): 174–86. https://doi.org/10.1017/s0022381611000123x.

Bafumi, Joseph, and Michael Herron. "Leapfrog Representation and Extremism: A Study of American Voters and Their Members of Congress." *American Political Science Review* 104, no. 3 (August 2010): 519–42. https://doi.org/10.1017/s0003055410000316.

Banfield, Edward C. *The Unheavenly City*. Little, Brown, 1970.

Banks, Antoine J., Ismail K. White, and Brian D. McKenzie. "Black Politics: How Anger Influences the Political Actions Blacks Pursue to Reduce Racial Inequality." *Political Behavior* 41, no. 4 (2019): 917–43.

Baradaran, Mehrsa. *The Color of Money*. Harvard University Press, 2017.

Barber, Benjamin. *Strong Democracy: Participatory Politics for a New Age*. University of California Press, 2003.

Barr, Jeremy. "Critical Race Theory Is the Hottest Topic on Fox." *Washington Post*, June 24, 2021. https://www.washingtonpost.com/media/2021/06/24/critical-race -theory-fox-news/.

Beavers, Olivia. "House Freedom Caucus Faces an Internal Purge Push." *Politico*, June 23, 2023. https://www.politico.com/news/2023/06/23/house-freedom-caucus -members-00103296.

Becker, Penny Edgell, and Pawan Dhingra. "Religious Involvement in Volunteering: Implications for Civil Society." *Sociology of Religion* 62, no. 3 (Autumn 2001): 315–35. https://doi.org/10.2307/3712353.

Beggs, John J., Valerie A. Haines, and Jeanne S. Hurlbert. "Revisiting the Rural-Urban Contrast: Personal Networks in Nonmetropolitan and Metropolitan Settings." *Rural Sociology* 61, no. 2 (1996): 306–25.

Bellah, Robert Neelly, Richard Madsen, William M. Sullivan, Ann Swidler, and Steven M. Tipton. *Habits of the Heart: Individualism and Commitment in American Life*. University of California Press, 2008.

Benedictis-Kessner, Justin de, Matthew A. Baum, Adam J. Berinsky, and Teppei Yamamoto. "Persuading the Enemy: Estimating the Persuasive Effects of Partisan Media with the Preference-Incorporating Choice and Assignment Design." *American Political Science Review* 113, no. 4 (2019): 902–16.

Berry, Jeffrey M., with David F. Arons. *A Voice for Nonprofits*. Brookings Institution Press, 2003.

Berry, Jeffrey M., James M. Glaser, and Deborah J. Schildkraut. "Ideology, Racial Resentment, and the Mass Media." Paper presented at the Annual Conference of the American Political Science Association, Washington, DC, September 2019.

Berry, Jeffrey M., James M. Glaser, and Deborah J. Schildkraut. "Race and Gender on Fox and MSNBC." *Forum* 18, no. 3 (2020): 297–317. https://doi.org/10.1515/for-2020-2011.

Berry, Jeffrey M., and Kent Portney. "The Group Basis of City Politics." In *Nonprofits and Advocacy*, edited by Robert J. Pekkanen, Steven Rathgeb Smith, and Yutaka Tsujinaka, 21–46. Johns Hopkins University Press. 2014.

Berry, Jeffrey M., and Sarah Sobieraj. *The Outrage Industry: Political Opinion Media and the New Incivility*. Oxford University Press, 2014.

Blake, Aaron. "The Rapid Decline of White Evangelical America." *Washington Post*, July 8, 2021. https://www.washingtonpost.com/politics/2021/07/08/rapid-decline -white-evangelical-america/.

Blum, Rachel. *How the Tea Party Captured the GOP: Insurgent Factions in American Politics*. University of Chicago Press, 2020.

Boatright, Robert G., Timothy J. Shaffer, Sarah Sobieraj, and Dannagal Goldthwaite Young, eds. *A Crisis of Civility? Political Discourse and Its Discontents*. Routledge, 2019.

Bode, Leticia. "Closing the Gap: Gender Parity in Political Engagement on Social Media." *Information, Communication & Society* 20, no. 4 (June 28, 2016): 587–603.

Bode, Leticia. "Pruning the News Feed: Unfriending and Unfollowing Political Content on Social Media." *Research & Politics* 3, no. 3 (August 12, 2016): 205316801666187. https://doi.org/10.1177/2053168016661873.

Bolzendahl, Catherine, and Hilde Coffe. "Are 'Good' Citizens 'Good' Participants? Testing Citizenship Norms and Political Participation Across 25 Nations." *Political Studies* 61, no. 1 (April 2013): 45–65. https://doi.org/10.1111/1467-9248.12010.

Borger, Julian. "'I Have Political Capital: I Intend to Spend It.'" *Guardian*, November 4, 2004. https://www.theguardian.com/world/2004/nov/05/uselections2004.usa5.

Bouie, Jamelle. "A Breathtaking Contempt for the People of Wisconsin." *New York Times*, sec. Opinion, September 8, 2023. https://www.nytimes.com/2023/09/08/opinion/wisconsin-judge-impeachment-democracy.html.

Bowman, Ann, and George Krause. "Power Shift: Measuring Policy Centralization in U.S. Intergovernmental Relations, 1947–1998." *American Politics Research* 31, no. 3 (2003): 301–25.

Brenan, Megan. "Americans' Trust in Media Dips to Second Lowest on Record." Gallup, October 7, 2021. https://news.gallup.com/poll/355526/americans-trust-media-dips-second-lowest-record.aspx.

Broockman, David, and Joshua Kalla. "Consuming Cross-Cutting Media Causes Learning and Moderates Attitudes: A Field Experiment with Fox News Viewers." Working paper, April 2023. https://doi.org/10.31219/osf.io/jrw26.

Broockman, David, and Joshua Kalla. "Selective Exposure and Partisan Echo Chambers in Television News Consumption: Evidence from Linked Viewership, Administrative, and Survey Data," January 8, 2024. https://doi.org/10.31219/osf.io/b54sx.

Broockman, David E., and Christopher Skovron. "Bias in Perceptions of Public Opinion Among Political Elites." *American Political Science Review* 112, no. 3 (August 2018): 542–63. https://doi.org/10.1017/S0003055418000011.

Brooks, Arthur C. *Who Really Cares*. Basic Books, 2006.

Bunch, Sonny. "Conservatives Are Dying to Own the Libs: Can Anyone Use That Logic to Get Them Vaccinated?" *Washington Post*, September 21, 2021. https://www.washingtonpost.com/opinions/2021/09/21/conservatives-are-dying-own-libs-can-anyone-use-that-logic-get-them-vaccinated/.

Bureau of Labor Statistics. "Volunteering in the United States—2015," February 25, 2016. https://www.bls.gov/news.release/pdf/volun.pdf.

Byler, David. "5 Myths About Politics, Busted by Data." *Washington Post*, July 17, 2023, sec. Opinions. https://www.washingtonpost.com/opinions/2023/07/17/political-myths-pew-research-center/.

"Cable News Fact Sheet." Pew Research Center, September 14, 2023. https://www.pewresearch.org/journalism/fact-sheet/cable-news/.

Campbell, Angus, Philip Converse, Warren Miller, and Donald Stokes. *The American Voter*. University of Chicago Press, 1960.

Campbell, David E., Geoffrey C. Layman, and John C. Green. *Secular Surge: A New Fault Line in American Politics*. Cambridge University Press, 2020.

Carlson, Taylor N., and Jamie E. Settle. *What Goes Without Saying: Navigating Political Discussion in America*. Cambridge University Press, 2022.

Carney, Dana R., John T. Jost, Samuel D. Gosling, and Jeff Potter. "The Secret Lives of Liberals and Conservatives: Personality Profiles, Interaction Styles, and the Things They Leave Behind." *Political Psychology* 29, no. 6 (October 23, 2008): 807–40. https://doi.org/10.1111/j.1467-9221.2008.00668.x.

Carraro, Luciana, Luigi Castrelli, and Claudia Macchiella. "The Automatic Conservative: Ideology-Based Attentional Asymmetries in the Processing of Valenced Information." *PLOS One* 6, no. 11 (2011): e26456. https://doi.org/10.1371/journal.pone.0026456.

Christensen, Devin J., John Lovett, and John A. Curiel. "Mainstream Media Recirculation of Trust-Reducing Social Media Messages." *American Politics Research* 50, no. 2 (March 1, 2022): 213–26. https://doi.org/10.1177/1532673X211023931.

Citrin, Jack. "Comment: The Political Relevance of Trust in Government." *American Political Science Review* 68, no. 3 (September 1974): 973–88.

Cochrane, Emily. "Sarah Huckabee Sanders Was Asked to Leave Restaurant over White House Work." *New York Times*, June 23, 2018. https://www.nytimes.com/2018/06/23/us/politics/sarah-huckabee-sanders-restaurant.html.

Cohen, Michael A. "Thanks, Red Hen, for Kicking Out Sarah Huckabee Sanders." *Boston Globe*, June 25, 2018. https://www.bostonglobe.com/opinion/2018/06/25/thanks-red-hen-for-kicking-out-sarah-huckabee-sanders/LrZ8CyqZvwtXkV6K7Cp3HN/story.html.

Coleman, Peter T., and Pearce Godwin. "Americans Are Tired of Political Division." *Time*, March 30, 2023. https://time.com/6266873/american-political-division-courage-challenge/.

Confessore, Nicholas. "How Tucker Carlson Reshaped Fox News—and Became Trump's Heir." *New York Times*, April 30, 2022. https://www.nytimes.com/2022/04/30/us/tucker-carlson-fox-news.html.

Confessore, Nicholas. "What to Know About Tucker Carlson's Rise." *New York Times*, April 30, 2022. https://www.nytimes.com/2022/04/30/business/media/tucker-carlson-fox-news-takeaways.html.

Conlan, Tim, and John Dinan. "Federalism, the Bush Administration, and the Transformation of American Conservatism." *Publius* 27, no. 3 (2007): 279–303.

Converse, Philip. "Change in the American Electorate." In *The Human Meaning of Social Change*, edited by Angus Campbell, 263–338. Russell Sage Foundation, 1972.

Converse, Philip. "The Nature of Belief Systems in Mass Publics." In *Ideology and Discontent*, edited by David Apter, 206–61. Free Press, 1964.

"Countries with Highest Numbers of Volunteers." Volunteer FDIP, January 1, 2023. https://www.volunteerfdip.org/countries-with-highest-numbers-of-volunteers-usa-canada-australia-uk-france#.

Cox, Daniel, and Robert P. Jones. "'Merry Christmas' vs. 'Happy Holidays': Republicans and Democrats Are Polar Opposites." *PRRI* (blog), December 19, 2016. https://www.prri.org/research/poll-post-election-holiday-war-christmas/.

Creswell, Julie. "Cheaper Than Water: Retailers Try to Unload Bud Light." *New York Times*, June 29, 2023. https://www.nytimes.com/2023/06/29/business/bud-light-sales.html?searchResultPosition=1.

Crews, Clyde Wayne. "Tens of Thousands of Pages and Rules in the Federal Register." Ten Thousand Commandments 2021. Competitive Enterprise Institute, June 30, 2021. https://cei.org/publication/tens-of-thousands-of-pages-and-rules-in-the-federal-register-2/.

Curato, Nicole, John S. Dryzek, Selen A. Ercan, Carolyn M. Hendriks, and Simon Niemeyer. "Twelve Key Findings in Deliberative Democracy Research." *Daedalus* 146, no. 3 (2017): 28–38.

Curry, James, and Francis Lee. *The Limits of Party: Congress and Lawmaking in a Polarized Era*. University of Chicago Press, 2020.

Dahl, Robert A. *Dilemmas of Pluralist Democracy: Autonomy vs. Control*. Yale University Press, 1983.

Dahl, Robert A. "Myth of the Presidential Mandate." *Political Science Quarterly* 105, no. 3 (1990): 355–72.

Dahl, Robert A. *On Democracy*. Yale University Press, 1998.

Dahl, Robert A. *Polyarchy: Participation and Opposition*. Yale University Press, 1971.

Dahl, Robert A. *A Preface to Democratic Theory*. University of Chicago Press, 1956.

Dahl, Robert A., and Edward R. Tufte. *Size and Democracy*. Stanford University Press, 1974.

Dalton, Russell J. *The Good Citizen*. 3rd ed. CQ Press, 2021.

Daniels, Alex. "As Charitable Giving Rates Sag, Foundations Back Ambitious New Effort to Ignite Generosity by All Americans." *Chronicle of Philanthropy*, October 12, 2021. https://www.philanthropy.com/article/as-charitable-giving -rates-sag-foundations-back-ambitious-new-effort-to-ignite-generosity-by-all -americans.

Darcy, Oliver. "How Fox News Is Making a Network out of Race Baiting." *CNN Business*, July 23, 2021. https://www.cnn.com/2021/07/23/media/fox-news-race -baiting/index.html.

Davenport, Coral. "Trump Defends Plan to Kill California's Auto-Emissions Authority." *New York Times*, September 18, 2019.

Davis, Nicholas T. "Identity Sorting and Political Compromise." *American Politics Research*, September 17, 2018, 391–414. http://journals.sagepub.com/doi/10.1177/ 1532673X18799273.

Davis, Nicholas T., Keith Gaddie, and Kirby Goidel. *Democracy's Meanings: How the Public Understands Democracy and Why It Matters*. University of Michigan Press, 2022.

Dawson, Michael C. *Black Visions: The Roots of Contemporary African-American Political Ideologies*. University of Chicago Press, 2001.

Delli Carpini, Michael, and Scott Keeter. *What Americans Know About Politics and Why It Matters*. Yale University Press, 1996.

Demaris, Alfred, and Renxin Yang. "Race, Alienation, and Interpersonal Mistrust." *Sociological Spectrum* 14, no. 4 (1994): 327–49. https://doi.org/10.1080/02732173 .1994.9982075.

Derthick, Martha. "American Federalism: Madison's Middle Ground in the 1980s." *Public Administration Review* 47, no. 1 (1987): 66–74.

Desilver, Drew. "The Polarization in Today's Congress Has Roots That Go Back Decades." Pew Research Center, March 10, 2022. https://www.pewresearch.org/ fact-tank/2022/03/10/the-polarization-in-todays-congress-has-roots-that-go-back -decades/.

Devine, Christopher J. "Ideological Social Identity: Psychological Attachment to Ideological In-Groups as a Political Phenomenon and a Behavioral Influence." *Political Behavior* 37, no. 3 (September 17, 2015): 509–35. https://doi.org/10.1007/ s11109-014-9280-6.

Dews, Fred. "Fox News' Incomparable Role on the Political Right." Brookings Institution, June 12, 2014. https://www.brookings.edu/articles/fox-news -incomparable-role-on-the-political-right/.

Dinan, John, and Jac C. Heckelman. "Stability and Contingency in Federalism Preferences." *Public Administration Review* 80, no. 4 (2020): 234–43.

Dionne, E. J., Norman J. Ornstein, and Thomas E. Mann. *One Nation After Trump: A Guide for the Perplexed, the Disillusioned, the Desperate, and the Not-Yet-Deported*. St. Martin's Press, 2017.

"Distribution of X (Formerly Twitter) Users Worldwide as of April 2024, by Age Group." Statista, April 2024. https://www.statista.com/statistics/283119/age -distribution-of-global-twitter-users.

Dorison, Charles A., Julia A. Minson, and Todd Rogers. "Selective Exposure Partly Relies on Faulty Affective Forecasts." *Cognition* 188 (2019): 98–107.

Douthat, Ross. "The Two Crises of Conservatism." *New York Times*, April 24, 2021. https://www.nytimes.com/2021/04/24/opinion/sunday/republicans-conservatism.html.

Druckman, James N., Samara Klar, Yanna Krupnikov, Matthew Levendusky, and John Barry Ryan. "(Mis)Estimating Affective Polarization." *Journal of Politics* 84, no. 2 (April 2022): 1106–17. https://doi.org/10.1086/715603.

Druckman, James N., Samara Klar, Yanna Krupnikov, Matthew Levendusky, and John Barry Ryan. *Partisan Hostility and American Democracy: Explaining Political Divisions and When They Matter*. University of Chicago Press, 2024.

Drutman, Lee. *Breaking the Two-Party Doom Loop: The Case for Multiparty Democracy in America*. Oxford University Press, USA, 2020.

Drutman, Lee. "How Much Longer Can This Era of Political Gridlock Last." FiveThirtyEight, March 4, 2021. https://fivethirtyeight.com/features/how-much-longer-can-this-era-of-political-gridlock-last/.

Eady, Gregory, Jonathan Nagler, Joshua A. Tucker, Andy Guess, and Jan Zilinsky. "How Many People Live in Political Bubbles on Social Media? Evidence from Linked Survey and Twitter Data." *Sage Open* 9, no. 1 (February 28, 2019). https://doi.org/10.1177/2158244019832705.

Eagly, Alice H., Mary C. Johannesen-Schmidt, and Marloes L. van Engen. "Transformational, Transactional, and Laissez-Faire Leadership Styles: A Meta-Analysis Comparing Women and Men." *Psychological Bulletin* 129, no. 4 (2003): 569–91. https://doi.org/10.1037/0033-2909.129.4.569.

Eliasoph, Nina. *Avoiding Politics: How Americans Produce Apathy in Everyday Life*. Cambridge University Press, 1998.

Ellis, Christopher, and James A. Stimson. *Ideology in America*. Cambridge University Press, 2012.

Emerson, Ralph Waldo. *Self-Reliance*. Peter Pauper Press, 1967.

Engelhardt, Andrew M. "Observational Equivalence in Explaining Attitude Change: Have White Racial Attitudes Genuinely Changed?" *American Journal of Political Science* 67, no. 2 (2023): 411–25. https://doi.org/10.1111/ajps.12665.

Farwell, Lisa, and Bernard Weiner. "Bleeding Hearts and the Heartless." *Personality and Social Psychology Bulletin* 26, no. 7 (September 2000): 845–52. https://doi.org/10.1177/0146167200269009.

Federico, Christopher M. "Ideology and Public Opinion." In *New Directions in Public Opinion*, 3rd ed., edited by Adam J. Berinsky, 75–98. Routledge, 2020.

Federico, Christopher M. "Race, Education, and Individualism Revisited." *Journal of Politics* 68, no. 3 (August 2006): 600–610. https://doi.org/10.1111/j.1468-2508.2006.00448.x.

Federico, Christopher M., Emily L. Fisher, and Grace Deason. "Expertise and the Ideological Consequences of the Authoritarian Predisposition." *Public Opinion Quarterly* 75, no. 4 (2011): 686–708. https://doi.org/10.1093/poq/nfr026.

Felton, Emmanuel. "Baltimore Mayor Weathers Racist Attacks After Bridge Collapse." *Washington Post*, March 31, 2024. https://www.washingtonpost.com/nation/2024/03/31/baltimore-bridge-collapse-mayor/.

Fishkin, James S., and Jane Mansbridge. "Introduction." *Daedalus* 146, no. 3 (2017): 6–13.

Forbes, Kevin F., and Ernest M. Zampelli. "The Impacts of Religion, Political Ideology, and Social Capital on Religious and Secular Giving: Evidence from the 2006 Social

Capital Community Survey." *Applied Economics* 45, no. 17 (June 1, 2013): 2481–90. https://doi.org/10.1080/00036846.2012.667555.

Forgey, Quint, and Josh Gerstein. "Trump: It's My Decision, Not Governors', to Reopen Country." *Politico*, April 13, 2020. https://www.politico.com/news/2020/04/13/trump-governors-decision-reopen-183405.

Froomkin, Dan. "Fox News Is Stoking Anti-Immigration Hysteria Again. Are We Ready to Defeat It This Time?" *Salon*, February 26, 2021. https://www.salon.com/2021/02/26/fox-news-is-stoking-anti-immigration-hysteria-again-are-we-ready-to-defeat-it-this-time/.

Gaines, Brian J., and James H. Kuklinski. "Experimental Estimation of Heterogeneous Treatment Effects Related to Self-Selection." *American Journal of Political Science* 55, no. 3 (July 2011): 724–36. https://doi.org/10.1111/j.1540-5907.2011.00518.x.

Gervais, Bryan T., and Irwin L. Morris. *Reactionary Republicanism: How the Tea Party in the House Paved the Way for Trump's Victory*. Oxford University Press, 2018.

"The Giving Environment: Understanding Pre-Pandemic Trends in Charitable Giving." Indiana University Lilly Family School of Philanthropy, 2021. https://scholarworks.iupui.edu/bitstream/handle/1805/26290/giving-environment210727.pdf.

"Giving USA: Total U.S. Charitable Giving Remained Strong in 2021, Reaching $484.85 Billion." Lilly Family School of Philanthropy, June 21, 2022. https://philanthropy.iupui.edu/news-events/news-item/giving-usa:--total-u.s.-charitable-giving-remained-strong-in-2021,-reaching-$484.85-billion.html?id=392.

Glaser, James M., and Jeffrey M. Berry. "Compromising Positions: Why Republican Partisans Are More Rigid Than Democrats." *Political Science Quarterly* 133, no. 1 (March 2018): 99–125. https://doi.org/10.1002/polq.12735.

Glaser, James M., Jeffrey M. Berry, and Deborah J. Schildkraut. "Education and the Curious Case of Conservative Compromise." *Political Research Quarterly* 74, no. 1 (2021): 59–75.

Glaser, James M., Jeffrey M. Berry, and Deborah J. Schildkraut. "Ideology and Support for Federalism in Theory—and in Practice." *Publius* 53, no. 4 (2023): 511–35. https://doi.org/10.1093/publius/pjad003.

González-Bailón, Sandra, David Lazer, Pablo Barberá, et al. "Asymmetric Ideological Segregation in Exposure to Political News on Facebook." *Science* 381, no. 6656 (2023): 392–98. https://doi.org/10.1126/science.ade7138.

Goodman, Sara Wallace. *Citizenship in Hard Times: How Ordinary People Respond to Democratic Threat*. Cambridge: Cambridge University Press, 2022.

Goodman, Sara Wallace. "'Good Citizens' in Democratic Hard Times." *Annals of the American Academy of Political and Social Science* 699, no. 1 (January 2022): 68–78. https://doi.org/10.1177/00027162211069729.

Granovetter, Mark S. "The Strength of Weak Ties." *American Journal of Sociology* 78, no. 6 (May 15, 1973): 1360–80. https://doi.org/10.1086/225469.

Grossmann, Matt, and David A. Hopkins. *Asymmetric Politics: Ideological Republicans and Group Interest Democrats*. Oxford University Press, 2016.

Grumbach, Jacob M. *Laboratories Against Democracy: How National Parties Transformed State Politics*. Princeton University Press, 2022.

Grynbaum, Michael M., and Tiffany Hsu. "Advertisers Are Fleeing Tucker Carlson. Fox News Viewers Have Stayed." *New York Times*, June 18, 2020. https://www.nytimes.com/2020/06/18/business/media/tucker-carlson-advertisers-ratings.html?searchResultPosition=1.

Guess, Andrew. "(Almost) Everything in Moderation: New Evidence on Americans' Online Media Diets." *American Journal of Political Science* 65, no. 2 (February 19, 2021): 1007–22. https://doi.org/10.1111/ajps.12589.

Gutmann, Amy, and Dennis Frank Thompson. *The Spirit of Compromise: Why Governing Demands It and Campaigning Undermines It.* Princeton University Press, 2014.

Haberman, Maggie. *Confidence Man.* Penguin Random House, 2022.

Hacker, Jacob S., and Paul Pierson. "Confronting Asymmetric Polarization." In *Solutions to Political Polarization in America*, edited by Nathaniel Persily, 59–71. Cambridge University Press, 2015.

Hagle, Courtney. "Six Weeks of Fox's Alexandria Ocasio-Cortez Obsession: 'Totalitarian,' 'Ignorant,' 'Scary,' and Waging a 'War on Cows.'" Media Matters for America, April 12, 2019. https://www.mediamatters.org/fox-news/six-weeks-foxs -alexandria-ocasio-cortez-obsession-totalitarian-ignorant-scary-and-waging.

Hamilton, Alexander, James Madison, and John Jay. *The Federalist Papers.* Dover Publications, 2014.

Hamilton, James T. *All the News That's Fit to Sell.* Princeton University Press, 2004.

Harbridge, Laurel, Neil Malhotra, and Brian F. Harrison. "Public Preferences for Bipartisanship in the Policymaking Process." *Legislative Studies Quarterly* 39, no. 3 (2014): 327–55.

Hartig, Hannah. "About Six-in-Ten Americans Say Abortion Should Be Legal in All or Most Cases." Pew Research Center, June 13, 2021. https://www.pewresearch.org /fact-tank/2022/06/13/about-six-in-ten-americans-say-abortion-should-be-legal-in -all-or-most-cases-2/.

Hartnett, Brendan, and Alexandra Haver. "Unconditional Support for Trump's Resistance Prior to Election Day." *PS: Political Science & Politics*, July 18, 2022, 1–7. https://doi.org/10.1017/S1049096522000695.

Heater, Derek. *A Brief History of Citizenship.* New York University Press, 2004.

Hersh, Eitan. "The Political Role of Business Leaders." *Annual Review of Political Science* 26 (2023): 97–115.

Hersh, Eitan. *Politics Is for Power: How to Move Beyond Political Hobbyism, Take Action, and Make Real Change.* Simon & Schuster, 2020.

Hetherington, Marc J., and John D. Nugent. "Explaining Public Support for Devolution: The Role of Political Trust." In *What Is It About Government That Americans Dislike?*, edited by John R. Hibbing and Elizabeth Theiss-Morse, 134–51. Cambridge University Press, 2001.

Hibbing, John R., Kevin B. Smith, and John R. Alford. "Differences in Negativity Bias Underlie Variations in Political Ideology." *Behavioral and Brain Sciences* 37 (June 27, 2014): 297–307. https://doi.org/doi:10.1017/S0140525X13001192.

Hibbing, John R., and Elizabeth Theiss-Morse. "Process Preferences and American Politics: What the People Want Government to Be." *American Political Science Review* 95, no. 1 (March 2001): 145–53. https://doi.org/10.1177/1065912918819860.

Hirschman, Albert O. *Exit, Voice, and Loyalty: Responses to Decline in Firms, Organizations, and States.* Harvard University Press, 1970.

Holbert, R. Lance, Yotam Ophir, Dror Walter, Josh Pasek, and Kathleen Hall Jamieson. "The Electorates' Communication Dynamics." In *Democracy amid Crises: Polarization, Pandemic, Protests, and Persuasion*, edited by Kathleen Hall Jamieson, Matthew Levendusky, Josh Pasek, R. Lance Holbert, Andrew Renninger, Yotam

Ophir, Dror Walter, et al. Oxford University Press, 2023. https://doi.org/10.1093
/oso/9780197644690.003.0004.

Hopkins, Daniel J. *The Increasingly United States: How and Why American Political
Behavior Nationalized*. University of Chicago Press, 2018. https://www.press
.uchicago.edu/ucp/books/book/chicago/I/bo27596045.html.

Hopkins, Daniel J., Yphtach Lelkes, and Samuel Wolken. "Increased Fox News
Viewership Is Not Associated with Heightened Anti-Black Prejudice." *SSRN*, April
17, 2023. https://papers.ssrn.com/sol3/papers.cfm?abstract_id=4420947.

"'How Democracies Die' Authors Say Trump Is a Symptom of 'Deeper Problems.'"
*Fresh Air*. National Public Radio, January 22, 2018. https://www.npr.org/2018/01
/22/579670528/how-democracies-die-authors-say-trump-is-a-symptom-of-deeper
-problems.

Huckfeldt, Robert, and John Sprague. "Networks in Context: The Social Flow of
Political Information." *American Political Science Review* 81, no. 4 (1987): 1197–1216.

"In U.S., Decline of Christianity Continues at Rapid Pace." Pew Research Center,
October 27, 2019. https://www.pewresearch.org/religion/2019/10/17/in-u-s
-decline-of-christianity-continues-at-rapid-pace/.

Institute of Politics and Public Service, Georgetown University. "Overwhelming
Number of Americans Frustrated with Incivility in Politics," April 24, 2019.
https://politics.georgetown.edu/2019/04/24/new-survey-overwhelming-number
-of-americans-frustrated-by-incivility-in-politics-but-conflicted-on-desire-for
-compromise-and-common-ground/.

Iyengar, Shanto, Yphtach Lelkes, Matthew Levendusky, Neil Malhotra, and Sean J.
Westwood. "The Origins and Consequences of Affective Polarization in the United
States." *Annual Review of Political Science* 22 (May 2019): 129–46. https://doi.org/10
.1146/annurev-polisci-051117-073034.

Iyengar, Shanto, and Sean J. Westwood. "Fear and Loathing Across Party Lines: New
Evidence on Group Polarization." *American Journal of Political Science* 59, no. 3
(2015): 690–707.

Jacobs, Jane. *The Death and Life of Great American Cities*. Random House, 1961.

Jacobs, Lawrence R. *Democracy Under Fire: Donald Trump and the Breaking of
American History*. Oxford University Press, 2022.

Jacobs, Nicholas. "An Experimental Test of How Americans Think About Federalism."
*Publius* 47, no. 4 (2017): 572–98.

Jacobs, Nicholas. "Federalism, Polarization, and Policy Responsibility During
COVID-19: Experimental and Observational Evidence from the United States."
*Publius* 51, no. 4 (2021): 693–719.

James, Russell N., III, and Deanna L. Sharpe. "The Nature and Causes of the U-Shaped
Charitable Giving Profile." *Nonprofit and Voluntary Sector Quarterly* 36, no. 2
(June 2007): 218–38. https://doi.org/10.1177/0899764006295993.

Jamieson, Kathleen Hall, and Doron Taussig. "Disruption, Demonization, Deliverance,
and Norm Destruction: The Rhetorical Signature of Donald J. Trump." *Political
Science Quarterly* 132, no. 4 (Winter 2017): 619–50.

Jardina, Ashley. *White Identity Politics*. Cambridge University Press, 2019.

Jefferson, Hakeem. "The Curious Case of Black 'Conservatives': Assessing the Validity
of the Liberal–Conservative Scale Among Black Americans." *Public Opinion
Quarterly* 88, no. 3 (2024): 909–32.

Jones, Keely S. "Giving and Volunteering as Distinct Forms of Civic Engagement." *Nonprofit and Voluntary Sector Quarterly* 35, no. 2 (June 2006): 249–66. https://doi .org/10.1177/0899764006287464.

Jurkowitz, Mark, Amy Mitchell, Elisa Shearer, and Mason Walker. "Americans Are Divided by Party in the Sources They Turn to for Political News." Pew Research Center's Journalism Project, January 24, 2020. https://www.pewresearch.org /journalism/2020/01/24/americans-are-divided-by-party-in-the-sources-they-turn -to-for-political-news/.

Kahn, Mattie. "No, Sarah Huckabee Sanders Shouldn't Be Able to Eat Dinner in Public." *Glamour*, June 26, 2018. https://www.glamour.com/story/sarah-huckabee -sanders-civility-politics.

Kahneman, Daniel, and Amos Tversky. "Choices, Values, and Frames." *American Psychologist* 39, no. 4 (1984): 341–50. https://doi.org/10.1037/0003-066X.39.4.341.

Kalla, Joshua L., and David E. Broockman. "Voter Outreach Campaigns Can Reduce Affective Polarization Among Implementing Political Activists: Evidence from Inside Three Campaigns." *American Political Science Review* 116, no. 4 (November 2022): 1516–22. https://doi.org/10.1017/S0003055422000132.

Kalmoe, Nathan P., and Lilliana Mason. *Radical American Partisanship: Mapping Violent Hostility, Its Causes, and the Consequences for Democracy*. University of Chicago Press, 2022.

Kam, Cindy D., and Robert A. Mikos. "Do Citizens Care About Federalism? An Experimental Test." *Journal of Empirical Legal Studies* 4, no. 3 (2007): 589–624.

Kam, Cindy D., and Carl L. Palmer. "Reconsidering the Effects of Education on Political Participation." *Journal of Politics* 70, no. 3 (July 2008): 612–31.

Kapur, Sahil, and Scott Wong. "Congress Is Passing a Wave of Bipartisan Bills as Biden's Big Plans Stall." NBC News, February 11, 2022. https://www.nbcnews.com /politics/congress-passing-wave-bipartisan-bills-bidens-big-plans-stall-rcna15798.

Karni, Annie, Robert Draper, and Luke Broadwater. "As Spending Fights Loom, Freedom Caucus Is at a Crossroads." *New York Times*, July 25, 2023.

Kim, Eunji, and Taylor Carlson. "An Era of Not-So-Minimal Effects? The Case of Fox News." 2023 MIT American Politics Conference, Cambridge, MA, 2023.

Kinder, Donald R., and Nathan P. Kalmoe. *Neither Liberal nor Conservative*. University of Chicago Press, 2017.

Klinkner, Philip A., and Rogers M. Smith. *The Unsteady March: The Rise and Decline of Racial Equality in America*. University of Chicago Press, 1999.

Konisky, David. "Public Preferences for Environmental Policy Responsibility." *Publius* 41, no. 1 (2011): 76–100.

Konisky, David, and Paul Nolette. "The State of American Federalism 2021–2022: Federal Courts, State Legislatures, and the Conservative Turn in the Law." *Publius* 52, no. 3 (2022): 353–81.

Krieg, Gregory. "Keurig Roasted? The Latest Effort to 'Own the Libs.'" CNN, November 14, 2017. https://www.cnn.com/2017/11/14/politics/keurig-protest -owning-the-libs-meme/index.html.

Krupnikov, Yanna, and John Barry Ryan. *The Other Divide: Polarization and Disengagement in American Politics*. Cambridge University Press, 2022.

Ksiazek, Thomas B., Edward C. Malthouse, and James G. Webster. "News-Seekers and Avoiders: Exploring Patterns of Total News Consumption Across Media and the

Relationship to Civic Participation." *Journal of Broadcasting & Electronic Media* 54, no. 4 (November 30, 2010): 551–68. https://doi.org/10.1080/08838151.2010.519808.

Ladd, Jonathan M. *Why Americans Hate the Media and How It Matters*. Princeton University Press, 2012.

Lazarsfeld, Paul, Bernard Berelson, and Hazel Gaudet. *The People's Choice: How the Voter Makes Up His Mind in a Presidential Campaign*. Duell, Sloan & Pearce, 1944.

Lee, Frances E. *Insecure Majorities: Congress and the Perpetual Campaign*. University of Chicago Press, 2016.

Lee, Younghwa, Sukki Yoon, Young Woo Lee, and Marla B. Royne. "How Liberals and Conservatives Respond to Equality-Based and Proportionality-Based Rewards in Charity Advertising." *Journal of Public Policy & Marketing* 37, no. 1 (April 1, 2018): 108–18. https://doi.org/10.1509/jppm.16.180.

Leetaru, Kalev. "Twitter Users Mostly Retweet Politicians and Celebrities: That's a Big Change." *Washington Post*, March 8, 2019. https://www.washingtonpost.com/politics/2019/03/08/twitter-users-mostly-retweet-politicians-celebrities-thats-big-change/?utm_term=.5affob0eac05.

Lepore, Jill. *These Truths*. W. W. Norton, 2018.

"Let the Trump Team Eat in Peace." Editorial Board. *Washington Post*, June 25, 2018. https://www.washingtonpost.com/opinions/let-the-trump-team-eat-in-peace/2018/06/24/46882e16-779a-11e8-80be-6d32e182a3bc_story.html.

Levendusky, Matthew. "Americans, Not Partisans: Can Priming American National Identity Reduce Affective Polarization?" *Journal of Politics* 80, no. 1 (2018): 59–70.

Levendusky, Matthew. *How Partisan Media Polarize America*. University of Chicago Press, 2013.

Levendusky, Matthew. *Our Common Bonds*. University of Chicago Press, 2023.

Levendusky, Matthew. *The Partisan Sort: How Liberals Became Democrats and Conservatives Became Republicans*. University of Chicago Press, 2009.

Levendusky, Matthew S., and Dominik A. Stecula. *We Need to Talk: How Cross-Party Dialogue Reduces Affective Polarization*. Elements in Experimental Political Science. Cambridge University Press, 2021. https://doi.org/10.1017/9781009042192.

Levine, Peter. *We Are the Ones We Have Been Waiting For*. Oxford University Press, 2013.

Levitsky, Steven, and Daniel Ziblatt. "End Minority Rule." *New York Times*, October 23, 2020, sec. Opinion. https://www.nytimes.com/2020/10/23/opinion/sunday/disenfranchisement-democracy-minority-rule.html.

Levitsky, Steven, and Daniel Ziblatt. *How Democracies Die*. Crown, 2018.

Levitsky, Steven, and Daniel Ziblatt. *Tyranny of the Minority: Why American Democracy Reached the Breaking Point*. Penguin Random House, 2023.

Lijphart, Arend. *Patterns of Democracy*. Yale University Press, 1999. https://yalebooks.yale.edu/book/9780300172027/patterns-democracy.

Lindsay, Drew. "Major Funders Bet Big on Rural America and 'Everyday Democracy.'" *Chronicle of Philanthropy*, June 17, 2024. https://www.philanthropy.com/commons/major-funders-bet-big-on-rural-america-and-everyday-democracy.

Lupia, Arthur, and Anne Norton. "Inequality Is Always in the Room: Language and Power in Deliberative Democracy." *Daedalus* 146, no. 3 (2017): 64–76.

Malka, Ariel, and Yphtach Lelkes. "More Than Ideology: Conservative–Liberal Identity and Receptivity to Political Cues." *Social Justice Research* 23, nos. 2–3 (September 22, 2010): 156–88. https://doi.org/10.1007/s11211-010-0114-3.

Mangum, Maurice. "Explaining Political Trust Among African Americans." *Journal of Public Management and Social Policy* 23, no. 2 (2016): 84–100.

Manin, Bernard. "Political Deliberation and the Adversarial Principle." *Daedalus* 146, no. 3 (2017): 39–50.

Mann, Thomas E., and Norman J. Ornstein. *It's Even Worse Than It Looks: How the American Constitutional System Collided with the New Politics of Extremism.* New York: Basic Books, 2016.

Marcus, George E., and Michael B. MacKuen. "Anxiety, Enthusiasm, and the Vote: The Emotional Underpinnings of Learning and Involvement During Presidential Campaigns." *American Political Science Review* 87, no. 3 (1993): 672–85.

Martin, Cathy Jo. "Negotiating Political Agreements." In *Political Negotiation: A Handbook*, edited by Jane Mansbridge and Cathie Jo Martin, 7–33. Brookings Institution, 2016.

Masket, Seth. "We Freaking Warned You." *Mischiefs of Faction* (blog), January 9, 2021. https://www.mischiefsoffaction.com/post/we-freaking-warned-you.

Mason, Lilliana. "Ideologues Without Issues: The Polarizing Consequences of Ideological Identities." *Public Opinion Quarterly* 82, no. S1 (April 11, 2018): 866–87. https://doi.org/10.1093/poq/nfy005.

Mason, Lilliana. *Uncivil Agreement: How Politics Became Our Identity.* Chicago: University of Chicago Press, 2018.

McBeth, Mark K., Robert J. Tokle, and Susan Schaefer. "Media Narratives Versus Evidence in Economic Policy Making: The 2008–2009 Financial Crisis." *Social Science Quarterly* 99, no. 2 (August 22, 2017): 791–806. https://doi.org/10.1111/ssqu.12456.

McClosky, Herbert. "Consensus and Ideology in American Politics." *American Political Science Review* 58, no. 2 (1964): 361–82.

McCoy, Jennifer, and Benjamin Press. "What Happens When Democracies Become Perniciously Polarized." Carnegie Endowment for International Peace, January 18, 2022. https://carnegieendowment.org/2022/01/18/what-happens-when-democracies-become-perniciously-polarized-pub-86190.

McInturff, Bill. "Polarization and a Deep Dive on Issues by Party." Public Opinion Strategies, n.d. https://pos.org/wp-content/uploads/2023/06/Deep-Dive-on-Issues-Short-Deck-d1g.pdf. Accessed May 22, 2025.

McLaughlin, Dan. "The Minnesota Democrats' Culture War." *National Review*, February 2, 2023.

Meer, Jonathan, and Benjamin A. Priday. *Tax Prices and Charitable Giving: Projected Changes in Donations Under the 2017 TCJA.* NBER Working Paper Series, no. w26452. Cambridge, MA: National Bureau of Economic Research, 2019.

Mercer, Jonathan. "Prospect Theory and Political Science." *Annual Review of Political Science* 8 (June 2005): 1–21. https://doi.org/10.1146/annurev.polisci.8.082103.104911.

Mettler, Suzanne, and Robert C. Lieberman. *Four Threats: The Recurring Crises of American Democracy.* St. Martin's Publishing Group, 2020.

Miller, Lisa L. "Up from Federalism." *Boston Review*, July 18, 2022. https://bostonreview.net/articles/up-from-federalism/.

Mitchell, Amy, Carrie Blazina, Jocelyn Kiley, and Katerina Eva Matsa. "Political Polarization and Media Habits." Pew Research Center, October 21, 2014. https://www.pewresearch.org/journalism/2014/10/21/political-polarization-media-habits/.

Mitchell, Amy, Mark Jurkowitz, J. Baxter Oliphant, and Elisa Shearer. "How Americans Navigated the News in 2020: A Tumultuous Year in Review." Pew Research Center, February 22, 2021. https://www.pewresearch.org/journalism/2021/02/22/how-americans-navigated-the-news-in-2020-a-tumultuous-year-in-review/.

Morris, Meredith Ringel, Scott Counts, Asta Roseway, Aaron Hoff, and Julia Schwarz. "Tweeting Is Believing? Understanding Microblog Credibility Perceptions." In *Proceedings of the ACM 2012 Conference on Computer Supported Cooperative Work—CSCW '12*, 441. ACM Press, 2012. https://doi.org/10.1145/2145204.2145274.

"Most Democrats, Republicans Have 'Just a Few' or No Friends in Opposing Party." Pew Research Center, October 4, 2017. http://www.people-press.org/2017/10/05/8-partisan-animosity-personal-politics-views-of-trump/8_02/.

Musa, Donald, Richard Schulz, Roderick Harris, Myrna Silverman, and Stephen B. Thomas. "Trust in the Health Care System and the Use of Preventive Health Services by Older Black and White Adults." *American Journal of Public Health* 99, no. 7 (2009): 1293–99. https://doi.org/10.2105/AJPH.2007.123927.

Mutz, Diana C. *Hearing the Other Side: Deliberative Versus Participatory Democracy.* Cambridge University Press, 2006.

Mutz, Diana C., and Byron Reeves. "The New Videomalaise: Effects of Televised Incivility on Political Trust." *American Political Science Review* 99, no. 1 (February 2005): 1–15.

Mwachiro, Mark. "Wednesday, April 10, 2024." TV Newser, April 12, 2024. https://www.adweek.com/tvnewser/wednesday-april-10-scoreboard-the-five-and-gutfeld-were-the-most-watched/.

Mwachiro, Mark. "Week of April 8 Evening News Ratings." TV Newser, April 16, 2024. https://www.adweek.com/tvnewser/week-of-april-8-evening-news-ratings-world-news-tonight-leads-newscasts/?ver=1713360959826.

Myrdal, Gunnar. *An American Dilemma.* McGraw-Hill, 1944.

Nathan, Richard P. "There Will Always Be a New Federalism." *Journal of Public Administration Research and Theory* 16, no. 4 (2006): 499–510.

"National Politics on Twitter: Small Share of U.S. Adults Produce Majority of Tweets." Pew Research Center—U.S. Politics & Policy, October 23, 2019. https://www.pewresearch.org/politics/2019/10/23/national-politics-on-twitter-small-share-of-u-s-adults-produce-majority-of-tweets/.

Neuman, Scott. "Fewer Than Half of U.S. Adults Belong to a Religious Congregation, New Poll Shows." National Public Radio, November 20, 2021. https://www.npr.org/2021/03/30/982671783/fewer-than-half-of-u-s-adults-belong-to-a-religious-congregation-new-poll-shows.

"The Next Generation of American Giving." Blackbaud Institute, 2018. https://cdn.fedweb.org/fed-115/2/2018-Next-Generation-of-Giving.pdf.

Noel, Hans. *Political Ideologies and Political Parties in America.* Cambridge University Press, 2014.

"Number of Nonprofit Organizations in the United States in 2021, by Subsector." Statista, n.d. https://www.statista.com/statistics/1373603/number-nonprofit-organizations-irs-subsection-us/.

Paarlberg, Laurie E., Rebecca Nesbit, Richard M. Clerkin, and Robert K. Christensen. "The Politics of Donations: Are Red Counties More Donative Than Blue Counties?" *Nonprofit and Voluntary Sector Quarterly* 48, no. 2 (2019): 283–308. https://doi.org/10.1177/0899764018804088.

Papandrea, Dawn. "56% of Americans Donated to Charity in 2021, at Average of $574." LendingTree, November 29, 2021. https://www.lendingtree.com/debt-consolidation/charitable-donations-survey-study.

Parker, Christopher, and Matt Barreto. *Change They Can't Believe In: The Tea Party and Reactionary Politics in America*. Princeton University Press, 2013.

Pasek, Josh, and Kathleen Hall Jamieson. "Law and Order vs. Law and Order with Racial Justice: Debating How to Understand the Summer's Protests." In *Democracy amid Crises: Polarization, Pandemic, Protests, and Persuasion*, edited by Kathleen Hall Jamieson, Matthew Levendusky, Josh Pasek, R. Lance Holbert, Andrew Renninger, Yotam Ophir, Dror Walter, et al., 219–54. Oxford University Press, 2023. https://doi.org/10.1093/oso/9780197644690.003.0009.

Pears, Emily. *Cords of Affection: Constructing Constitutional Union in Early American History*. University Press of Kansas, 2021.

Persson, Mikael. "Review Article: Education and Political Participation." *British Journal of Political Science* 45, no. 3 (July 2015): 689–703.

Pettigrew, Thomas F., and Linda R. Tropp. "How Does Intergroup Contact Reduce Prejudice? Meta-Analytic Tests of Three Mediators." *European Journal of Social Psychology* 38, no. 6 (2008): 922–34. https://doi.org/10.1002/ejsp.504.

Pettigrew, Thomas F., Linda R. Tropp, Ulrich Wagner, and Oliver Christ. "Recent Advances in Intergroup Contact Theory." *International Journal of Intercultural Relations* 35, no. 3 (May 2011): 271–80.

Phillips, Kevin. *The Emerging Republican Majority*. Arlington House, 1969.

Philpot, Tasha S. *Conservative but Not Republican: The Paradox of Party Identification and Ideology Among African Americans*. Cambridge University Press, 2017.

Phoenix, Davin. *The Anger Gap: How Race Shapes Emotion in Politics*. Cambridge University Press, 2019.

Piliavin, Jane Allyn, and Erica Siegl. "Health Benefits of Volunteering in the Wisconsin Longitudinal Study." *Journal of Health and Social Behavior* 48, no. 4 (December 2007): 450–64. https://doi.org/10.1177/002214650704800408.

Polsby, Nelson. *Political Innovation in America*. Yale University Press, 1984.

Popper, Karl R. *The Open Society and Its Enemies*. New 1-vol. ed. Princeton University Press, 2013.

Price, Gregg. "Fox News's Audience Almost Exclusively White as Network Faces Backlash over Immigration." *Newsweek*, August 10, 2018. https://www.newsweek.com/fox-news-white-audience-immigration-1067807.

Przeworski, Adam. *Democracy and the Market: Political and Economic Reforms in Eastern Europe and Latin America*. Cambridge University Press, 1991. https://doi.org/10.1017/CBO9781139172493.

Putnam, Robert D. *Bowling Alone: The Collapse and Revival of American Community*. Simon & Schuster, 2000.

Putnam, Robert D., and David E. Campbell. *American Grace: How Religion Divides and Unites Us*. Simon & Schuster, 2010.

Rendleman, Hunter, and Jon C. Rogowski. "Americans' Attitudes Toward Federalism." *Political Behavior* 46, no. 1 (2024): 111–34. https://doi.org/10.1007/s11109-022-09820-3.

Ring, Trudy. "11 Times Marjorie Taylor Greene Was the Worst." *Advocate*, August 12, 2022. https://www.advocate.com/politics/2022/8/12/11-times-marjorie-taylor-green-was-worst.

Robertson, Derek. "How 'Owning the Libs' Became the GOP's Core Belief." *Politico*, March 21, 2021. https://www.politico.com/news/magazine/2021/03/21/owning -the-libs-history-trump-politics-pop-culture-477203.

Rohlinger, Deana A. "American Media and Deliberative Democratic Processes." *Sociological Theory* 25, no. 2 (June 24, 2007): 122–48. https://doi.org/10.1111/j.1467 -9558.2007.00301.x.

Romano, Aja. "'OK Boomer' Isn't Just About the Past: It's About Our Apocalyptic Future." *Vox*, November 19, 2019. https://www.vox.com/2019/11/19/20963757/what -is-ok-boomer-meme-about-meaning-gen-z-millennials.

Rosener, J. B. "Ways Women Lead." *Harvard Business Review* 68, no. 6 (1990): 119–25.

Rosenstone, Steven, and John Mark Hansen. *Mobilization, Participation, and Democracy in America*. Macmillan, 1993.

Rossiter, Erin L., and Taylor N. Carlson. "Cross-Partisan Conversation Reduced Affective Polarization for Republicans and Democrats Even After the Contentious 2020 Election." *Journal of Politics* 86, no. 4 (October 2024): 1608–12. https://doi .org/10.1086/729931.

Rothstein, Richard. *The Color of Law*. Liveright, 2017.

Royal Swedish Academy of Sciences. Press release. October 9, 2002. https://www .nobelprize.org/prizes/economic-sciences/2002/press-release/.

Saksa, Jim. "What If Congress Isn't Hopelessly Locked in Partisan Gridlock? What If It's Getting a Lot Done?" Roll Call, March 3, 2022. https://www.rollcall.com/2022 /03/03/congress-gridlock-getting-stuff-done/.

Samuel, Sigal. "Why Every Generation Thinks People Were Nicer in the Past." *Vox*, June 19, 2023. https://www.vox.com/future-perfect/23762261/moral-decline -philosophy-ethics-religion-spirituality.

Samuels, Alex, and Neil Lewis, Jr. "How White Victimhood Fuels Republican Politics." FiveThirtyEight, March 21, 2022. https://fivethirtyeight.com/features/how-white -victimhood-fuels-republican-politics/.

Sanders, Lynn M. "Against Deliberation." *Political Theory* 25, no. 3 (1997): 347–76.

Santoro, Erik, and David E. Broockman. "The Promise and Pitfalls of Cross-Partisan Conversations for Reducing Affective Polarization: Evidence from Randomized Experiments." *Science Advances* 8, no. 25 (2022): eabn5515. https://doi.org/10.1126/ sciadv.abn5515.

Schaffner, Brian F., Matthew MacWilliams, and Tatishe Nteta. "Understanding White Polarization in the 2016 Vote for President: The Sobering Role of Racism and Sexism." *Political Science Quarterly* 133, no. 1 (Spring 2018): 9–34. https://doi.org/10 .1002/polq.12737.

Schildkraut, Deborah J., Jeffrey M. Berry, and James M. Glaser. "Charge and Retreat: Asymmetric Patterns of Political Engagement Among Liberals and Conservatives." In *Dynamics of American Democracy: Partisan Polarization, Political Competition and Government Performance*, edited by Eric M. Patashnik and Wendy J. Schiller, 200–224. University Press of Kansas, 2020.

Schlozman, Kay Lehman, Nancy Burns, and Sidney Verba. "Gender and the Pathways to Participation: The Role of Resources." *Journal of Politics* 56, no. 4 (November 1994): 963–90. https://doi.org/10.2307/2132069.

Schneider, Saundra K., William G. Jacoby, and Daniel C. Lewis. "Public Opinion Toward Intergovernmental Policy Responsibilities." *Publius* 41, no. 1 (2011): 1–30. https://doi.org/10.1093/publius/pjq036.

Schnell, Mychael, and Emily Brooks. "5 Takeaways: Biden, McCarthy Strike Deal to Raise Debt Limit." *Hill*, May 28, 2023. https://thehill.com/homenews/house/4024521-5-takeaways-biden-mccarthy-strike-deal-to-raise-debt-limit/.

Selk, Avi, and Sarah Murray. "The Owner of the Red Hen Explains Why She Asked Sarah Huckabee Sanders to Leave." *Washington Post*, October 23, 2021. https://www.washingtonpost.com/news/local/wp/2018/06/23/why-a-small-town-restaurant-owner-asked-sarah-huckabee-sanders-to-leave-and-would-do-it-again/.

Shaw, Greg M., and Stephanie L. Reinhart. "Trends: Devolution and Confidence in Government." *Public Opinion Quarterly* 65, no. 3 (2001): 369–88. https://doi.org/10.1086/322849.

Shook, Natalie J., and Russell H. Fazio. "Political Ideology, Exploration of Novel Stimuli, and Attitude Formation." *Journal of Experimental Social Psychology* 45 (July 2009): 995–98. https://doi.org/10.1016/j.jesp.2009.04.003.

Sides, John, Chris Tausanovitch, and Lynn Vavreck. *The Bitter End: The 2020 Presidential Campaign and the Challenge to American Democracy*. Princeton, NJ: Princeton University Press, 2022.

Sides, John, Michael Tesler, and Lynn Vavreck. *Identity Crisis: The 2016 Presidential Campaign and the Battle for the Meaning of America*. Princeton, NJ: Princeton University Press, 2018.

Simas, Elizabeth N. *In Defense of Ideology*. Cambridge University Press, 2023.

Simonetti, Isabella, and Joe Flint. "TV Networks Embrace Their Aging Audience with a New Mantra: Age Doesn't Matter." *Wall Street Journal*, May 22, 2024. https://www.wsj.com/business/media/tv-networks-embrace-their-aging-audience-with-a-new-mantra-age-doesnt-matter-63badbd1.

Sniderman, Paul M., Phillip E. Tetlock, James M. Glaser, Donald Phillip Green, and Michael Hout. "Principled Tolerance and the American Mass Public." *British Journal of Political Science* 19, no. 1 (January 1989): 25–45.

Soskis, Benjamin. "Republicans Used to Celebrate Voluntarism and Service: What Happened?" *Washington Post*, August 3, 2018. https://www.washingtonpost.com/outlook/republicans-used-to-celebrate-volunteerism-and-service-what-happened/2018/08/03/7544bfe4-95bd-11e8-a679-b09212fb69c2_story.html.

Spector, Nicole. "'OK Boomer' Is Dividing Generations: What Does It Mean?" *NBC News*, November 6, 2019. https://www.nbcnews.com/better/lifestyle/ok-boomer-dividing-generation-what-does-it-mean-ncna1077261.

Spinner-Halev, Jeff, and Elizabeth Theiss-Morse. *Respect and Loathing in American Democracy: Polarization, Moralization, and the Undermining of Equality*. University of Chicago Press, 2024.

"State Minimum Wages." National Conference of State Legislatures, n.d. http://www.ncsl.org/research/labor-and-employment/state-minimum-wage-chart.aspx. Accessed March 28, 2017.

Steinberg, Brian. "TV Networks Put Harder Sell Behind Hard News as 2020 Election Draws Closer." *Variety*, January 7, 2020. https://variety.com/2020/tv/news/tv-news-hard-sell-advertising-fox-news-msnbc-1203458945/.

Stelter, Brian. "Lachlan Murdoch Finally Says It Aloud: Fox Is the 'Loyal Opposition.'" *CNN Business*, March 5, 2021. https://www.cnn.com/2021/03/04/media/lachlan-murdoch-fox-reliable-sources/index.html.

Stewart, Emily. "The Past 72 Hours in Sarah Sanders's Dinner and the Civility Debate, Explained." *Vox*, June 25, 2018. https://www.vox.com/policy-and-politics/2018/6/25/17500988/sarah-sanders-red-hen-civility.

Stroud, Natalie Jomini. *Niche News*. Oxford University Press, 2011.

Sullivan, John L., James Piereson, and George E. Marcus. *Political Tolerance and American Democracy*. Chicago: University of Chicago Press, 1982.

Sullivan, Kathleen. "From States' Rights Blues to Blue States' Rights: Federalism After the Rehnquist Court." *Fordham Law Review* 75 (2006): 799–813.

Sullivan, Margaret. "Tucker Carlson's Attacks on Sen. Tammy Duckworth Are as Disgusting as They Are Predictable." *Washington Post*, July 8, 2020. https://www.washingtonpost.com/lifestyle/media/tucker-carlsons-attacks-on-sen-tammy-duckworth-are-as-disgusting-as-they-are-predictable/2020/07/08/5c9fd6fa-c12a-11ea-b4f6-cb39cd8940fb_story.html.

Susan G. Komen. "Susan G. Komen® Announces the Return of MORE THAN PINK Walk, Race for the Cure." June 11, 2022. https://www.komen.org/news/2022-race-walk-announcement/.

Sydnor, Emily. *Disrespectful Democracy: The Psychology of Incivility*. Columbia University Press, 2019.

Theriault, Sean M. *The Gingrich Senators: The Roots of Partisan Warfare in Congress*. Oxford University Press, 2013.

"Thurmond Says States' Rights Is Only Bar to Establishment of 'Kremlin' in Washington." *New York Times*, October 27, 1948.

Tilly, Charles. *Democracy*. Cambridge: Cambridge University Press, 2007.

Tocqueville, Alexis de. *Democracy in America*. Vintage Books, 1835.

Tocqueville, Alexis de, and Isaac Kramnick. *Democracy in America: An Annotated Text, Backgrounds, Interpretations*. Norton critical ed. W. W. Norton, 2007. https://books.google.com/books?id=DBokAQAAIAAJ.

Tversky, Amos, and Daniel Kahneman. "Loss Aversion in Riskless Choice: A Reference-Dependent Model." *Quarterly Journal of Economics* 106, no. 4 (November 1991): 1039–61.

United States Census Bureau. "National Volunteer Week," December 2, 2018. https://www.thenonprofittimes.com/npt_articles/volunteer-hours-now-worth-167-billion-annually/.

Vaidyanathan, Brandon, Jonathan P. Hill, and Christian Smith. "Religion and Charitable Financial Giving to Religious and Secular Causes: Does Political Ideology Matter?" *Journal for the Scientific Study of Religion* 50, no. 3 (September 2011): 450–69. https://doi.org/10.1111/j.1468-5906.2011.01584.x.

Valentino, Nicholas A., Ted Brader, Eric W. Groenendyk, Krysha Gregorowicz, and Vincent L. Hutchings. "Election Night's Alright for Fighting: The Role of Emotions in Political Participation." *Journal of Politics* 73, no. 1 (January 1, 2011): 156–70. https://doi.org/10.1017/S0022381610000939.

Valentino, Nicholas A., Fabian G. Neuner, and L. Matthew Vandenbroek. "The Changing Norms of Racial Political Rhetoric and the End of Racial Priming." *Journal of Politics* 80, no. 3 (July 2018): 757–71. https://doi.org/10.1086/694845.

Vigil, Jacob M. "Political Leanings Vary with Facial Expression Processing and Psychosocial Functioning." *Group Processes and Intergroup Relations* 13 (September 2010): 547–58. https://doi.org/10.1017/pls.2019.18.

Ward, Paul R., Emma Miller, Alex R. Pearce, and Samantha B. Meyer. "Predictors and Extent of Institutional Trust in Government, Banks, the Media and Religious Organisations: Evidence from Cross-Sectional Surveys in Six Asia-Pacific Countries." *PLOS One* 11, no. 10 (October 4, 2016). https://doi.org/10.1371/journal.pone.0164096.

"Wave 19 of the American Trends Panel Survey, Conducted July 12–August 8, 2016." Pew Research Center, 2016. http://www.people-press.org/dataset/american-trends-panel-wave-19/.

Webster, Steven W. *American Rage: How Anger Shapes Our Politics.* Cambridge University Press, 2020.

Wemple, Erik. "Tucker Carlson Said Immigration Makes America 'Dirtier.'" *Washington Post,* December 15, 2018. https://www.washingtonpost.com/opinions/2018/12/15/tucker-carlson-said-immigration-makes-america-dirtier-so-an-advertiser-took-action/.

"What Is the National Debt?" US Treasury Department, n.d. https://fiscaldata.treasury.gov/americas-finance-guide/national-debt/. Accessed July 22, 2023.

What's Next Project. "What's Next for American Democracy?" *Democracy Journal,* 2023. https://democracyjournal.org/magazine/whats-next-for-american-democracy/.

Wike, Richard, Laura Silver, and Laura Clancy. "What Makes Someone a Good Member of Society." Pew Research Center, November 16, 2022. https://www.pewresearch.org/global/2022/11/16/what-makes-someone-a-good-member-of-society/.

Williams, Mark. "Pink Back in Style as Komen Race for the Cure Returns to Downtown Columbus After COVID-19." *Columbus Dispatch,* May 14, 2022. https://www.dispatch.com/story/news/2022/05/14/columbus-komen-race-cure-raises-1-m-draws-7-k-participants/9708422002/.

Winterich, Karen Page, Vikas Mittal, and William T. Ross Jr. "Donation Behavior Toward In-Groups and Out-Groups: The Role of Gender and Moral Identity." *Journal of Consumer Research* 36, no. 2 (August 2009): 199–214. https://doi.org/10.1086/596720.

Winterich, Karen Page, Zhang Yinlong, and Mittal Vikas. "How Political Identity and Charity Positioning Increase Donations." *International Journal of Research in Marketing* 29, no. 4 (2012): 346–54.

Wittenberg, Chloe, Matthew A. Baum, J. Berinsky Adam, Justin de Benedictis-Kessner, and Teppei Yamamoto. "Media Measurement Matters: Estimating the Persuasive Effects of Partisan Media with Survey and Behavioral Data." *Journal of Politics* 85, no. 4 (2023): 1275–90. https://www.journals.uchicago.edu/doi/10.1086/724960.

Wolak, Jennifer. *Compromise in an Age of Party Polarization.* Oxford University Press, 2020.

Wolak, Jennifer. "Core Values and Partisan Thinking About Devolution." *Publius* 46, no. 4 (2016): 463–85. https://doi.org/10.1093/publius/pjw021.

Woon, Jonathan. "Primaries and Candidate Polarization: Behavioral Theory and Experimental Evidence." *American Political Science Review* 112, no. 4 (2018): 826–43.

Yang, Yongzheng, and Peixu Liu. "Are Conservatives More Charitable Than Liberals in the U.S.? A Meta-Analysis of Political Ideology and Charitable Giving." *Social Science Research* 99 (2021). https://doi.org/10.1016/j.ssresearch.2021.102598.

Yen, Steven T., and Ernest M. Zampelli. "What Drives Charitable Donations of Time and Money? The Roles of Political Ideology, Religiosity, and Involvement." *Journal of Behavioral and Experimental Economics* 50 (June 2014): 58–67. https://doi.org/10.1016/j.socec.2014.01.002.

Young, Dannagal G. *Irony and Outrage: The Polarized Landscape of Rage, Fear, and Laughter in the United States.* Oxford University Press, 2020.

Young, Dannagal G., and Katherine Anderson. "Media Diet Homogeneity in a Fragmented Media Landscape." *Atlantic Journal of Communication* 25, no. 1 (January 31, 2017): 33–47. https://doi.org/10.1080/15456870.2017.1251434.

Young, Ernest A. "Welcome to the Dark Side: Liberals Rediscover Federalism in the Wake of the War on Terror." *Brooklyn Law Review* 69, no. 4 (2004): 1277–1311.

Zaller, John. *The Nature and Origins of Mass Opinion.* Cambridge University Press, 1992.

Zhou, Li. "Why There's Been a Surge of Bipartisan Activity in Congress." *Vox*, February 15, 2022. https://www.vox.com/2022/2/15/22927345/congress-bipartisan-bills-forced-arbitration-postal-reform.

# Index

*Figures and tables are indicated by "f" and "t" following page numbers.*

federalist attitudes and, 103, 109,
112–19, 113–14t, 117t, 190n24; gender
influences on, 125; operational, 39–
40, 180–81nn69–70; partisanship in
relation to, 8, 39; political worldviews
and, 8–9, 12, 26, 160; racial and ethnic
influences on, 12, 114, 125; symbolic,
39, 40; values as manifestations of, 140;
volunteerism and, 133–35, 134f, 138. *See
also* conservatives; liberals; moderates
immigrants and immigration: citizenship
for children of, 180–81n69; keyword
search terms for, 44, 181n76; legal
status granted to illegal immigrants,
181n70; media coverage of, 57, 57t, 59,
67; social service organizations for,
129; Trump's racist language toward,
14; voting and, 150
incivility. *See* civility; hatred and hateful
(toxic) exchanges
inequality, 25, 92, 98, 129. *See also*
discrimination and bias
Ingraham, Laura, 51, 55, 59, 150, 179n49
Institute of Politics and Public Service at
Georgetown, 74t, 76
Iyengar, Shanto, 55

Jackson, Andrew, 144
Jacobs, Jane, 156
Jacobs, Nicholas, 116
Jamieson, Kathleen Hall, 64
Jeffries, Hakeem, 58
Jim Crow era, 99, 100, 118, 190n37
Johnson, Martin, 63
Jones, Van, 179n49

Kahneman, Daniel, 17, 81, 83, 86, 186n21
Kaiser Family Foundation surveys, 104t,
105–6
Kalla, Joshua, 52, 66
Kalmoe, Nathan, 7
Kam, Cindy, 121
Kansas-Nebraska Act (1854), 144
Keeter, Scott, 87
Keurig company, 22
Knight, Phil and Penny, 130
Konisky, David, 110
Korean War, 144

Lee, Francis E., 194n11
Lee, Younghwa, 141
Lepore, Jill, 145
Levendusky, Matthew, 63, 151
Levine, Peter, 24
Levitsky, Steven, 7, 50, 168
Lewis, John, 58
liberal media, 11, 26, 61, 69. *See also
specific media outlets*
liberals: charitable donations, 9, 18,
126–32, 128f, 131t, 137–43, 138t, 139f,
155, 161; classic conceptualizations
of, 10; on compromise, 9, 17, 72–80,
74–75t, 78t, 80f, 89f, 90, 93–95t,
97, 147, 161; conflict orientation
and, 23, 37–39, 37f, 38t; emotional
reactions to political debate, 23,
33–37, 34f, 35t; engagement with
political opponents, 15–16, 21–23,
26–43, 30f, 69; federalism and, 10, 18,
99–110, 102f, 104–5t, 109t, 121, 152;
government interactions with, 110–12,
111t; hypocrisy accusations by Brooks,
124; ideological consistency and, 40;
income tax rate experiment and, 86,
87t; minimum wage rate experiment
and, 84–85, 85t; progressives, 21, 22,
82, 83, 85; racial resentment among,
65, 65t; on states' rights, 117t, 119, 120t;
stereotypes associated with, 123; as
survey respondents, 179n47; Twitter
networks of, 24, 30–33, 31t, 32f;
volunteerism and, 9, 19, 133–35, 134f,
138, 142, 155; on welfare system, 10,
129. *See also* Democrats
Lieberman, Robert, 7–8, 13, 50, 149, 162
Limbaugh, Rush, 36, 52–53t
Lindell, Mike, 60
Liu, Peixu, 192n16
local associations. *See* neighborhood and
local associations
local government: access to, 165;
attitudes on devolution of power to,
11, 18, 99–110, 104–5t, 116, 117t, 118, 121;
trust in, 110–12. *See also* federalism;
states' rights
loss aversion, 81, 84, 96, 97
Lupia, Arthur, 25

Twitter (now X): civility on, 16, 43–46, 45t, 150, 151; elite account followers, 30–33, 31t, 32f, 179n49, 179n51; engagement with political opponents on, 27; ideological bubbles on, 30–33, 31t, 32f; name-calling on, 44, 46, 150, 182n82; toxic language on, 24, 44–46, 45t, 150, 151; user demographics, 69

US Capitol insurrection (2021), 1, 50, 159
US Constitution: institutional boundaries of, 2, 17, 99–100, 168; replacing Articles of Confederation, 144

Verba, Sidney, 136
Vietnam War, 12, 144
volunteerism: community and, 6, 133, 135, 136, 155–57; conservatives and, 9, 19, 123–25, 133–35, 134f, 155; contact theory and, 157–58; in COVID-19 pandemic, 135; demographics of, 133; gender differences and, 135–37, 136f; habits of the heart and, 7, 132, 133, 141; health-related, 134, 134f, 136f, 137, 156; ideology and, 133–35, 134f, 138; liberals and, 9, 19, 133–35, 134f, 138, 142, 155; moderates and, 133, 134f, 157, 161; motivations for, 132, 138, 156; nonprofits and, 6, 9, 132–33, 134f, 136–38, 136f, 141, 156–57, 166; partisanship and, 133; political participation and, 124, 132–35, 156, 159, 164, 166; racial influences on, 135; religion and, 134–38, 134f, 136f, 142; social services and, 134, 134f, 136f, 137, 156–57; unpaid labor through, 133

voting: access to, 99, 159; good citizenship and, 14, 158, 196n45; immigrant threat and, 150; minority experiences of, 162; mobilization for, 124; poll worker, taking role of, 164; in primaries, 163; recommendations for, 163–64; registration, 132, 163, 164. *See also* elections

Wagner, Alex, 51
*Washington Post*, 14, 52–53t, 68
Watergate scandal, 12, 144
Watters, Jesse, 51, 60
web-scraping tools, 43–44, 182n77
Webster, Steven, 63
Weiner, Bernard, 141
welfare system, 10, 123, 129
Wemple, Erik, 68
Wheeler, Andrew, 106
white privilege, 62, 62f
Wilkinson, Stephanie, 21–22
Wolak, Jennifer, 71, 72, 109–10, 148
women. *See* abortion; gender
World War II, 12, 144, 155

X. *See* Twitter

Yang, Yongzheng, 192n16
Yen, Steven, 133
YouGov surveys, 79, 80f, 186n16
Young, Dannagal, 49
YouTube, 53, 61, 69

Zampelli, Ernest, 133
Ziblatt, Daniel, 7, 168

# Chicago Studies in American Politics

A series edited by Susan Herbst, Lawrence R. Jacobs, Adam J. Berinsky, and Frances Lee; Benjamin I. Page, editor emeritus

www.ingramcontent.com/pod-product-compliance
Lightning Source LLC
Chambersburg PA
CBHW032131020426
42334CB00016B/1113